Floyd Off the Farm

Floyd Off the Farm

An Autobiography by Floyd Wachs

2004
Galde Press, Inc.
Lakeville, Minnesota, U.S.A.

Floyd Off the Farm

Printed in the United States of America

First Edition
First Printing, 2004

Illustrations by Floyd Wachs
Cover design by Andrew Wood

Library of Congress Cataloging-in-Publication Data

Wachs, Floyd
Floyd off the farm : an autobiography / by Floyd Wachs.-- 1st ed.
p. cm.
ISBN 1-931942-15-3 (trade pbk.)
1. Wachs, Floyd, 1927- 2. Farm life--Minnesota. 3. Executives--Minnesota--Minneapolis--Biography. 4. Executives--Illinois--Chicago--Biography. 5. Sears, Roebuck and Company--Officials and employees--Biography. 6. Oral biography. 7. Minneapolis (Minn.)--Biography. 8. Chicago (Ill.)--Biography. I. Title.
CT275.W14A3 2003
977.6'05'092--dc22

2003024396

Galde Press, Inc.
PO Box 460
Lakeville, Minnesota 55044–0460

This book about my life is dedicated to my wife Jeanne,
my two children, William and Jennifer,
and my grandchildren.

They are my life.

Introduction

Today is March 3, 1994. It is the first day of the rest of my life and since I will be 67 years old in three days, if I am going to do anything with my life, I had better get on with it. What I would really like to do is write a book about my life, an autobiography, my memoirs, my update of a diary or whatever you want to call it. If that sounds a bit nuts, it's because I probably am, and it would be perfectly understandable if your reaction was something like this: "Write a book? Floyd, you're not a writer, your brother was a writer, but you barely passed high school English!"

All of this is true; I am not a writer, which will be abundantly clear to you even after the first few pages, so please keep this in mind if you care to go on. There will be misspelled words, barnyard vocabulary, incorrect grammar, punctuation errors, improper sentence structure, and so on. But I don't know that a perfect piece of prose is all that necessary to convey a message from the heart of some of the crazy events in my past. Furthermore, this book will not win any Pulitzer Prizes, even in Pine River, Minnesota, or make the bestseller list at Backus. In fact, only a few copies will be made, just enough to pass on to the offspring of my family. This means I won't have to suck up to any critic or publishing house; I just have to have the courage to say this is my life, take it or leave it.

My brother Douglas was a writer, and in my opinion a very good humorous writer. He was a graduate of the School of Journalism at the University of Minnesota, worked as a reporter on several different newspapers, and retired from the 3M Company where he was a public relations writer for trade magazines. I wish I had his talent and education, and I wish that he was still around to help me now. It is a rotten shame that he never got around to do some "fun" writing. It would have been a joy to read.

It is also true that I came so close to flunking English that I may have the only Washington High School diploma with an asterisk on it, meaning that there is some question as to whether or not I really deserved the diploma. But that is a chapter by itself, and we'll get into that later.

So what is this book all about?

I haven't the slightest idea at this point. I haven't planned that far ahead. It might be easier to tell you what it is not. It will not be the typical memoir of the type that famous statesmen, politicians, or other well known people might do. They are in many cases, like a plugged-up toilet that overflows, simply an outlet for their egos, without admitting that their success was due to a great deal of luck, being in the right place at the right time.

Although I'll have to admit, it is a bit difficult to write an entire book about yourself without boasting a little. That in itself sounds egotistical. So if you find that I have gotten carried away to the point where you want to stick your finger down your throat, I apologize. But if you will just stop and quietly listen, you might hear one of my favorite songs:

Oh Lord, it's hard to be humble when you're perfect in every way...

I've always said I'd rather be lucky than good, whether it be in a golf match, a card game, in business, or in choosing a mate. And I will be the first to admit that Lady Luck has been on my side more than I deserve. Yes, I still have an ego—who doesn't? Actually there is very little in my life that I have the right to brag about, but at the same time, I don't plan to look for things that I should apologize for just to balance the scale.

This book will not be a confession of all my sins in my past 67 years in the hopes that this will cool the fires of hell. That might take volumes instead of just one book, and I don't think there's enough energy left in my lifetime for me to get it all written down.

Likewise, this will not be a hot, sexy account of all my love-making conquests. That might require all of five or six pages of double spaced type. Oops! There I go bragging already. My dear wife would just as soon not hear about any of this and I therefore agree, anyone else who bothers to read this shouldn't either.

So, the reason I want to tell my story is simply this: I want my children, my grandchildren, their children's children, and wherever their tree branches might grow, to know a little bit about their ancestry. What was it like for old Floyd back in the 20th century? Does his life help explain the way we are today? Could we, as they say, "Take a page out of his book," to help prevent some of the blunders he made from happening to us?

I don't have a lot to leave my children but I would like for them to know who I was, why I became the person I did and that my life was very rewarding in the end because of the good fortune of my family and because God gave me the right attitude to appreciate this good fortune.

I never was very good at communicating this message to my children and maybe this is a roundabout way of correcting this, but I know of no other way at this point other than to write it down as I feel. Fact is, I never really got to know my own parents, at least not the way I would have liked. There always seemed to be a great deal of secrecy about their lives. They avoided communicating with each other like it was a contagious disease, and for the life of me, I cannot ever remember them laughing or having any fun together. They were simply very unhappy people. I'm sure they were good people; they didn't abuse their children, at least not physically, but their otherwise wasted life would have meant so much more if they could have shared some joy with each other and their children.

Most children today also get to know their grandparents, maybe even their great-grandparents, and if the relationship I have been able to enjoy living so close to my granddaughter is any indication, then wow! It should be remembered and preserved as a most wonderful experience.

I have no memories at all of my grandparents except one, my father's father, and that is a very thin thread of a memory. All this I consider a void in my life. Ideally I believe that every parent, regardless of how inept they may be at telling their life story, as I am, should do it anyway. Wouldn't it be cool, even at this point in time, to find an old chest stored in an attic someplace, and inside there would be a couple of dusty old books and on the cover sheet would be written, "This is the story of my life," by Ed Wachs, or Lorena Wachs, or Christ Wachs, or any one of my many ancestors.

The first part of my life story you will soon find is anything but glamorous, but if you think I am complaining, feeling sorry for myself, or want you to feel sorry for me, forget it. Put it back on the shelf. I will let you in on something, however: I expect it to have a happy ending.

Incidentally, it will be my style of writing to begin each chapter in response to a question and form the events of the story of my life around these questions as if I were having a conversation with you, the reader. I have never seen this done before but I am sure it is not original.

In this way I hope I can anticipate the questions you may have as events unfold, and hopefully make a rather uneventful life become more interesting in story form. If I'm wrong about this, just forget the questions and read whatever you feel like in your own way.

Nothing that is memorable ever passes...

...for in memory the past is ever present.

Chapter 1

Most everyone has some special event that occurred when they were a small child that seems to be preserved in their memory bank forever. What is the first thing you can remember as a child in your early days on the farm?

FOR SOMEONE who cannot remember what he had for breakfast this morning, this could be a difficult question. However, as they say, a good place to start is at the beginning, so let's give it a try. I believe your personal life really begins at a point where memory begins. In other words, if you can only remember things that happened ten years ago and nothing before that, then for you, your life began just ten years ago.

People with Alzheimer's disease who cannot remember anything—and I don't think I'm there yet—really have no life at all. Then there are others who at about my age claim they can remember things that happened when they were two or even a year old, or maybe there is someone who will claim they can remember when they were first born. Two years old maybe, but I have my doubts about anything before that.

When you think about it, memory may be the most wonderful thing about life. That's why Alzheimer's is so devastating. Memory serves as a base point in your mind to relate other events to and make comparisons of good or bad, happiness or sadness, love or hate and so on. For someone who is very poor, winning a thousand dollars in a lottery may be the most memorable event in their lifetime, but to a rich person it may be meaningless and crowded out of their memory bank by other events.

The mysterious mind is a wonderful mass of magic. Your mind also has the ability to suppress or erase certain events from your memory bank that are simply too painful for a sane person to cope with, so some inner body switch just blanks it out. A person who has been horribly abused as a child or witnessed some terrible event may not have the ability to retrieve this memory without the aid of a trained professional through hypnosis, drugs or other means. With such people there is often some strange characteristic giving evidence to a problem occurring some time in their life, but the stored memory may be remotely suppressed and the problem never revealed.

I'm sure there has been no drastic event in my young life that my mind has purposely hidden the memory of, although I do not know that for certain. There are a few people who think my characteristics are strange enough that something gruesome must have happened to me as a child. No, I think my memory blackouts are all very natural, sometimes conveniently so.

Someday I suppose there will be advancement in medical science that will allow professionals to go into your mind and retrieve not only what's been suppressed, but all memory items regardless of their magnitude or events of horror. The good side of this would serve a purpose in resolving matters of dishonesty, solving crimes, testing students, etc. The scary part may be the next step when the average person has the ability to see inside your mind and know what you are thinking about. Thank God this will not happen in my lifetime or I would end up getting my face slapped several times a day. Even Bill Clinton would have a problem with that one.

Getting back to the question of the first thing I can remember as a child: There are a few things I can remember when I was either three or four, but a particular event occurred, I am almost certain, during the summer of 1930, when I was three. Maybe it was 1931 when I was four, but it makes little difference. It is one of those things you can call up from your memory bank and it's just as clear as if it happened last week.

My mother had received a letter from her sister, Hazel Gilligan, who lived in North Dakota, announcing that she was coming to visit. This was a special event because I am sure Mother had never met either of her two sisters, or if she did, she had no memory of either one. Mother and her sisters were placed in an orphanage in Lake City, Minnesota, when they were small children. Her sister Florence was the oldest, I believe, and Mother was the middle child. Hazel was definitely the youngest. There is no record of a father that anyone has been able to find, but we presume his name was Flink because that is the name Mother used as her maiden name. There is also very little knowledge about Mrs. Flink (her mother) except that she died in the mid-1930s. Mother had no recollection of her mother either.

It was Mother's aunt, Emma Snow, a younger sister of her mother, who made an effort to keep track of the three sisters from the orphanage, but she also had little knowledge of their parents, the Flink family. Mother had never met her Aunt Emma, but later in life she would meet her and live with her briefly.

Somehow Emma Snow was able to stay in touch with the other two sisters, Hazel and Florence, and eventually she would locate Mother when she was in her early twenties. She wrote to Mother and told her, for the first time, about her two sisters. It was a few years after this that Mother got the letter from Hazel announcing her intended visit. You can imagine this would be one very emotional and special event.

Emma's letters to Mother said that her sister Florence was adopted by some rich family from California and had studied to be an actress but didn't know if she had gotten in any movies. She said Florence had stopped answering her letters, but Emma did receive a picture from Florence which she sent on to Mother. It was a large, framed picture taken by a professional photographer, and she was indeed beautiful. Unfortunately, it was only a few years later that Mother received word from her Aunt Emma that Florence had died: no details, no information about her family, she had just died at a very young age. That was it.

Hazel, likewise, was adopted by a well-to-do family from North Dakota. Perhaps all this good fortune of being adopted by families with money didn't sound all that wonderful to Mother, who considered herself very poor and stuck on a backwoods farm away from the rest of the world. She avoided any further correspondence with her aunt and only replied to her sister Hazel that she was happy she was coming to see her.

The preparation for this great event couldn't have been any more involved had President Hoover himself been coming. On the other hand, I think my parents were Democrats, so they might have put up a "Not Welcome" sign for Hoover. As much as we could afford at the time, all resources were devoted to this preparation, with everyone working from morning 'til night to get the tired old farm to look as rich as possible. New wallpaper was put up, along with new curtains, varnish for the woodwork, and so on. Mother scrubbed the kitchen floor every other day until the boards were nearly white. Then she nagged Dad to fix the screen door, fix the pump, fix the chair, fix this, fix that. Mom was the world's champion nagger and Dad was the world's champion procrastinator.

Finally the day arrived when Dad would crank up the old Model T Ford—it was a 1926 or older vintage—and we motored to Staples, Minnesota, where we met the train that was bringing Aunt Hazel from North Dakota. Staples was a long trip, maybe thirty miles or so, and with our not-so-dependable Model T, we allowed a couple hours. Eventually the train arrived and there was a surprise. Aunt Hazel was not alone. She brought her little daughter Joanne along. If this wasn't a surprise to Mother it certainly was for me, and I was thrilled. Joanne was about my age, and while I didn't know much about what little girls were supposed to look like, because there were none around where we lived, my instincts told me she was a knockout. It was a case of love at first sight.

On the way home I sat in the front seat with my brother and my dad while my Mother, Aunt Hazel, and this little cute chick, Joanne, sat in the back. I was much too shy to talk or even get caught looking at this newfound cousin, but every now and than I would sneak a peak across the top of the seat and hope that she wouldn't be looking my way at the same time.

After our family and the two newly discovered relatives got home, Joanne and I changed into running clothes. My summer attire consisted of a pair of bib overalls that I wore every day until they could stand in the corner by themselves, no shirt, no socks, no shoes and most of the time not even any underwear. Joanne was much neater, with shoes, socks, short pants, and a top. Once I was alone with this gorgeous creature I wasn't so shy anymore. In fact, I was trying to be the real macho man, thinking this poor girl probably had never been on a farm before and I could give her a real education.

"Out here is the barn where we keep all the cows and horses, but if you see a big cow with a ring in his nose, stay away from him. He is called a bull and he can be very mean. They're all out in the pasture now so we can go in there and play or even go up in the hay mow if you want to."

"Not now," Joanne replied.

"Over there is the pig barn but that even smells worse than the cow barn so let's not go over there."

Next I showed her the tractor, a Fordson, but I wasn't allowed to play around it so we moved on. "This little building is the smoke house," I said.

"What's a smoke house?"

"It's a place where you hang hams and bacon over a smoky fire and it makes them taste really good. Over here are the grain bins, and this is my favorite place to play, the machine shed." It was a big building open on one side where the farm implements were stored. I would climb on the seats of the cultivator, the mower, the rake, or the big grain binder and wish that I was old enough to operate them myself. A wish, I'm sorry to say, that came true much too soon.

Joanne and I were now out by the garden and I offered to pull up a radish or carrot for her to eat, but she refused. I said, "Over there are the beehives and sometimes they bite so let's not go there. Maybe I can get Dad to cut off a chunk of honey for us. He's not afraid of the bees."

We had wandered quite a ways from the main house, out where the remains of the original homestead log house were partially standing, surrounded by tall grass and weeds. Suddenly she announced, "I have to go to the toilet."

Toilet was not a word I was totally familiar with but I was pretty sure I knew what she meant. I said, "We don't have a toilet, but we have a backhouse."

"What's a backhouse?"

"Everybody has a backhouse," I said. "It's a little building with a moon in the door that sits in back of our house." I guess that's why it's called a backhouse, because it was always positioned in back of the main house. "But it's full of spiders and flies so I only go there if I have to take a dump. If I have to take a leak I just do it anywhere outside wherever I happen to be." "Taking a dump" or "taking a leak" were the acceptable words for kids to use on the farm to describe the process of waste elimination from the human body.

"I have to wee-wee," Joanne said.

"Well, then just do it right here." She gave me a puzzled look. "Here, let me show you. Just unbutton your pants, take out your little thing and let it go." I had to go also so I was now demonstrating by spraying all over the old logs we were standing by.

Joanne just stood there. Finally she said, "I don't have any buttons on my pants."

Zippers on pants were not very common yet but I couldn't understand pants without any buttons. *Where does this girl come from anyway?* "Well then, just pull your pants down."

Joanne proceeded to pull her pants down and her underwear came with them. " Ye Gods! You don't even have a little thing!" And already her overwhelming need to wee-wee was running down her legs, soaking her underwear, pants, shoes, and socks. *What a mess*, I thought, *and I'll bet somehow I'll get blamed for it.*

We immediately went back to the house and Joanne's mother was furious. She had probably just got through telling Mother how well trained and dependable her little daughter was. Joanne was sent upstairs and I didn't get to play with her the rest of the day. My new discovery gave me a lot to think about. I was proud of my little cousin because she didn't squeal on me.

I wanted to find Dad to ask him about the difference between little boys and girls but he would have just said, "You better go ask your mother." So I waited to get Mom alone.

"Mom, are all girls different from boys or just those from North Dakota?" At this point I had to confess what happened. I said, "It was my fault that Joanne wet her pants. She had to take a leak and I told her to do it outside where we were in the weeds. But she doesn't have a little thing. She's different."

"Oh, so that's what happened, and thank you for telling me," Mom said. "Yes, all girls are different, not just those from North Dakota."

"Why?"

"Because God made them that way."

"Why?"

"So that girls, when they grow up, can have babies. Only mothers can have babies, fathers cannot. Just like the mother cow can have a baby calf but the bull can't. The sow pig can have little pigs, but the boar pig can't, and the hen chicken can have little chicks, but the rooster can't."

"But I thought you told me that little chicks came from eggs."

"Well, yes they do. In fact all little babies, people babies and animal babies, sort of start out as eggs in the beginning."

Boy, this is getting complicated. "Let's talk about it some other time, Mom."

That was the full extent of my sex education either at home or in school from that time on. It was a subject that was avoided like the plague.

For a number of different reasons there were never any repeat visits between Mother and her sister for many years, so I only saw cousin Joanne two or three times again when, she was in her early twenties. We never discussed that incident back on the farm and I wonder if she remembers it as well as I do. I know I will never forget it.

THE BACK HOUSE

Time is the most valuable coin in your life.

You and you alone will determine how that coin will be spent.

Be careful that you do not let other people spend it for you.

Chapter 2

It would appear that the efforts of Emma Snow to get your mother and her sisters together did not develop into much beyond the first meeting with Hazel. Can you explain why and can you tell us anything more about your mother's background?

WHAT HAPPENED during that summer visit to the farm by Mother's sister Hazel? Although it was a bit difficult to travel back and forth between our northern Minnesota location and Hazel's North Dakota residence—I'm not sure where in North Dakota it was—I don't believe they corresponded again or even sent a Christmas card after that first meeting. Money was also a problem.

It would be at least fifteen or twenty years later before they got together again. It certainly wasn't for the lack of enthusiasm to begin with, because Mother really planned and looked forward to finally being united with at least one of her two sisters. And, of course, we know the other sister died before there was a chance to get any connection established. I believe something must have happened between Hazel and Mother during that visit that turned them off.

It is true that Mother had a problem staying friendly with people very long. There would be a close relationship for a while and then something would happen where they would not speak to one another again. I know of only one person, Vera Broad (now Vera Swenson) a few years younger than Mother: she was her friend before Mother got married and remained her friend until the day Mother died. Vera was a very special person.

Much of this, I am sure, had to do with the circumstances of Mother's family background: being sent to an orphanage at a very young age, being adopted into the Wachs family and then marrying one of the sons. A certain amount of resentment about life's plan for her is perhaps understandable, but it also resulted in an attitude that seemed to make it difficult for her to latch on to anything positive.

There is a great deal I don't know about either of my parents, especially my mother. When she was young, perhaps five, six, or seven, she was adopted by my father's parents while they were still living in Wabasha, Minnesota. There were two theories about why my father's parents adopted Lorena, neither of which I can verify as fact: but as people like to expound on the dramatic, there are those who say that one or the other scenario is God's truth. If either my mother or father actually knew the truth, and they are the only ones on which I would place any reliance, they certainly made no effort to divulge it to their children.

The first theory is that people from the old country, Germany, Poland, and other European nations, would choose mates for their sons and daughters well in advance of the time they would marry. Everything was planned so they didn't have to spend their time and energy on such silly things as courtship and competing with others for their partners in life. Furthermore, in following my grandparents' plan to eventually move to northern Minnesota, there would no longer be time for such things and certainly little or no opportunity. There simply wasn't anyone within miles to provide for that potential courtship. Under the circumstances the whole idea would seem to make sense to my grandparents and it certainly was a lot simpler. After all, it was good enough for them when they were young, so it should work for their children also. I personally don't subscribe to any of this as the way it was, but what do I know?

The second theory, which may be more likely, is the fact that my grandparents had a daughter who died at a young age, perhaps nine or ten, in 1906 or 1907.

It was shortly after this that my mother was adopted from the orphanage. It is possible that my grandparents could no longer have children and since there were already two boys in the family, acquiring a daughter to replace the one who died seemed like a natural step to take. The only thing my mother did reveal to me was that her foster mother was a slave driver: mean, overweight, and apparently not in good health. Mother at times hinted that it was for this reason that Grandmother Wachs wanted to adopt her, to have another female to help with household chores, particularly after moving to the farm where there was enough work for dozens of hands.

Had Mother been given an address where she could have corresponded with her sister Florence, she certainly would have done so. For some reason Florence became Mother's idol. She desperately wanted to meet her, but unfortunately Florence died before they could arrange a meeting.

When the information about Florence first surfaced, Mother was pregnant with me. The fact that she was pregnant at all made her about as happy as having the hogs eat up a winning lottery ticket. (Yes, there was a form of lottery back then too, a national sweepstakes out of Canada.) Nevertheless, she took some comfort in her hope and overwhelming desire that I would be a girl.

Before going too far, let's back up and get my father and mother married. Was Mother destined to marry my father already at the early age when she was adopted from the orphanage? I still don't believe that my grandparents planned this arrangement, yet the marriage may have been unavoidable from the beginning.

When the Wachs family, now including young Lorena (my mother) moved to the farm in northern Minnesota, it was a real pioneering project. There were very few people living in the area and little opportunity to meet anyone, let alone have a courtship or a romance. It is understandable if two young adults of the opposite sex and similar age might have had a little tumble in the hay. Regardless of their apparent incompatibility, their lack of physical attraction, or their efforts to avoid involvement, I believe it quite natural for two people in these circumstances to satisfy their sexual desires with each other. And I believe it was just that and nothing more.

There was no romance, no love, no courtship, no wedding plans, but getting pregnant happened anyway. Marriage was therefore an absolute must. Having a baby out of wedlock was totally unacceptable. Having sex before marriage was a sin right close behind the act of committing murder. I think we have a problem here: fetus happens.

I am not exactly sure when the wedding took place, where it took place, who conducted the ceremony or anything about it. My parents kept no evidence of their wedding: no wedding announcements, no copies of a license, nothing pressed in a Bible someplace. It was as if it never happened.

But there was a wedding picture taken (I believe only one), by what appears to be a professional photographer. In it Mother is sitting down with a large bouquet of flowers in her lap and Dad is sort of sitting on the arm of the chair behind her. Others have suggested – and it could be true – that the reason Mother is sitting down with the flowers in her lap is to conceal her swollen waistline. I'm guessing the wedding took place in the fall of 1922 and the conception took place in early summer: that's when hay is at its best. (Before completing this book I made a trip to the Cass County Courthouse to examine marriage records and discovered that the license for Edwin Wachs and Lorena Flink was dated August 22, 1922.)

The whole affair was probably kept hush-hush among other relatives or neighbors who might have questioned the time between the wedding date and the firstborn. Considering the terrible stigma of premarital sex and pregnancy of that time, it must have been devastating to live with their apparent sin and coverup. Perhaps the worst part, for Mother at least, was getting married without the love and romance a normal young woman dreams about.

Brother Douglas was born on March 24, 1923. Moving back a few months, Mom would have been married at nineteen and Dad twenty-seven, reasonable ages to begin married life, but not with a baby in your belly already. All this made little difference to Doug and me: we were both happy to be here, even though neither one of us would have made it had birth control pills, contraception, or abortion been available at that time.

Many years later Mother found it too painful to keep this inside her any longer so she finally unloaded part of the story to my brother Doug's wife, Lois Mae. I doubt that Doug knew anything about this side of the story before then, any more than I did. All of this is no big deal today, but I think it was one of the very weighty issues that created so much unhappiness with Mom and Dad, and made an already doomed marriage a hopeless disaster.

In connection with this, I also recall an incident when I was six or seven: a big fight between two young men at a McKinley Hall community dance. The Hall was built after the township was first formed, to serve as a meeting place for community functions, social events, dances, etc. (A township consisted of an area of about 36 square miles, the smallest unit of government at that time.) The town hall wasn't very big but large enough to hold most of the settlers for a social gathering, and to be sure, everyone who could stand up got there, because it was the only place to go and meet anyone.

We lived about three miles away and Mother loved to dance, although Dad refused to even make an attempt at it. He would take her there, but then he would just stand and watch. I went along when they would let me, even though there were seldom any other kids there. It could be a bitterly cold night, a blizzard blowing, but Dad would still hitch up a team of horses, pile some hay on the sled and we would take off. We kept warm down in the hay but I used to feel sorry for the horses who had to stand out in the cold.

Once a month there would be a dance, ice cream social, ladies aid, summer picnic, or something to get people together. It eventually became the hangout where beer was brought in by the keg and the whiskey bottle was passed around from mouth to mouth. Most of the time it was a relatively clean and respectable place to go, and as the population grew a few romances got started. Occasionally (and not unexpectedly) a fight might break out.

On this particular warm summer night, the fight I referred to earlier involved the Wachs family. One of the local citizens decided to start a rumor that Dad was not the real father of Douglas and that he had married Mother just to save embarrassment to the family. Such gossip, regardless of how absurd it might be, caused some excitement and spread around fast. "Have you heard about Rena and Ed and their first son? She had her child you know, shortly after they were married. He sort of looks like Rena but I see no resemblance to Ed."

The source of the rumor was finally traced to Homer Clews, a very fat tobacco-chewing know-it-all. The one thing I remember about him is that he could not put two words together without inserting a swear word. Along with the tobacco juice oozing out of his mouth while he talked, it was a beautiful language.

All this did not faze my dad too much, and although he had a terrible temper, he just wasn't a scrapper. But Mom, she was furious. She hired a fighter (not really hired, she merely asked a young guy), Roy Mitchell, to beat up on Homer Clews until he retracted what he was saying and apologized. With a couple of drinks in Mitchell the idea of beating up on Homer Clews sort of appealed to him. But swearin' fat Homer was no dummy; he got his friend Bud Holmes to stand in for him and fight Mitchell.

It was a dandy bare-knuckle bloody fight that kept on going in front of a full cheering section, and nobody tried to stop it. Finally Holmes, with only one eye open and too tired to get off the ground, said, "I've had enough."

Mitchell replied, "As soon as your friend Homer apologizes to Rena, I'll let you up, otherwise I'll pound his face in the mud also." I didn't see it but I understand the affable Clews did make some kind of apology to Mom and that was the end of that.

Mom thought I was too young to understand all this and never bothered to explain anything to me, but I wormed around and listened to every conversation (and that was the only thing talked about for a long time) until I figured out what was going on. My brother, Douglas, was not at the dance so I don't know if he ever learned that this fight involved him. I never discussed it with him.

This certainly did not do much for the relationship between Mom and Dad, even though the rumor was totally false and they knew it. Mom's interest in going to dances cooled considerably, and Dad obviously didn't care to go anyway. I don't suggest that this became a turning point in their marriage: that occurred right after the justice of the peace said, "I now pronounce you man and wife." Maybe the downhill trend accelerated a little faster.

THE FAMILY FORD

THE WATKINS WAGON

God does not accept the plea…

…that others have sinned against me.

Chapter 3

How did it come about that your grandparents picked this remote location in northern Minnesota to begin their life as farmers?

IF YOU WERE to take a map of an area of northern Minnesota and select a location as the least likely place in the early twentieth century to raise a family, find happiness, and begin a successful career in farming, this would be one of the spots. I honestly don't know how or why my grandparents selected this place to live. I'm sure it looked a lot different to them than it does to me now, but even when I was struggling to grow up at that time, I could see the futility of it all.

Perhaps there was a good reason. Since the state was trying to bring settlers into this area, the land was being offered at a very low cost or even free. It is possible the incentive to move to McKinley Township in northern Minnesota came at the time they emigrated from Germany. Could there have been a commitment or contract tied in with their immigration, forcing them to take the land sight unseen? Whatever happened, my grandfather wasn't the type to admit he'd made a mistake, and so the "grin and bear it" life went on.

My grandfather, Christ Wachs, had three brothers, August, Gustoff, and Otto, who had immigrated from northeastern Germany, close to the Polish border, at the same time. With the borders in that part of the world changing frequently, I could easily be of Polish descent. The three brother settled in northeastern Kansas, and from what I learned later on in life, they had developed rather successful grain farms. The fact that my grandfather first settled in Wabasha, Minnesota, which had climate and other characteristics resembling northern Germany, may have been one reason why he broke away from the three Kansas brothers.

My grandfather had experience as a brewery worker in Germany, and the fact that he was able to continue this line of work in Wabasha may have been another reason why he came to Minnesota. I don't know why he couldn't have made a career out of making beer, and then passed this trade on to his descendants. There is no doubt I'd have found happiness much easier growing up around a brewery than with a bunch of cows: is there any argument that beer is better than butter?

The "farm" Grandpa Wachs got stuck with was 280 acres of woods, swamp, brush, and rock, not a bad size but low quality land outside of nowhere. It was located eighteen miles southwest of Backus, the closest town with a population of more than thirty-five people, twenty miles northwest of Pine River and twenty-two miles east of Sebeka. Nimrod was only eleven miles west, but it was not easy to get to, and when you did get there, there were only about ten people you could talk to or do business with. The other ten or twelve people were Finnish and couldn't speak English. It's not unusual to find people, even Minnesotans, who have never heard of any of these places.

To begin life on a farm at a place unheard of is pioneering in its most primitive sense. "Stubborn, gutsy, and a glutton for punishment" can be added to the description of my grandfather, and that is why the Wachs family began there.

The farm was actually two farms. One was 160 acres (a quarter section of land) and the other a bit smaller at 120 acres. It was my grandfather's intent that one farm would eventually go to his son Ed, and the other to his son Charles. There was apparently no plan to give anything to their adopted daughter Lorena. No contracts were ever drawn up on the agreement, and this caused some problems between the two brothers—mainly between their wives.

Dad's brother Charles (Uncle Charlie to me) never really had any interest in farming. Maybe he was the smart one. I have little knowledge of his role in the family settlement in northern Minnesota, except that he got married and suddenly his wife died during the birth of their child, Dorothy. After that he moved to St. Paul to work for the railroad. He soon married again and brought Dorothy to live with him and his new wife.

He had no interest in the farm; that is, until Grandpa died. Then, all of a sudden he—or I should say, his second wife, Martha—discovered that one of those hopeless parcels of rock and swamp actually belonged to him. My dad's attitude was, "Come and live on it if you want it so bad, but for damn sure I am not going to sell it and give you the money for it." Nothing was ever done, of course, and nothing changed, including the bad feelings.

A great deal of work went into converting this primitive countryside into land where crops could be harvested, livestock raised, and where a family could grow up. I am amazed that it could even be accomplished. No one in their right mind would consider it today. With nothing but horses to work with, trees, stumps, brush, and rock had to be cleared to prepare an open field for planting and cultivation. They had a platform-type sled built just to haul away the rocks that were piled up into a mound the size of a house. By the time I came along all of this had been done, but imagining how the fields of straight rows of corn and potatoes were once nothing but trees, brush and rock, you could see what my family had performed when they set up the farm.

Logs from the trees on the farm were used to build their first house. There is still a picture or two of this structure around someplace, but the only thing I remember is the remains and a few logs, four or five rows still standing when I was a small boy, where I used to play, and where my cute little cousin Joanne and I made some monumental discoveries about the differences between boys and girls.

Perhaps the most depressing thing on the farm for me (and perhaps other members of the family as well) was the complete isolation of it all. You could go for days or even weeks without seeing another person, unless you made it a point to travel someplace—not easy to do, especially in the winter. To the north and west of us was nothing but trees, brush, and swamp, and I was not allowed to wander there for any reason. To the south was the Thorpe Brothers ranch, consisting of about four or five square miles of more trees, brush, and swamp. There were some sheep and cattle on the ranch so I was not allowed to venture there either. To the east was the only corridor into civilization: a two-rut dirt road not used by anyone for the first mile or so except by our family.

The closest neighbor was about a mile away, but for some reason my parents didn't speak to them. They had no children anyway so it didn't make any difference to me: families with any children were about three or four miles away (most of them were older than I) so it was not unusual to go for months without seeing another boy or girl close to my age. If by chance I did get together with anyone I couldn't get myself to play with them: I simply didn't know how, I was so damned timid.

In the wintertime I would beg my parents to let me go with them into Backus or Nimrod whenever they made such a trip, just to see some other people. But it was risky and I was seldom given this opportunity.

I was thrilled when someone came to our house, such as the Watkins man with his horse and wagon. He would stop in four or five times a year and try to sell some of his products of spices, extracts, serums, and so on. We rarely bought anything other than maybe a bottle of nectar extract, which I thought was a real treat.

He was a jolly man and joked with me about a lot of things, including my big ears. And then one day he said, "I'll bet I can pick you up by those ears." Before I knew it he had hold of my ears and at the same time cupped his hands around my face. He actually picked me up by my head, but it appeared as if he was lifting me by my ears only. I didn't think this was at all funny; I thought he was going to pull my head off. I let out a bloody scream until he put me down.

That ruined my anticipation of seeing any strange visitors at our door. From that time on when he did show up I would plead with my mother to tell him she didn't know where I was. I was hiding in the bedroom—under the bed.

Once a year, though, I really did look forward to one group of men that came to our house. It was the threshing crew that arrived each year to thresh the grain that had been stacked up by the barn. This consisted of three or four guys who traveled with the steam engine and threshing machine wherever it went. Lodging and food had to be provided, and they always seemed to show up at our house in the afternoon, in time for the evening meal. That was because they knew Mom was such a good cook, and for those few days out of the year we always went overboard to have an ample amount of the best food possible. They always gave Mom a lot of attention in return and she loved it. That was perhaps the main reason I looked forward to their visits.

The other reason was that the steam engine driver, Johnny Peterson, blew his whistle when he was in sight of our house and I would run down the road to meet them. Then he'd stop the engine and hoist me up on the platform behind the firebox, letting me ride into our yard with them and their big machines. Then he would let me blow the whistle. This was about my happiest time, along with Christmas. It was never a disappointment.

My brother, who was four years older than I, was my only playmate. I worshiped him, did everything I could for him, pleaded and begged with him to play with me. He must have been sick of me: you can imagine the interest differences between two kids four years apart when it comes to play time.

Doug was a robust lad, big for his age, and he actually enjoyed the farm. His favorite farm chore was to go out with Dad and spread fertilizer. The "spreader" was a sled with the cow shit piled as high as the horses could pull. You used a pitchfork to sling it off into the fields for fertilizer. Doug would come in the house and brag about how far he could sling the shit. It looked to me like he got most of it on himself, and he smelled as if he had been sleeping in it. It was so bad the dog didn't want to get close to him.

I didn't understand a lot of things about my brother, and the manure spreader routine was one of them. I was content being in the house with Mom, baking bread or cookies, washing and ironing, and even sewing. It wasn't that I enjoyed it that much, it was just something to do that I thought was a heck of a lot better then slinging shit out in the freezing cold.

Doug loved to be around the farm animals. He would lose his temper with them, just like Dad, and swear a blue streak. This sometimes called for punishment, where he would be sent to his bedroom without any supper, but then after the meal was finished and the family settled down I would sneak him some cold potatoes to eat. Occasionally he would feel sorry for me and play with me, but more often than not Mom would force him to, which was not enjoyable for either one of us. All my life I idolized my brother and tried to follow in his footsteps, but from the beginning it was obvious that we did not have the same interests.

In the early stages the farm actually progressed quite well. There was plenty of livestock, including milk cows, work horses, hogs, sheep, chickens, geese, and a wonderful collie dog named Boots who thought the farm would never survive without him. Come to think of it, it didn't survive after Boots died.

I am also amazed, as I look back now, at all the farm machinery that had been acquired to operate the farm. Either Grandpa had saved a lot of money from his brewery job to buy this machinery or else it was heavily mortgaged. The latter is more likely to be true. There were plows, disks, seeders, cultivators, mowers, rakes, wagons, sleds, and even a binder for harvesting grain: everything one needed to run a complete farm.

When I was very young a Fordson tractor was delivered to the farm. Boy, was I impressed. This for sure was purchased on contract, because after two or three years the same truck that delivered it came back and repossessed it. This was the one event that signaled a steady and sharp decline of the farm and all the hard work that went into trying to make it a success. My Mom had a good cry, my big brother went off someplace to be alone, and my Dad disappeared into the barn to swear at the cows. I didn't understand what was happening.

While my grandfather was still alive the deterioration of Dad and Mom's "forced" marriage was not so obvious. Grandpa liked my mother, and she liked him. To some degree it seemed to make up for the absence of affection between my parents. Grandpa somehow held things together for the entire family.

One of the real joys I had as a little boy was to climb up on my grandpa's lap, help him clean and stuff his corncob pipe with Prince Albert tobacco, and then sit there while he smoked it. I can't understand why I never started smoking myself; I really liked the smell of that tobacco smoke. Regardless of how tired my grandpa would be after a long hard day in the fields, he never refused to let me climb up on his lap.

He would tell me stories: Much of the time it was old German philosophy about life, and I would ask him question after question until I thought I understood it or until he would say, "You're drivin' me kratzy." He would sing "Ach du Lieber Augustine," and he had a number of clichés he would say in German and then explain the meaning. One was: "Remember, after laffa comes kriffa," meaning that when you are very happy, laughing and having a good time, you can expect that it will soon end in tears.

I thought about this many times, to the point where I was afraid of letting myself get too happy because I knew this would be followed by a letdown of being sad and unhappy, taking away all the good fun feelings I had. It's amazing how often this seems to be true in day-to-day life.

Grandpa Wachs died in the summer of 1933, when I was six years old, in an unfortunate accident. You might even say it was the result of his desire to be good to his adopted daughter and to make things more pleasant for her. He was that kind of person. The accident occurred when my dad and Grandpa were coming into the yard with a large wagonload of hay pulled by a team of horses. They passed under the telephone wires going into the house from the road. The telephone wires often got twisted together due to high winds, and when this happened the telephone was inoperative. Typically Mom would stew when the telephone wasn't working, and typically Dad would procrastinate on fixing it in spite of her nagging.

Telephones were not necessarily the most essential piece of equipment in a household in those days, primarily because of their limited power to make a call of any distance and because of their undependability. Like everything else, they operated on dry-cell batteries, which had to be replaced frequently.

Not everyone had a telephone, nor did everyone want one: wherever they were installed they were hooked up to a party line with about fifteen or twenty other households. There were no exceptions to this. Everyone on the line had their own code and with the little crank on the side of the big box mounted on the wall. To make a call, you send out a code for who you wanted to talk to. Our code was two long and three short rings. But of course, this same code rang on every telephone in the party line area. Although you were not supposed to, there were at least five or six people listening in on every conversation. If more people than that decided to listen in at the same time, there would be such a power drain that you could hardly hear anyone speak. Then you had to holler at people to get off the line.

This was a source of entertainment to a lot of people, and Mom was no exception. After all, there wasn't much else to do on the farm, and some of the households provided such juicy gossip, you would be sure to remember their codes. Where we lived, isolated from much of the world, it was the only way Mom had of finding out what was going on in the world, her world being the twenty- or thirty-mile radius of the party line.

On this particular warm summer day, ideal for bringing hay into the barn, Grandpa told Dad to stop the horses and he would try to reach up and untangle the telephone wires with a pitchfork from where he stood on top of the load of hay. No doubt he felt sorry for Mom because her pleas to get the telephone fixed were being ignored by Dad. Grandpa stood on the back edge of the hay load while Dad in the front of the load was telling him where to use the pitchfork to get the wires straightened out. Meanwhile, the horses, anxious to get into the barn and finish their day's work, suddenly lunged forward. Grandpa lost his balance and plunge to the ground.

I was watching all of this from the kitchen window and saw Grandpa fall. I came running out of the house and screamed at Dad who was paying attention to the horses and didn't even know that Grandpa had fallen. The driveway going into the yard was simply two deep wheel ruts with a hard ridge in between. Grandpa had fallen on his back across this hard ridge, breaking three or four ribs and puncturing one lung. This would not generally be a fatal accident in our time, with x-rays, hospitals, and surgery, but none of this was readily available back then. A doctor was called in Pine River, twenty miles away,—the telephone lines had been untangled and the telephone was now working. The doctor drove out to the farm (house calls were quite common at that time). The doctor taped Grandpa's back and ribs but this did little good.

Another doctor was called. He came to the farm and said the first doctor had taped him all wrong. By this time pneumonia had set in, and it eventually killed Grandpa. Malpractice might have applied here, but I don't know if there was even such a word then.

Grandpa apparently realized he was going to die so he insisted on going to see his son Charles in St. Paul. An ambulance or a hearse-type car was hired, and he was transported to St. Paul. It was a difficult trip and certainly must have been very painful for Grandpa. He died a couple days later at Uncle Charlie and Aunt Martha's house.

It was the first time I had ever seen anyone die or observed a dead body. Dead animals were no problem, but a dead person, and particularly someone so close to me, was very frightening and more than I could handle. I couldn't understand what was happening and nobody was able to explain it to me to my satisfaction. At that time it was the custom to have the funeral in the living room of the immediate family. So here was Grandpa lying in this fancy, long box with hundreds of flowers all over the room, looking very white and ghostlike. I took one look at this scene and wouldn't go near the room again. They tried to force me to attend the funeral, but I kicked and screamed and made such a fuss, they finally let me have my way.

Grandpa was buried at a cemetery in Wabasha, Minnesota, next to his wife Emma, although I am not sure about this. I was very sad and cried most of the way back to the farm, realizing for the first time that I would never see my Grandpa again. Neither would I be able to climb up on his lap at the end of the day, listen to his old German stories and fill his corncob pipe. Mom and Dad were not the type to let me climb on their lap and besides, they didn't smoke a corncob pipe.

MINNESOTA

Certificate of Citizenship.

OF AMERICA.

District Court, County of Wabasha,

State of Minnesota.

Be it Remembered, *That on the* 8 *day of* April *in the year of our Lord One Thousand Eight Hundred and Ninety* eight

Napoleon Nagels

appeared in the District Court, said Court being a Court of Record, having common law jurisdiction and a Clerk and Seal and applied to the said Court to be admitted to become

A CITIZEN OF THE UNITED STATES OF AMERICA,

pursuant to the provisions of the several Acts of the Congress of the United States of America, for that purpose made and provided and the said applicant having thereupon produced to the Court such evidence and taken such oaths as are by the said acts required. Thereupon it was ordered by the said Court, that the said Applicant be admitted, and he was accordingly admitted by the said Court to be

A CITIZEN OF THE UNITED STATES OF AMERICA.

In Testimony Whereof, *The Seal of the said Court is hereunto affixed this* 8 *day of* April *One Thousand Eight Hundred and Ninety* eight *in the* 123 *year of our Independence.*

Chas. J. Stauff *Clerk.*

By .... *Deputy.*

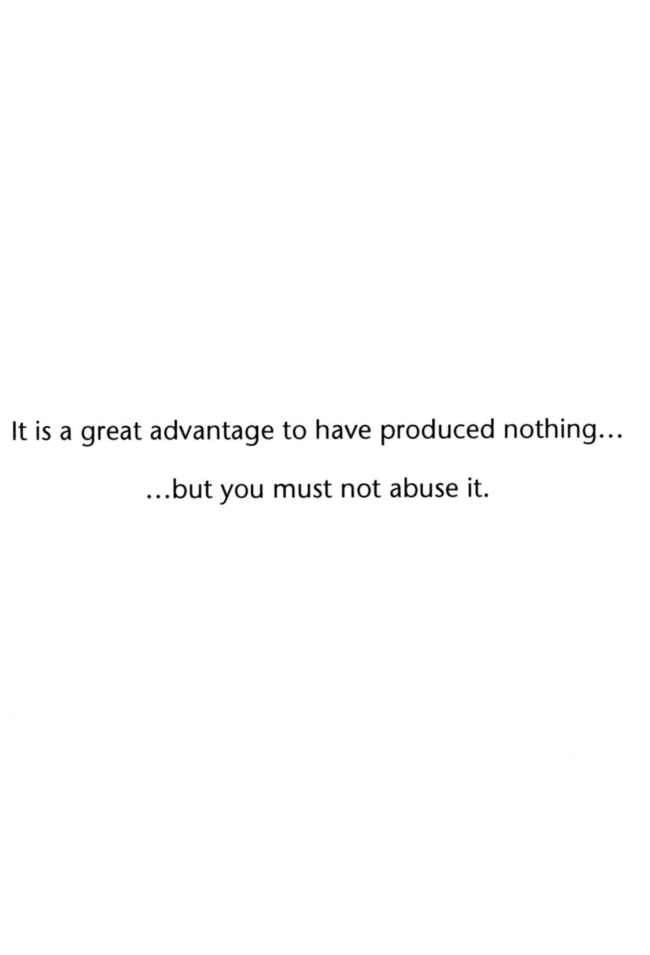

It is a great advantage to have produced nothing…

…but you must not abuse it.

Chapter 4

Beginning school is usually a big event in a child's life and this must have been a gratifying change from the quiet life you were living on the farm. Where were the schools in your area and what were they like?

THE LITTLE OLD COUNTRY schools were actually much better than you might imagine. I give all the credit to the true dedication of the teachers. The conditions they had to teach in were deplorable, but they had no union to run to and their patience was incredible. I can't say enough about the three different teachers I had in the little one-room country school.

Before turning to the subject of school, I would like to point out that there were some fun and memorable times on the farm, contrary to the desolate way I've made things sound up to now. I believe it's possible to accept most any circumstances or living conditions if you don't know any better.Prior to going to school, I was definitely not exposed to any different way of life. As someone once said, "You can even get used to hanging if you hang long enough."

Work was a way of life on the farm, but for me it wasn't hard labor like it was for Dad and Mom, and to some extent for my older brother. Oh, I had my routine household chores, plus carrying wood, pumping water, dumping ashes, feeding chickens, gathering eggs, and weeding the garden. Milking cows and shoveling shit was yet to come. During the summer days, at least, I spent as much time as I could outside, sitting up high with my dad on the tractor or other machinery. Dad was good about that, though maybe not as accident-conscious as he should have been.

Planting a garden, a hot bed for tomatoes, cabbage and a few other things, were some of the busy little tasks that kept me from being bored.

Just about anything you buy in a grocery store today, we tried to grow on the farm and it was exciting when something turned out successful. There were always many failures, but you couldn't afford to lose patience. We made things like different kinds of pickles, sauerkraut, horseradish, beer, root beer, wine, grape juice, and many other good things.

A colorful scene involving grape juice makes me smile as I remember it now. There was a fairly good arbor of concord grapes in the backyard that provided for many unsuccessful attempts at making wine, though we did make some delicious grape juice.

Once, during the winter when I was recovering from one of those long childhood sessions with the flu, Mom said, "Just tell me what you would like to eat and I will fix it for you."

I said, "I don't feel like eating, but I would like some grape juice."

Mom ordered Dad to go to the cellar to get some grape juice, but Dad said, "We finished the last bottle over a month ago."

Mom didn't accept this, and challenged Dad: "Go look in the cellar again. There must be some there someplace." Dad looked and sure enough he found an old bottle tucked back in a corner, one that was left over from several seasons before. He brought it up, sat it on the kitchen table, wiped a half inch of dust off the bottle and proceeded to remove the cork or whatever it was capped with.

What followed was a sight to behold, an explosion like an oil well gusher, not black but a beautiful purple grape juice color. How a one-quart bottle of juice could so thoroughly cover the kitchen ceiling and part of the walls, I will never know. The bottle did not break but it had been fermenting in there so long that every drop tried desperately to escape that container all at once. I could only stand back and laugh while it rained purple grape juice all over us.

The purple stain that penetrated the painted kitchen ceiling could never be removed in spite of our efforts. I know it was painted over and repainted several times with the water paint they called calsomine, but to no avail: the reminder of that colorful event came through the paint every time. Needless to say I never got my grape juice, but it was still the best medicine I could have received.

By the time I was six years old I had been ready to go to school for about two years, but rules were rules: no one was allowed to go to school until they had reached their sixth birthday. Because my older brother had now been going to school for three years, I had read his books, learned to write what he wrote, and even did some of his arithmetic. There was very little a first- or second-grader was doing that I had not already learned from my brother and could do for myself. It wasn't that I was any smarter than other five-year-olds, it's just that there wasn't anything else for me to do at home alone, and it was my challenge to prove to that I was ready for school.

In spite of my pleading, Mother said I wasn't allowed to go to school until I was six. I finally accepted this because the family promised that, on March 6, 1933, (when I would be six years old), my wish would be granted and I would be off to school. I know my parents had in mind that I wouldn't actually start until the following fall—the beginning of a regular school year—but they didn't have the courage to tell me that. Finally I prevailed.

After constant pressure on my mother, she had a visit with the teacher and the teacher reluctantly agreed. It was understood that I couldn't officially enroll in school, but the teacher would allow me to sit with the first graders even though I couldn't participate. Well, I didn't know I couldn't or shouldn't participate, so for the three months of March, April, and May, I dug in and made my way along with the three or four other first graders in the class. It was, in fact, woefully easy for me to compete. I could already read and write fairly well at that level, I knew my numbers, and I could do just about everything the other first graders could do because I had the advantage of learning from my older brother.

All this was not going to alter the position of the stodgy old school board or the teachers about my first grade status. Come next fall I would still be a first grader and that was that. It's hard to believe that I could be exposed to the bureaucracy of government and the school system at such an early age, but I have since learned it is unavoidable, and it becomes even more of an obstacle as life goes on.

A lucky break developed the next term when I got back to school in the fall, at least I think it was a lucky break. I was the only kid for the first grade class. I'm sure this wasn't the first time a similar situation had come before the school board, but apparently never before had they made an exception.

I'm not sure if the teacher, Mrs. Newman, tried to persuade the school board to make an exception and allow me to enroll as a second grader. All I know is that a couple days after school started, I was given the books and assignments right along with the second graders. Mrs. Newman was a hard-nosed individual in her fifties, with plenty of experience and probably could have arm-wrestled any school board member into allowing her to do what she wanted. But she also may have said, "to hell with them" and put me in the second grade without telling anyone.

By the time I got to third grade there was a new teacher and all the concern about what grade I should be in was forgotten. All my life I've had to lie when filling out forms where it asks how many years of school have you completed. I state "twelve" when it actually should only be eleven; I never completed the first grade. Someday I am going to have to go back to school and take first grade. I wonder if I could pass it. Don't answer that!

There has been a great deal of study done on the subject of allowing students to advance to the level they appear to be capable of regardless of their age, at least recently. Anyone can point to a number of brilliant scholars—the genius, the rocket scientist, or brain surgeon—to prove this is the right thing to do, but I was certainly not in that category and, as it turned out, it may not have been the right thing for me after all.

A major turning point in my life occurred while in the third grade, and with twenty-twenty hindsight it is easy to say it all happened because I was too young to compete at that school level. That may very well have been the case, but I personally don't think so. Physically I was tall enough but very skinny, and didn't have near the strength of other boys my age, or even the girls for that matter. I found this out one day when three third grade girls dragged me off into the woods behind the school. They wrestled me to the ground and two of them held me down while the other one took my pants down. All they wanted to do was look at my penis. They must have been disappointed because they let me up right away. Of course, they made all kinds of threats on my life if I told anyone what they had done.

In addition to being physically immature, I was extremely shy, sheltered and unexposed to the facts of life, well behind others at the same age or grade level. All through school, at least at the early stage, this was a problem and it all came down on me like a ton of bricks while in the third grade at age seven.

One day in late fall, Miss Rourick, now the new teacher of our little one-room school, was presiding over the third grade class in a reading session. I believe there was a total of five kids in the third grade including myself. The day before we had been given poetry pages to review, but unfortunately I had procrastinated and never got around to reading. Lo and behold, she called on me to get up in front of the class (or should I say the entire school) and read this particular poem.

Wait a minute! Never before had we ever been asked to stand up in front of the class, to read aloud. We were always allowed to do this sitting at our desks. This was a major departure, one for which I was not prepared.

I was very adequate in reading whether I had read the material before or not, and reading aloud was no problem, but this thing of standing up in front of twenty-five or thirty other students in the school, most of whom were much older than me, well I just didn't know how I could do that. Anyway I slowly wandered up to the front of the room and opened my book to the designated page. I can even remember some of the story yet today.

It was about Abou Ben Adam, an East Indian boy. Sounds like it may have been Kipling. It is a bit of a tongue-twister, particularly if you are nervous as I was. I made a stab at it and after a couple of tries I finally got the title out. And then I froze. Nothing would come out of my mouth.

I began to hyperventilate and the more I tried to talk the worse it got. I knew of two things that were about to happen, I was either going to cry or wet my pants. Either way juices were going to shoot out of my body someplace. Thank goodness they came out of the top rather than the bottom.

"Floyd," Miss Rourick asked, "What seems to be the matter?"

"I don't know, (sob, sob). I guess I'm just hungry, (sob sob)." Why I said that, I will never know. I wasn't any more hungry than our four-hundred-pound pregnant sow, but I couldn't think of anything else I could get out of my mouth between sobs. What a mess I was!

Miss Rourick, however, was a very compassionate person and sensed that I wanted to just get the hell out of there, and quick. "It will soon be lunch time," she said, "but why don't you go into the library and get a sandwich or something out of your lunch pail?" I ran and didn't stop to question if she really meant that or not, because ordinarily giving special privileges was not her style.

I couldn't believe what had just happened. I had broken down and cried in front of all those kids. A boy was not supposed to cry. I was conditioned that boys my age were just not supposed to cry regardless of how bad they were hurt or how ashamed they were. It was okay for girls to cry, but not boys.

The library was a small room, about eight feet by eight feet, in the corner of the building where everybody hung their coats and stored their lunch buckets on the shelves. It contained a few library books as well. I found my lunch pail and choked down a peanut butter sandwich. You know, there is nothing harder to force down your esophagus when you are crying than a peanut butter sandwich, but I made sure I ate something in case Miss Rourick checked. I locked myself in the library until just before lunch time, perhaps close to an hour, and before the noon recess I sneaked out and ran as fast as I could the two and one half miles home.

I was still sobbing when I got home, or maybe I started up all over again when I saw my mother. She used many different techniques to try and get out of me what had happened, but it seemed much too humiliating for me to even tell my mother. The next day I absolutely refused to go back to school. So after school was over, my dad had to drive Mom to school to talk to Miss Rourick. Both my dad and mom (especially my dad) had the kind of compassion that went something like, "You get your butt back down the road to that school house or it's going to be blistered with the buggy whip." I didn't care. The buggy whip could create blisters on your butt, but at that moment, I knew it would be less painful than facing all those kids in school.

Thank God for Miss Rourick. She had a better understanding of my problem than my parents would ever have, and said to my mother, "It's just a couple weeks before Christmas vacation. Why don't you let Floyd stay home after Christmas vacation? He'll feel much better."

At first my mom, as well as my dad (what do you know, they agreed on something) would not hear of such a thing. Finally Miss Rourick told my mom, "Your son could be having a nervous breakdown and unless we handle this properly he could end up with some serious disorder the rest of his life."

Nobody knew exactly what was meant by a "nervous breakdown," and whether I really was a candidate for one is hard to tell. I think Miss Rourick may have just made this up to get my mom's attention, because in that part of the country and at that time, people who were a little strange, (and there were plenty of them,) were diagnosed by their peers as having had a nervous breakdown sometime in their life.

Heaven forbid, I am sure my parents reasoned. *We can't have the neighbors talking about Floyd as having a nervous breakdown.* So I then got some attention and daily analysis by my parents of my behavior to prove to themselves that Miss Rourick didn't know what she was talking about. I was kept at home, in fact I was virtually quarantined at home, out of sight from anyone, just in case one of the neighbors might observe me and come to the conclusion that I was acting a little strange.

Christmas that year was a blur. All I could think about was the day when I eventually would have to go back to school and face my classmates again. Both Mom and Dad were getting annoyed with me hanging around the house. As my dad put it, "The boy belongs in school."

But I finally got Mom to go talk to Miss Rourick again and have her promise that I would never have to stand up in front of the school and read again. Miss Rourick agreed to this which was somewhat comforting, but I still had to face the other kids.

After Christmas vacation and a few days after school had started up again, Dad and Mom insisted I get back to school, apparently convinced there was nothing wrong with me. I fought them all the way but I had no alternative. Dad had to take me in the car and in spite of my pleading and begging, he pushed me out of the car and locked the door. I clung to the side of the car but he drove off and left me standing in the schoolyard alone and sobbing again. It was very cold out so as soon as I got my eyes dried I walked in.

What happened next was very strange, at least I thought so at the time. Not one of the twenty-five or thirty kids in the school ever brought up the incident I was so worried about. One or two kids asked where I had been, and I simply told them I had been sick, but nothing more was ever said. What I had thought was the most horrifying experience that ever happened to me apparently was no big deal to anyone else. Life went on as if it never happened, yet I could not erase the fear from my mind of what I would do the next time.

The school year ended with no further problems and I was happy. But then I learned during the summer that Miss Rourick, my lifesaver, was not going to return and teach the next year and was instead being replaced by a Miss Fisher. My worries started all over again: would this new teacher be as understanding? Would she make us get up and read in front of the entire school?

The day school started in the fall I arrived very early to meet Miss Fisher and to quiz her about her methods of teaching. Did she require students to read in front of the class? She was noncommittal, and even though she was never apprised of my problem, (at least I don't think she was) she never made this a requirement of anyone. She continued to be my teacher for the next three years until I was through the sixth grade.

Much was learned from this experience. The question must be asked whether or not it is a good idea to push an ordinary student with average intelligence, but woefully immature, beyond their expected grade level. In my case it would appear that this was not such a good idea, and perhaps it contributed to my problem. On the other hand, what this forced me to do at a very young age may have prepared me better than anything for life's challenges at a later date.

My phobia of public speaking, or whatever you want to call it, was still going to be there. But I had to face up to it, because in the seventh grade I would be starting school at Backus. When I started there, I took a bus to that huge school with a hundred or more kids in grades seven through twelve from all over the area. Surely the problem would present itself again. This sounds rather silly to someone like my little granddaughter, who probably has ten times that many kids in her school, with a couple hundred or more all in the first grade. Still, I bet she would understand my concern.

Sometime after starting the seventh grade, someone told me that the way to overcome fear of any kind was to do what you feared the most and continue to repeat doing it until it was no longer a fear. For example, if you were afraid of the dark, force yourself to go to sleep in a dark room every night. If you had a fear of water, jump in over your head every chance you get. If you are afraid of heights, keep climbing a ladder every day and a little bit higher each time. (I never did conquer that ladder business.)

This seemed to make sense, so whenever I got the chance, I raised my hand to orally respond in class to the teacher's questions. Not only did this help to overcome my public speaking phobia, but it impressed the teachers and good grades started to come easier. When I was finally called upon to do something in front of the class, I got through it and didn't even realize what I had accomplished.

From then on I did everything I could to be out in front of a group. Some natural leadership traits started to develop. I joined the choir. I was terrible at all sports but I could sing. As a freshman I was the lead singer in the male quartet. As a sophomore I became the president of the class, all of about twenty-five kids, which I held until I left Backus. In my junior year I had the lead role in our class play and during that same year I was elected president of the student council, which was a position normally only given to seniors.

None of this was an ego trip for me. It was all done with one thing in mind: to rid myself of this God-awful fear of speaking in front of a group. I doubt that I would have done any of this at all if not for that terrible experience back in the third grade. As my Grandpa might have said, "What makes you feel bad today may be the thing that makes you feel good tomorrow."

Murphy's Law: If anything can go wrong it will.

Murphy's Corollary: If nothing can go wrong it still will.

Murphy is an optimist.

Floyd

Chapter 5

Back to the earlier days of your childhood, you seem to parallel the arrival of the Great Depression in the late 1920s and early 1930s. How did this affect your life and life on the farm?

FROM THE TIME I can first remember, I know we were very poor and as I got older conditions only got worse. But this was not so much of a hardship as one might think, simply because we didn't know any better, and we were not exposed to many other people who had it any better. In fact we were the envy of some people in the neighborhood because of the house we lived in, probably bigger than any house within a thirty-mile radius, which gave the illusion of being better off. It was definitely an illusion.

During our more prosperous days (the early or mid-1920s), a large house was built, very large by northern Minnesota standards, replacing the old two-room log house of the original homestead. How my grandparents were able to build this big house I will never know. We must go back to the time they arrived in this area from Wabasha. Apparently my grandfather's brewery job allowed him to make some money. With a very frugal lifestyle, he was able to put some away for the day when he could start running his own farm. It was a goal for most European immigrants to become independent regardless of how meager this existence might be.

My grandfather apparently acquired this land through some incentive for immigrants to homestead and develop property in this desolate part of Minnesota. It may very well have been a land grant at very little cost or maybe even no cost to him. All he had to do was move his family there, build a house of some kind and prove that he could live off the land while developing it. Old movies portray how difficult it was for settlers to find a suitable plot of ground, build a log cabin and try to make a go of it facing one hardship after another. I'm sure my grandparents' venture to northern Minnesota was not unlike this, although I don't think fighting Indians was one of the hardships they had to endure.

The original two room log house was built from timber on the land where Christ and Emma, their two sons Ed and Charlie and their adopted daughter Lorena settled and began the task of making a home and developing the land. Apparently there was money left to buy some work horses, a few cows, a pig or two, chickens, some farm machinery, and then build the buildings necessary to house the animals and other things.

That was the way it was done if you were ever going to be successful. The animals came first and would be better cared for than the families. There was no car—no need for one because roads were virtually nonexistent. Furniture was maybe handmade or hand-me-down, and clothes were mostly handmade. Kitchen dishes, cooking utensils, and silverware were all moved with the families from wherever they lived before. In other words, all resources were devoted to what was necessary to sustain life, and for the advancement of the farm.

Whatever the master plan was, it never seemed to come together. Call it persistence or plain old German bullheadedness, they kept on going, waiting for the day when all their hard work and self-sacrifice would pay off. It never did.

The big house was obviously a goal of my grandfather's. Even though his wife died before he could get it built, it appears that he wanted to do the things for his two sons and adopted daughter that he never accomplished for his wife. Since his son Ed was destined to marry Lorena—and he was likely the son who would continue on with the farm—he wanted this house for them. In fact, there seems to have been a devotion on his part to enhance the life of his adopted daughter. Maybe there was some feeling of guilt, or at least a stronger effort was made to satisfy her needs as opposed to the two sons.

This was definitely not the case while Grandpa's wife was still living, because Emma and Lorena were not happy campers. Lorena, in Emma's mind, was simply the working female of the household and very possibly was adopted because a daughter of Christ and Emma's died shortly before Lorena was adopted. As far as Emma was concerned she deserved no privileges and less consideration than her two sons. Grandfather, I believe, was trying to correct this disparity.

Other buildings on the farm had been constructed before the big house. Exactly when and in which order I don't know, but they were all done with specific purpose to fulfill the needs for sustaining life of the animals and the future growth of the farm. The barn was large enough to hold about ten or twelve cows, three or four horses, and a bull who did nothing but eat, sleep, service his cow harem, and scare the dickens out of me when he was loose. The barn also had a large hay mow to store winter hay and straw which served as one of the fun places to play when I was a little kid. One of the other large buildings was a machine shed necessary to cover the farm machinery and protect them from the elements.

A second, much smaller barn was for the pigs, maybe some sheep, and the new calves being milk fed to be sold as veal. There was a chicken coop and another very tiny building called the smoke house. I only saw the smoke house used once, but when a hog was butchered, usually in the fall, one way of preserving the meat was to soak it in salt brine for a period of time and then hang it in the smoke house over a constantly smoldering oak log fire. Since the smoke house was closed up tight, the fire never flamed, but spewed out a considerable amount of smoke. After a few days it produced the best ham and bacon, which could be stored in a cool place for months.

We also had a food storage place called a root cellar, because that was where all the root vegetables from the garden were stored, such as potatoes, onions, carrots, and rutabagas. It was dug underground deep enough so that winter frost couldn't get to it, but if you didn't clean it out in the spring the remaining vegetables would start to rot and it would smell to high heaven. I never went into it because there were always lots of spiderwebs hanging from the ceiling and maybe a family of mice also spending the winter with their endless food supply. Jars of canned goods, bottles of home brew, wine, and other home-processed foods were always stored in the basement, where there was less danger of frost.

Another interesting building was the granary for storing grain used for feed or for sale if there was any excess. Coupled with the granary was an ice house, believe it or not, that was intended to store ice for use in the summertime. Ice was harvested from a lake in the middle of the winter and, if it was properly packed in the ice house under mounds of sawdust, it could be stored all summer. The biggest problem was that we lived a long ways from a lake, and to haul it home in the middle of the winter was a major undertaking.

There was only one summer that I can remember when we actually had ice, which was great because on some special occasions we could have homemade ice cream. We had an ice cream maker and it was always a mystery to me how you could make cream freeze by putting rock salt on the ice around the freezer and forcing it to melt. This special treat was very infrequent because it required a lot of cream and eggs, and those were things that could be sold. More obvious was the fact that Mother and Father didn't have a desire to spend time and material on things just to have fun. Then again, I guess it's pretty hard to have fun with someone you hate, and there wasn't much question about their feelings toward one another, even at this early stage.

Oh yes, we must not forget one of the most important buildings on the farm, the backhouse, referred to in the first chapter. It was a three holer, two large ones, and one small one for me that was just big enough so I wouldn't fall in. The thought of that still gives me chills.

The old Sears Roebuck catalogs could always be found there, and with a reasonable amount of conservatism the spring and summer catalog would make it until the fall and winter one appeared.

All these buildings were well constructed and painted the typical barn red with white trim. Most of the lumber for the buildings was produced from logs cut down on the farm land. Even so, the construction demanded many things you couldn't produce yourself, so there was still a great deal of expense involved. And for the big house, with a little class to it, a considerable amount of the building material had to be purchased.

It would seem obvious that some outside financial assistance was necessary. At this stage of the homestead settlement the property was developing into a workable, even profitable farm. So a loan from the bank was the logical source for the needed cash. This I know because I remember when the bank foreclosed on the property when the debt could not be repaid.

All this is a rather lengthy response to the question regarding the Great Depression, but it shows that the family was not in a position of poverty in the twenties and early thirties, at least it did not appear that way on the surface. If you were resourceful enough to raise a garden, can or preserve your own food, make your own clothes, cut down trees to heat your house, there was not a great deal of expense involved to sustain life. Income of any significant amount was always dumped back into the farm to produce more animals, more grain, more equipment, more buildings, etc. Sort of like reinvesting your dividends.

For some reason, however, these dividends began to get less and less. Now there was not only the need to forego the reinvestment of dividends, but to dip into our income-producing assets as well. In other words, grain had to be sold rather than used as feed for the livestock, which meant some livestock had to be disposed of. Eggs were sold instead of being used as food. Milk and cream had to be sold. Potatoes were raised as a sale crop, but they were not worth a lot.

Then there was another obstacle: you had to do all this with one hand tied behind your back, because the friendly banker who loaned you the money wanted it paid back. I have disliked bankers and mortgage companies ever since. Was this the result of the market crash and the Great Depression that followed in 1929? I don't think so.

The 1929 Crash and Depression had little to do with the family circumstances at that point, we were going to end up with economic disaster anyway. Perhaps the Depression was a catalyst for what eventually happened, or maybe a convenient excuse, but the farm failure had more to do with a defeatist attitude, poor management, and a seemingly concerted effort on the part of both my mother and father to work against each other in whatever goal they may have been trying to reach.

Sitting down to the family dinner was not the happy time it had once been. There was no longer the chicken dinner on Sunday as there used to be, unless Dad happened to run over one in the garage when he was parking the old car. Chickens used to dust themselves on the dirt floor of the garage, and with Dad's big feet he could never find the brake pedal just when he wanted to; the bulged-out back wall of the garage was evidence of that.

Earlier he had picked out an old hen that wasn't producing many eggs and chop her head off before she died of old age. This could be made into chicken soup or chicken and dumplings, which was one of my favorite dishes. Not any more. No longer was a young pig butchered for meat during the winter, and the smoke house didn't have that good smell of hams and bacon smoldering away. Our little pigs went to market, and we went wee-wee-wee all the way home.

No longer did we have those skin-on frankfurters, Mom's favorite, that were bought at Bailey's Meat Market when we drove into Backus, along with some fresh baked bread on Sunday mornings. The bread was still being made, but without butter. We were required to use pork fat on the bread, which I didn't like so I went without. Such luxuries were just not necessary. In fact, we couldn't even afford the luxury of driving to Backus anymore. Gas was too expensive (up to fifteen cents a gallon) and the tires were wearing out. Yes, the Depression was blamed for all of this or was used as the excuse anyway. But by damn we were not going to join the WPA (Works Progress Administration), the Democratic welfare program of that time, and get free handouts like most of the other people in the neighborhood were doing. We were going to make it on our own. I was kind of proud of my parents for their stubborn principles.

So how did we do on our own? Well, we had a lot of potato soup, made with skim milk, potatoes, and onions, and that's about all. To this day, I still have trouble eating potato soup, regardless of how well it may be made. Skim milk, you understand, was used rather than whole milk, not because it was less fattening, but because the cream had to be separated and sold for making butter. The hand cream separator, bolted to the kitchen floor, was the most used kitchen appliance and the cream, stored in cans and kept in a cool place, was picked up once a week by the creamery truck. In the summer time the cream got sour because we didn't have a good cool place to store it. But the creamery took it anyway and just gave us a lower price. Some of the skim milk was used for drinking or cooking and the rest went as slop for the pigs.

For some time there were a few other garden vegetables, but Mother was losing interest in maintaining a garden, so there wasn't the winter supply of sweet corn, beans, peas, tomatoes, or carrots there had once been. A couple dozen quarts of canned peaches was something we could depend on in the past, but we could no longer afford them.

Flour was cheap as long as you bought it in hundred-pound sacks: then Mom could make clothes, underwear at least, from the flour sacks. There was a brand of flour called "Sun Rise" with a picture of a big yellow sun rising over the horizon printed on the sack, and when this was laid out properly on the pattern the sun would appear on the back side of a pair of bloomers. A joke among the old farmers was, "When she bent over you could see the sun rise."

A lot of bread, pancakes, dumplings, and other things could be made from one hundred pounds of flour, so these items were worked into the menus quite regularly. If we ever got invited to someone's house for dinner, it was a real treat if they had something like roast beef or maybe a pork chop.

Winters were very long and dreary. We had two or three kerosene lamps for the entire seven-room house, which gave about as much light as my six-year-old birthday cake. If you wanted to use the light for reading you had to sit no more than a couple feet away.

One day someone gave Mother an Aladdin lamp, as they were called, and when we came home from school we were invited into the living room to see it lighted for the first time. It was amazing how much light it produced (probably no more than a forty-watt bulb), but we were thrilled to pieces. To us this was a big event in the household. Would that be a big event for our children today? Hardly. But it makes me feel very rich and lucky when I think about it now.

Then one beautiful warm summer day a large, flatbed semi-truck pulled into our yard: a most unusual occurrence indeed. I was impressed but could only watch from inside the house. Mom and Dad were not impressed—depressed, more likely. Dad went to the door and talked to the two men from the truck and then simply came back in the house. He sat in his usual chair and didn't say a word. Watching out the window, I saw one of the men start the tractor and drive it up the ramps they set up on the back of the semi flatbed.

"What's going on Dad?" I asked my father. "Why are these men loading up our tractor on to the truck?"

Dad just looked at me and didn't say a word. Mother finally said, "You're too young to understand." True, I was too young to understand the entire picture then, but later I would. Our tractor had just been repossessed, and soon I realized that this was the beginning of the end.

Whether or not this economic setback was the direct or indirect result of the Great Depression makes little difference, but was it also one of the elements that led to the deterioration of the marriage of Ed and Lorena? I can say without hesitation that our very poor economic status at this point and the further decline that followed had very little, if anything, to do with the ultimate separation of Mother and Dad. My overall view of their relationship was that their marriage was doomed from the beginning, and it became the goal of each of them to sever their ties at some date when it seemed respectable to them to do so.

So why did they get together in the first place? It was not just the proper thing to do in those days: it was the only thing to do. As I mentioned earlier, it probably started with a tumble in the hay, maybe once, maybe twice, maybe a dozen times. No one will ever know and so what, it is nothing so very unusual. Mom was not a bad looking chick and Dad was a big strapping young man. I doubt that either one ever experienced sex with anyone else before and I doubt that they knew very much about how babies are produced or, at least, how to prevent them from being produced. It happened and when it happened you got married as quick as you could, no ifs, ands or buts. The sad part is I don't believe there ever was any love before and certainly not after they were forced to marry.

Sometimes a newborn child may be the right prescription to rekindle the dawning love in a marriage, but it is hardly a solid formula for getting love started if there wasn't anything there to begin with. Nevertheless, little Douglas was well accepted. After all he was a boy and all German men wanted their firstborn to be a boy. Dad loved his son and allowed him to do just about anything he wanted to on the farm, because it was the usual hope that the sons would inherit the farm and carry on the traditions, it had been done in the last generation and the generation before that, and on and on.

This didn't help the marriage, though. I'm sure it was Mother's intention to make the best of her mistake, put up with Ed until her child was old enough to be on his own, and then split. I don't believe she ever had or ever expected to have any hope for the marriage. After all, she didn't really a model for a successful marriage. Maybe this was as good as it gets.

Things were going along pretty good and then—damn, how could this happen? She got pregnant again. Sorry about that, Mom. I know you didn't want me to begin with but I'm certainly glad you did what you did, and I hope I eventually provided you with a little happiness.

Once again this apparently was the way these things were supposed to be, and what could you do about it anyway? Furthermore, this gave Mom the chance to have the daughter she always wanted.

About this time Mother found out about her sisters. By way of her Aunt Emma Snow, Mother was sent a picture of her sister Florence in California. As a result, Mother decided her baby would be named Florence. Maybe the newborn would be beautiful and famous also. She was so sure that it would be a girl that no boys' names were even considered.

My arrival must have been a real downer, although nothing of this was ever directly confessed to me in later years. They did admit that the hospital had to push my parents to come up with a name to put on my birth certificate, and thank God Mother got off the Florence handle. Floyd was apparently the closest thing to Florence she could think of, and Dad didn't care much one way or the other. I believe the doctor also carried out a little surgical routine at the request of Mother, to ensure no more unwanted children would be added to the family.

Winter is still pretty severe in northern Minnesota by the 6th of March, and 1927 apparently was no exception. I'm told that I was brought home by horse and sled during a blizzard. I doubt that it would have been all the way from Sebeka, over twenty miles away, but it would have been at least several miles since it was usually quite dangerous and most often impossible to travel by car during a snowstorm in our remote area of the country.

I don't know if it was because of my mother's strong desire to have a girl, but in a lot of ways I know I was treated more like a girl than my brother was. I was kept in the house more, I did girl things like helping to make cookies, bread, playing with cooking dishes, while my brother did all the outside things. That was okay with me: I had no desire to wade around in the cow shit up to my knees like my brother did.

The repossession of the tractor was just the beginning of the financial disasters to follow. A tractor is a most essential piece of equipment on the farm, particularly if you do not have work horses to take its place. Any farm needs about six good work horses to take the place of one tractor, and then how much you can work them and the kind of farm implements you can use are limited. We had only two mediocre work horses. They could be used to pull a sled, wagon, cultivator, mower, rake, or a one-furrow plow. A tractor could pull a three- or four-furrow plow, which means it would take three or four times as long to plow a field with a team of horses. And, of course, you couldn't work horses twelve to sixteen hours a day like you could a tractor. A grain binder, a combine, a corn picker, and other field jobs were simply out of the question with only one team of horses, and anyway there was no money to acquire any more horses.

We were forced, therefore, to change our type of farming from grain to livestock. Jobs like sawing wood, grinding corn, or pulling out stumps and rocks had to be hired out or somehow done by hand. A dairy or meat producing farm didn't require the use of a tractor as much as a grain farm, although the machine age cycle was also beginning to effect these farms as well.

A family of two adults and two kids doing as much work as possible could only milk so many cows and take care of the feeding and shit shoveling that went along with this, which limited the size of the operation. Farms with electricity were now using milking machines and utilizing equipment for feeding and cleaning; a farm of our size, without electricity, could in no way compete. Prices were declining as productivity went up, so unless you could produce more volume, you were left behind. What were we to do?

It took years of decline before our parents would begin to see the writing on the wall. Couple that with a sizable degree of stubbornness and it spelled disaster, failure, and frustration. This added immensely to the weight of the cross to bear. How long can one accept the blame for your failure without coming apart? How long can you go without the bare necessities of life without asking why, without blaming someone other than yourself? It gets your attention to continually bang your head against the wall, but it also hurts.

The hurt turned into hatred. Mother was a nagger, always pointing out everyone's mistakes, casting blame for each failure. She could drive anyone berserk. Dad was a quiet one, a brooder, a procrastinator, yes, but he would simply blow apart when the pressure got too great. He was a very big man, exceptionally strong. He had a loud voice and could not argue without swearing every third word. He wanted desperately to use his strength to replace his inability to respond to an accusation, but somehow was able to control it without lashing out and hurting somebody or something, for the most part anyway.

I don't think he ever laid a hand on Mother or one of us kids, but he could take his frustration out on the farm animals. I saw him beat a cow with a club, where the cow was locked in a stanchion and couldn't escape, until the cow literally laid down and bawled. One particular cow, although a good producer, did not like to be milked and would occasionally kick the pail and the person milking her across the barn floor. It was always after she was almost completely milked and the pail was nearly full that she decided to unload. The milk would go flying and Dad would slide in the cow-shit-filled gutter. It looked funny at first, until Dad got up and beat the poor cow unmercifully.

Dad would put shackles on the cow's hind legs so that she could not kick without falling down, but then the cow learned how to kick with both legs tied together, providing Dad with more excuses to beat her. One day Dad shot the cow.

"Why did you shoot old Bessy, Dad?" I asked.

"She broke her leg," he replied. "She can't live with a broken leg and we can't sell her, so we're going to have her butchered."

The next day a butcher came out from Backus, strung up the cow with a block and tackle from the peak of the barn roof, butchered her, and bought the meat, probably made it all into hamburger. We only kept the liver, but I couldn't eat any of it. I swear Bessy didn't break her leg accidentally.

Most people saw my father as a very gentle man, and I believe he really was once he was separated from Mother. But how was a seven- or eight-year-old boy supposed to know that his father would not do something to Mother similar to what he did to the cow, or to one of his kids? The thought of killing each other seemed to be on the minds of both of my parents, and it was not just my imagination. Common sense might not have considered this a serious possibility, but who can predict what a vicious temper will do in a given set of circumstances?

I recall one instance when Mother kept badgering Dad about one thing or another. "If you weren't so damn stubborn and bullheaded you would talk to the banker about extending the loan."

"It won't do no good."

"The banker probably thinks you're too damn lazy to come in and talk to him," Mother continued. "You're too damn lazy to fix this or that. You're too damn lazy to shave your ugly face." He shaved every Sunday, no more, no less. "You're too damn lazy to go out to the can so you fart in bed all night."

Dad would counter with, "By God you wouldn't be saying that if I had a club in my hand."

Any time Dad lost his temper with anyone, he would always say, "It was a good thing there wasn't a club I could have got my hands on." I know he never used a club on anyone or ever would, except the cow, but how was a young kid with these wild thoughts supposed to know that?

After the threat with the club, Mother said, "If you weren't too lazy to get your fat ass off that chair, you could go out and find a club."

With that Dad jumped up, grabbed the chair he was sitting on and slammed it down on the floor. It broke into several pieces and he was left with the splintered chair leg still in his hand. A club. He now had the club he wanted to use on Mother. I ran and hid. No blows were landed, of course, but Mother did shut up. The next day Dad spent the entire morning wiring the chair back together again.

I would eavesdrop on all their bitter battles every chance I could until I was too scared to listen anymore. How could I help but think the worst was going to happen. Dad listened to a radio program called "True Detective Stories." Today you are reminded many times not to allow your children to watch violence on TV, but no one told my parents that kids should not be listening to the gruesome violence portrayed on the radio. The programs were vividly dramatized, with very good sound effects. You could hear the knife slashing someone's throat and the blood bubbling out while the victim gasped for breath. Nightmares were common for me, mainly because I knew something like this was going to happen to one of my parents.

On one occasion after a tirade from Mother, Dad said, "Some day you are going to find yourself at the bottom of the well." Sure enough, that is exactly what happened to a man's wife on one of the "True Detective Stories."

Our well had no water in it, but it was dug down about twenty feet with a board frame to keep it from caving in. When it was determined that it was impractical to dig down far enough to find water, the well was finished by drilling the rest of the way. In total it was nearly one hundred feet down to the water level. Boards covered the platform on top of the well where the long handled pump sat, but should anyone be dumped down this hole, they might not be found for months.

On another occasion, Dad was trying to get the gas lantern to work and Mother was nagging about why he waited until it got dark to fix it. It seemed to always be out of order, plus the fact it was dangerous to operate if it wasn't working just right or if you really didn't know what you were doing. After a period of frustration over not being able to get it working, along with continuous nagging by Mother, Dad got up and threw the lantern against the wall on the other side of the kitchen.

"My God you stupid fool," Mother screamed. "You'll burn the house down."

Dad replied, "Well I'll make sure you're still in it if I do." My imagination told me I would probably be in it too.

After one huge argument Mother told Dad, "You better check your oatmeal in the morning because I found where you hid the rat poison." Poisoning was also a frequent method of murder on "True Detective Stories."

All night long I thought about this, and the next morning everyone had forgotten about the threat except me. Mom dished up the oatmeal for everyone, except she didn't take any. She said she wasn't hungry. *Oh, oh,* I thought, *this is it. She is going to do us all in.* I made some excuse that I wasn't feeling good and didn't eat any oatmeal. Even though I was hungry I didn't get anything else to eat. Going hungry was my choice.

Would Mom or Dad go so far as to kill each other? No, I don't think so, that is, *now* I don't think so. I think it is possible however, for a normal sane person to be trapped in such a web of hatred and hostility, and be provoked to the point of doing something abnormal, yes, even homicide. It does happen.

When spring came it was usually a happier time of the year, except for this spring the second ax fell. The bank foreclosed on the farm and we were forced to move to the little house on the small farm, the farm originally planned for Uncle Charlie and his family.

If you want to be a man

If you can keep your head, when all about you are losing theirs and blaming it on you,

If you can trust yourself when all men doubt you, but make allowance for their doubting too,

If you can dream and not make dreams your master. If you can think and not make thoughts your aim,

If you can meet with Triumph and Disaster and treat those two impostors just the same,

If you can make one heap of all your winnings and risk it on one turn of pitch and toss,

And lose and start again at your beginnings and never breath a word about your loss,

If you can walk with crowds and keep your virtue, or walk with kings nor lose the common touch,

If neither foes nor loving friends can hurt you, if all men count with you but none too much,

If you can fill the unforgiving minute with sixty seconds worth of distance run,

Yours is the earth and everything that's in it, and, which is more, you'll be a man, my son!

THE FORDSON TRACTOR GOT REPOSSESSED

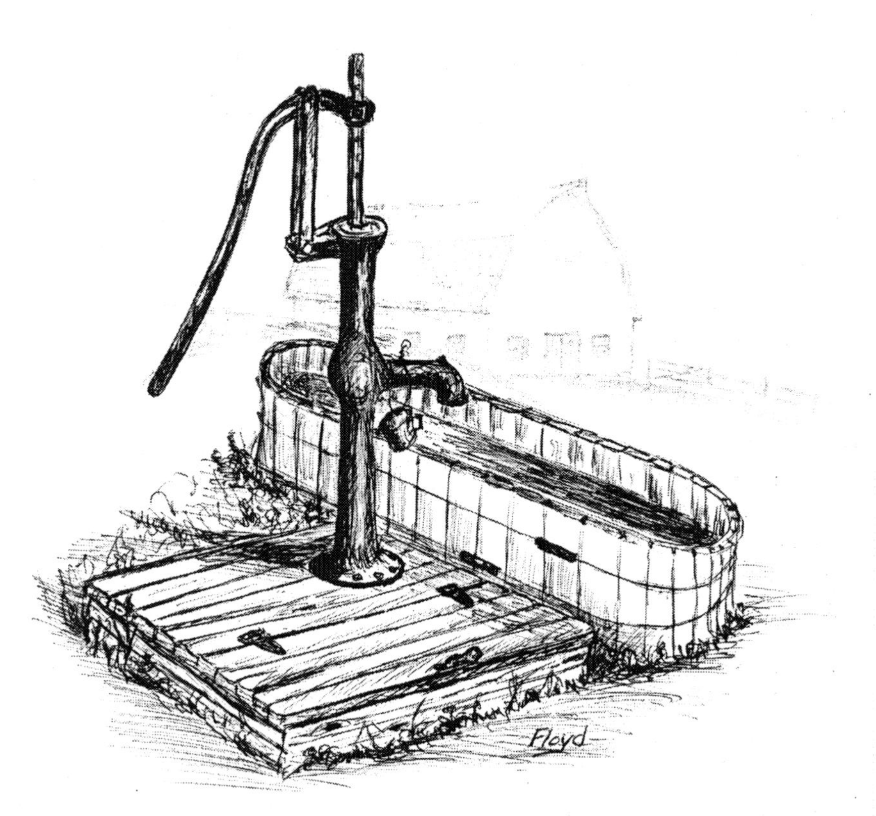
Floyd

Chapter 6

Earlier you stated that it was your grandfather's intention to leave the large farm to your dad, because he stayed home and continued farming, but the small house was to be your Uncle Charlie's, even though he had left home to work in St. Paul. Although this desire may not have been in writing, how was the bank able to separate the two properties, and did your family have the privilege of moving to the small farm after losing the big one?

PRIOR TO THE ACTION by the bank, some negotiation went on but I had no idea what was happening. Dad made a few trips to the bank in Backus. I would go along, but was made to sit out in the lobby while Dad and the banker went into the back room. Neither Mother nor Dad told me what was going on. I was considered too young to understand such things. All I knew was that Dad and Mother were always bitter and gloomy after a visit to the bank.

One day a fancy car pulled into the yard and I was very excited because it was a visit from my Uncle Charlie, Dad's brother, and my Aunt Martha from St. Paul. They were very kind to me when I was at their house for Grandpa's funeral, and I thought a great deal of them. I thought they were rich. Actually they lived in a very poor area of St. Paul. Charlie worked for the railroad as a yard man, but by means of a conservative lifestyle, they acquired some nice things, and once in a while purchased a new car.

On this particular day they were not in a friendly mood. They hardly talked to me. I was sent into the house and Mother and Dad talked to them in the front yard. They refused to come into the house. After a couple hours of conversation—Aunt Martha did most of the talking—they got back into their car and left for St. Paul. I thought this was very strange indeed, but once again I got no explanation from my parents.

There may have been two separate deeds on the properties and the bank had their mortgage only on the large farm, by far the more valuable of the two. The small farm was free and clear. Or, the bank may have had a mortgage on both properties, with two separate deeds, or there may have been only one deed. In the foreclosure process, Dad may have negotiated a separation of the properties and the bank only took over the large farm.

Mother or Dad may have written to Charlie and Martha to explain what was happening, or it is possible that the bank contacted them, which would have made it a more unhappy surprise. Either way, Aunt Martha and Uncle Charlie were very disturbed about the situation. Later on in life it was hinted in local gossip that Ed and Rena as much as stole the property that rightfully belonged to Charlie, but it doesn't look like anything was ever done about it, if in fact this was the case.

The only thing I was ever told was that we were moving to the small farm. This was indeed a big disappointment to me, to leave the big house and all the other fun buildings on the big farm, and move to a place where there was only a small house and absolutely nothing else. We tried to make it as exciting as possible. After the die was finally cast, amazingly my parents' attitude became a little more positive.

Speaking of stealing, I don't know if it was legal or not, but a couple of buildings were actually taken from the big farm and moved to the smaller place. The machine shed was moved to the small farm. It was a large building but not heavy, so it could be pulled down the road on rollers by a team of horses, with the car pushing from behind.

The shed was more or less rebuilt and converted into a barn large enough to accommodate a team of horses and about eight milk cows. A ceiling was put in to hold a small quantity of hay which helped to keep it warm and supply a couple months of feed during the winter. A well was dug inside the barn to provide water without the cows going outside. It was an adequate barn.

We also "stole" the backhouse (a most important building) and parts of another building that we used to construct a garage. A small building used as a pig shed may also have been taken. No one seemed to complain about it, or maybe they just didn't know. It seemed odd, although it might have been legitimate.

A shed was built out of poles and straw to house the sheep in the winter. Dad planned to give up a lot of the farming routine of the past and concentrate on raising chickens, a few sheep, a couple of pigs, and a few milk cows. None of these required a great deal of work or machinery.

Someone sold Dad on the idea of raising capons from male chickens, as there was a big market for them and he would make lots of money. A capon is simply a castrated rooster. For that reason a rather decent chicken coop was built with a raised wood floor and a low-down window where the sun streamed in from the south. A barrel stove was put in for heat.

The little chicks were purchased from a mail order breeding house and shipped to us by rail. About ten percent died en route. About half of the remaining were male chicks and half were females, so out of a purchase of about two hundred chicks, there were probably ninety potential capons. The females were raised until they were big enough to be fryers and then most of them were sold. Some were kept for producing eggs.

The process for castrating a young rooster was simple but extremely crude. A man showed Dad how to do it by putting a string loop with a weight on it around the chicken's wings and then another string loop with a weight on it around their feet. Then you stretched the chicken across a wide board with the weights on either side. This exposed their body between the wings and their legs. Then you cut a little slit in their side about a half inch or so and you searched inside the body for a little pink pea and cut it out. You did this on both sides, put a little disinfectant on the wounds and turned the nutless chicken loose. Dad was supposed to have done this himself, but after he butchered a few young chickens with his big hands, he gave up and got someone else to do it.

The chickens that survived this gruesome surgery grew into birds of enormous size in a short time. They were as big as turkeys. For a while the market was big on capons, but then, as the big producers got involved, it was no longer a profitable venture for a backyard chicken farmer. Naturally, as the neutered chickens grew they ate a tremendous amount of food, which Dad hadn't considered in the equation. After one chicken season Dad gave up on it. I believe you can still find capon in some meat markets today, but they are not that popular.

In spite of all this, there seemed to be just a little bit more money available after moving to the small farm. From what I gather, the property was free and clear: not much income, but also no debts. To my knowledge, my dad never bought anything without paying cash from that day forward. He had learned a hard lesson and did without rather than have a debt of any kind.

Mom wanted the new little house fixed up and Dad, unbelievable as it was, seemed to go along with it. They bought linoleum for the kitchen and a few gallons of paint. Maybe there was some effort, a half-assed effort at least, to get their marriage back together again. Try as they might, it was not to be.

Dad started to paint the south side of the house where the sun dried out the wood but he soon found that many of the boards were rotten and had to be replaced. I am certain the house had never been painted. It was built for Charles and his first wife, and when she died it was never finished and never used. It had no paint on the exterior, no finish on the plaster on the inside, or any of the necessary amenities. So each week Dad would buy some more siding boards and a couple gallons of paint. The dry wood really soaked it up. After about three hundred feet of siding and about six or seven gallons of paint, the south end of the house was done. Then Dad gave up. Nothing more was done to repair the house.

The money supply, meager as it was, once again dried up and the marriage, whatever trickle of compatibility that had surfaced, also dried up. It was back to fighting and cursing and the scary threats of deadly harm, maybe even more severe than in the past. My hopes of their survival, my survival and everything around us vanished. Even our dog, my best friend, was hit by a car on the road and killed. At this point I didn't care if they killed me while they killed each other.

But then something happened that gave hope for changing things. Change they did.

The bank that foreclosed on the bigger farm was now in a position to lease it. New neighbors moved in, Frank and Emma Paul. (Emma must have been a popular girl's name early in the twentieth century.) I have no idea where they came from, but they were very nice people, hard working and eager to make a go of it on the farm that our family couldn't. They had a daughter named Blanche, about a year younger than I was. Blanche was really "blanch." The word to describes a method of cooking vegetables, changing their appearance and making them limp without being overcooked. That may not be totally correct, but Blanche was like a limp vegetable.

At this point in my life I had never had a friend of any kind, boy or girl, that lived anywhere in our vicinity. Although I would much rather have seen a boy my age move onto our old farm, a girl would have to do. She was no raving beauty, even I knew that much. Her mother used a hot iron curler on her colorless hair that didn't curl, only crinkled it. The end result was a head of hair that stood straight out from the scalp and looked like Little Orphan Annie after she had just said "Leapin' lizards!" Emma did the same thing to her own hair and she looked like an old Little Orphan Annie, except it was black hair, a very solid cold black, and she was even less of a raving beauty. Other than that Emma was totally colorless.

Frank Paul, a Bohemian, was the handsome type, the type Mother always dreamed about, with dark hair, dark skin, and a big white toothy smile. He was a very friendly person but kind of shy. Dad also got along with the new neighbors, although it was difficult for him to accept the fact that his old farm was now taken over by someone who would make a success of it. Mother was just bubbly.

Things worked out well. During the summer the two families got together, had horseshoe parties and made bonfires to disburse the mosquitoes. During the winter they played a card game called "500," which was also festive. Whatever games they played, Frank and Mother were always partners and Dad was stuck with Emma. Poor Dad. They drank home brew and had coffee and cake or something before they went home. I always tagged along and everyone seemed to have a good time.

I learned to play 500 at about eight or nine because Emma didn't like to play cards that well. I would sit in and be Dad's partner. I got to be rather good at the game. In fact, there was a big 500 tournament in Backus once that Frank, Emma, Mom, and Dad entered, and because Blanche and I were too young to stay home alone, we went along. It turned out that one of the participants didn't show up at the tournament; they were a player short to make up sets of four at each table. There were at least ten or twelve tables. Mother said, "Floyd can play 500," and even though they were reluctant to allow this little kid to play in an adult tournament, they finally did. Everyone maintained their own personal score and you changed partners on a prearranged schedule. Well, I ended up winning the tournament, which made headlines in a regional newspaper of that area. "NINE YEAR OLD BOY WINS BACKUS 500." It sounded like I was a race car driver and had just won a five-hundred-mile race at Backus.

While our folks were out playing horseshoes, Blanche and I would sometimes play in the house. We would go upstairs and wrestle in one of the bedrooms on a straw tick bed. (A straw tick mattress was simply a big sack filled with straw that you slept on, not very comfortable when a straw was sticking through into your side, but it was warm even though it kept you scratching.)

One Sunday afternoon Blanche and I were wrestling—she was pretty strong for her age—and the sun was pouring through the window on to the bed, making it very warm and relaxing. Suddenly I felt something strange down in my pants. Could it be? I'll bet I was getting what I'd heard some of the big boys talk about in school—a hard-on!—glory be! If I had ever experienced anything like this before, I didn't recall, but with a girl next to you, this was a very new experience. We kept on wrestling and I put a move on Blanche that caused her hand to slip down by my groin. She immediately jumped back and got a strange look on her face. "Have you got a candy bar in your pocket?" Then she must have figured out the answer to her own question because she got up and said, "I don't want to wrestle anymore."

I suppose that means I was guilty of my first attempt at sexual harassment, a term never heard of at that time. But, hey, I was only ten. We never did wrestle again, in fact we didn't play much together at all after that. Blanche went back to being a limp vegetable. That's okay: there will be other "candy bars."

Mother, who never did much in the line of farm work except help milk cows, was suddenly becoming enthusiastic about working in the fields, driving the horses, racking hay, building haystacks, and so on. Charming Frank was the reason. They seemed to always be paired off working together as a team. Dad and Douglas were another team, but Emma seemed to stay around the house, like Mother used to do.

One day the Rena-and-Frank twosome were finishing with a haystack, with Mom on the top and Frank down below. He had to help her down from the tall hay stack, but they didn't know that I was watching from around the corner. Frank reached up with his hand and let Mom brace her foot on it while she slid down. Well, Frank's hand just happened to slip and it went up Mom's dress along her thigh. Mother never wore anything but dresses even while working in the fields. He held his hand there for a while, she giggled, they hugged and then he kissed her on the lips. Mom giggled some more. Wow! Sure hope Dad isn't watching. He would kill Frank, and Mom too no doubt—if he had a club in his hand, that is.

After that I paid particular attention to Frank and Mother and there were a few other similar instances. A couple of times when the card game was at the Pauls' house, Dad walked home by himself afterwards, but Frank would bring Mother home in his car. A real gentleman, that Frank was. My bedroom window was right by the driveway in the front yard, and though it was very dark, I was awake and would watch what was going on. They were kissing in the car.

My sex education was limited to watching a couple of horses go at it (which was awesome), and looking at a Whiz Bang comic book that some of the bigger boys had at school. If they rated comic books, these would receive a triple-X rating for sure. I still didn't know how babies were made or what actually took place in sexual intercourse. I had never heard of the term "having an affair," but I have no doubt now that's what Frank and Mother were doing.

I don't see how Dad could have not been aware of what was going on. He probably was, but right at that point he didn't seem to care anymore. Emma, on the other hand, may not have suspected a thing. She was one of those hard-working, dull farm ladies, oblivious to what was going on around her. Although she too may have figured out Frank's philandering, she was smart enough to realize that she and Blanche would not have an easy time finding another nest.

If I really knew for sure what was going on then, I believe I still would have said, "So what?" It was the first time in my life that I had seen my mother happy. She had finally met a man she really liked, who liked her and was giving her some attention; something to look forward to in her life.

So Mom, I know you went through a period of hell living with a guilty conscience, because, after all, having a relationship with another man was one of the unforgivable sins carved in stone, probably found right alongside the Viking Rune Stone from that part of the county. But even though I was still very naive about such things, I was happy for you, Mom. You were a totally different person: joyful, energetic, enthusiastic, walking around with a smiling face, not nagging Dad so much, and even making a batch of cookies once in awhile.

Dad no longer wanted to participate in the card games or horseshoes, and he didn't share in the field work with Frank. In fact, he and Frank didn't speak to one another any longer. This made it difficult for Mother and Frank to get together, for if they did it would have been too obvious. Their relationship cooled a little, at least for a while.

During all of this, Mother moved out of the bedroom and was sleeping on a little homemade cot in the living room. She and Dad were no longer fighting much because they were not speaking to each other at all. This was even scarier because I was sure they were now quietly plotting how they were going to kill each other. Doug and I were the messengers between them.

"Tell your dad dinner is ready," she would say, even if he was only fifteen feet away. "Ask your dad if he will pick up some flour when he drives into Backus."

Dad may have heard this and would say, "Tell your mother I am not going to town. There is a flat tire on the car."

After repeating this to Mother, she would say to no one in particular, "I wish he would get off his ass and fix the damn tire. He sure as hell will complain if there is no flour to make bread."

Everything came to a head in the spring of 1939. One day a car pulled into the yard with a man and a woman in it. Mother came out of the house and talked to them briefly, then she called me over from where I was watching. She said, "Floyd, this is Mr. and Mrs. Peterson," or whatever their names were. "They own the hotel and restaurant in Pine River and they want me to be their cook for a while."

I didn't say anything, still very shy, but I wondered what "a while" meant—a week, a month, two months, or what. I had no idea when she would return home again, although I am certain she knew all along: never.

I had just turned twelve, and by all standards a very immature and inexperienced twelve, but I was old enough now, in my mother's mind at least, that she could leave home without making it a guilt trip for herself.

"Tell your dad to bring you kids in to see me after I get settled," she said. Dad was not home at the time, Doug was in the house and she apparently told him the same thing. She went back in the house and came out with a suitcase already packed. She had had this all planned without our knowledge and was going to wait until the last minute to tell us.

When Mom left, sitting in the back seat of the car from Pine River, there was just a simple "good-bye," no tears, no kisses, I don't even recall a hug, and she was gone—never to return again. I remember feeling very sad, alone and crapped on by what I sensed was the beginning of the end, but I also knew this was the best for everyone concerned. In fact I hoped she wouldn't return, because now it would be more difficult for Mom and Dad to kill each other. Maybe the nightmares would go away.

Once the toothpaste is out of the tube...

...It is awfully hard to get it back in.

Chapter 7

You don't talk about your brother a great deal during the period of crises with you parents. What was his attitude? How did he perceive their constant battles and threats on each other?

YES, I DO WANT to bring Doug into the picture, but before I do, it should be known that around home, my brother was never referred to by that name. Mother insisted that he be called "Douglas" and I would be severely reprimanded if I called him anything else. I think I was at least forty years old before I ever called him to his face by the name of Doug, and even then it seemed a bit clumsy. Yet, outside the family, among all his friends or anyone he ever met, there wasn't a soul who didn't immediately call him Doug.

For people like Douglas MacArthur or Douglas Fairbanks, it seems natural that they should be called Douglas, but Doug Wachs was no MacArthur or Fairbanks. He was an old shoe, and speaking of that, he had the biggest feet of anyone I have ever known. Long before he reached his full stature of six feet three, he wore a size 13 or better.

Perhaps formal nomenclature, of Douglas rather than Doug, had something to do with the tremendous respect and admiration I had for my big brother. Regardless, he was my idol, my role model. I wanted to do everything he did, to be as good as he was and to be liked by friends the way his friends liked him. He was my hero in so many ways. No, not a sports hero: Doug was no athlete by any stretch of the imagination. Come to think of it, that is one area where I was quite successful in copying my brother. I didn't come close to becoming an athlete in any sport either. I guess it must be in the genes and I am sorry if I've passed some of these genes on to my children or grandchildren. But who said you have to be good in every room of the house?

One of my true regrets in life is that, in spite of my admiration for my brother, I never really got close to him, even after we left the farm and had our own families. The fact that I couldn't refer to him as Doug, as my friend as any other friend would, even behind my mother's back, maybe that had something to do with it.

I believe he was just disgusted with the way things were going on the farm, for which I don't blame him, and wanted as little to do with the family as possible, and that included me.

The four-year difference in our age may have also been a factor, particularly when we were young. Mother had to force Douglas to play with me because I always bugged her for something to do and she got tired of it. It was the easiest solution for her, but I could sense his resentful attitude. I always wanted to play with cars, or puzzles, or simple games, but he was too old for that. He wanted to be outdoors, chopping wood, feeding the cows or the pigs, or riding that Godforsaken stinking manure wagon.

With the exception of a few mosquito- or wood-tick-free weeks of summer, I was content to stay in the house and do things. These differences were certainly enough for Doug to seek out other friends rather than count on me, and I accept that. The fact that we were not close is more my fault than any shortcoming on his part.

Doug was very outgoing around other people, but at home he was quite the opposite. He spent his time outdoors, alone, as much as he could: in the woods, in the barn or other buildings. He was a dreamer. When I would get desperate for something to do and needed my brother, I would spend a half day or more looking for him and eventually find him up in the barn hay mow, back in a corner reading a book, or working on some piece of junk from the garage, or just hiding someplace doing nothing. I wanted to be around him but I didn't want Mom to force him to play with me.

Airplanes were Doug's passion. Passion may not be the right word: it was an obsession. From the time I can remember he was always doing something with airplanes, paper planes, kites, model planes, anything that would simulate flying. In this area at least, he did fulfill his dream. Because when the war came along, he had the opportunity to be a pilot, and I might add, a very good one. He eventually got to college, where he took flying lessons. No doubt this was a big asset in his efforts to get into the Army Air Corps. I may have resented this a little because I knew I would not have the same opportunities, but it didn't stop me from being very proud of my big brother.

He saved all the money he could, or did extra work for a few nickels whenever he could, just to buy a model airplane kit and build it. They were cheap little balsa wood kits built to fly with a wound-up long rubber band. They did fly a hundred feet or so and that was quite an accomplishment. Each one he built was better than the last one and I, of course, tried to do the same thing, but never was as successful as my hero brother.

Before Doug left high school, he and his best friend John Hopkins were serious about building their own single-seat airplane that they could actually fly. Hopkins said he could get his hands on a small gasoline engine, like a chainsaw engine, but they would have to buy a factory-made propeller. The rest they would build themselves.

Neither of the two sets of parents seemed to object too much, no doubt because they were sure it would never be completed, but I was scared to death they were going to finish it and get killed trying to fly it. Doug had most of the tail assembly completed before the idea was trashed.

At the time of their dream of flying there was no such thing as the Ultra Light single-seat planes made today, but that is precisely what they had in mind. In fact, I understand the early version of the Ultra Lights were actually powered by a chainsaw engine.

Doug was never as concerned as I was about the terrible fights our parents had. When he sensed a fight was developing, he would just disappear, while I would find a nearby hiding place and listen to the whole thing. I only discussed my concerns with my brother a couple of times, because he scoffed at my fears that they were going to kill each other and do us in at the same time.

"There you go having nightmares again," he would say.

"But I heard them," I would reply. "Mom said she was going to put rat poison in the oatmeal and Dad is going to bash her head in with a big club."

"Oh don't pay any attention to that kind of talk," Doug countered. "Besides, I don't believe they really said that."

Sure, I thought, *you would never stick around to hear them so how would you know?*

My big brother seemed to understand the whole family scene much better than I did. He found it disgusting and used every excuse in the book to stay away from home as much as he could.

My fears of some gruesome murders in the Wachs family never did go away, and I continued to reinforce those fears by listening to "True Detective Stories" whenever the radio was working. So that day when Mom got into the back seat of the car with the people from the restaurant in Pine River and waved good-bye to me standing in the front yard, a major change in my life began. For the most part I knew it would be for the better.

It takes your enemy and friend, working together, to hurt you to the heart; the one to slander you and the other to get the news to you.

Chapter 8

It doesn't sound like your dad and you two boys were very well prepared for your mother's departure. How did you manage all the household duties, the farm work and going to school at the same time?

WHEN DAD CAME home from wherever he was the day Mom left and learned of her departure, there was no emotion on his part. Mother left no note to explain things, not even where she had gone, but Dad was too stubborn, or maybe too ashamed, to question us kids. Although he had no warning of her escape plans, he showed no anger. It was like, "Let's get on with the rest of the day, get the chores done [the normal routine on every farm], and then we'll get supper." I don't remember what supper was, but I'm sure it was something pretty simple, and at supper we informed Dad where Mother was. Still no emotion.

"Mom said you should drive us into Pine River next week and she would take us to a movie." Pine River had the only movie theater for many miles around, so it was a very special treat if we ever got to a movie.

Dad said, "We'll see."

And he did. About every other week, at least in the beginning, Dad would drive us into Pine River and while he walked the streets or sat in his car, Doug and I would go see Mom, get a couple of quarters, and go to the movie. After the movie we would go to the restaurant where Mom worked and she would make us each a huge malted milk. I had never tasted anything that good in my entire life, so I really looked forward to the routine of going to Pine River, seeing a movie, and then gorging myself on a malted that filled at least two 16-ounce glasses of thick creamy chocolate.

As bachelors we seemed to fall into the routine quite well. Dad and Doug continued to do their outside work with the farm animals as they always had. I milked a cow or two every morning and night, but as a twelve-year-old I was still a little young and frail to be much good with the heavy work. My routine was to do a lot of the cooking, wash dishes, sweep the floor once in awhile, and take care of most of the laundry. I had never really done any of these things before, but I hung around the house long enough and observed what Mom did.

Cooking was the hardest part, but there wasn't that much variety on what there was available to eat. I could peel potatoes and boil or fry them, I could fry meat and eggs and make gravy, but I hadn't yet figured out how to get the lumps out of the gravy. Breakfast was either pancakes or oatmeal, which wasn't difficult. Lunch was hit-and-miss, usually something cold. The evening meal is where I had to do a lot of experimenting to provide some variety to the boiled potatoes and whatever there was available to go with them.

Doug, when he decided to stay home, complained about the food a lot, but Dad was smart enough to tell me I was a better cook than my mother, and that was all the encouragement I needed to keep me going.

My biggest concern was to try and carry on life as if nothing had changed. For some reason it was a huge embarrassment to me that Mother had deserted us and that we were living in this household without a mother or any other female. I could never admit to my friends in school that my mother wasn't living at home and that I was the one who was washing my clothes and ironing my shirts and pants just like she did so I wouldn't look funny.

The other kids never learned about our situation for a long time, but when they did they could have cared less anyway. Even though our family life was a mess, it bothered me a great deal that anyone might be critical of my parents, or to feel sorry for Doug and me. I was always overly concerned about what other people thought, and I wondered if they thought that we may have been part of the cause. I did not know of a single family in that part of the country where anything similar had ever happened. It just wasn't done, which does not mean marriage problems were any less. I just wanted to carry on as if none of this had happened.

So far I seemed to be recovering adequately from my perceived problems in school, in spite of the mixed-up home life that I was ashamed to talk about. I think this just caused me to bury myself deeper into school life. As an eighth grader I was starting to grow up, even though I was generally a year younger than my classmates and a lot younger in terms of junior-high savvy. I look at twelve-year-olds today and say, "Boy, you are a lot older than I was at twelve."

I was beginning to pay more attention to sexy girls, but I was too shy to look them in the eye or let them know in any way that I thought they were sexy. They were starting to pay attention to me too, and when my face would turn red over some flirtatious remark, that seemed to turn them on more.

All the good-looking girls were starting to pair off with other boys, most of whom were athletes. Since I was no athlete, I knew I didn't have a chance. Actually I could have competed with the other boys but didn't realize it until too late. I eventually learned that some of the good-looking girls appreciated a guy who had some smarts even though he may have been a stiff as a jock.

I tried and tried to join the football and basketball teams but I was constantly getting nosebleeds. The coaches were disgusted with me because my blood was making such a mess with the uniforms and the in locker room. I bet if I were a good jock they wouldn't have cared how much of a mess I made. Finally I gave up and started to concentrate on academics.

I soon discovered I could really compete here and could make friends with the big jocks, because I helped them with their schoolwork. Competing against girls didn't inspire me but there was another eighth-grade boy who moved to Backus who was not an athlete either because he was as blind as a bat without his half-inch-thick glasses. I forgot his first name because everybody called him "Specs." Specs Logan was very smart and we became the best of friends. He was only in school through the tenth grade and had we both finished school at Backus, I'm sure he would have beaten me out as the top student. There were only eighteen kids in our class so it's no big deal, but Specs and I made a game out of getting better grades than all the girls.

Doug was in the twelfth grade at the same school when I was in the eighth grade, and I was generally referred to as Doug's little brother. But that was okay, I still admired him a great deal even though he more or less ignored me in school. During his senior year he found more and more excuses for not coming home after school, for which I couldn't blame him even though I was bored to death home alone with just my dad.

He would look me up in school and say, "Tell Dad I won't be home tonight. I'm having play practice, or basketball practice, or something, and I'm staying over at the Hopkin's." His friend John Hopkins was involved in everything and he got Doug to join him. He was practically living with the Hopkins family but that seemed to be okay with them.

Doug was not much more of an athlete than I was even though he was a lot bigger, but he was still very popular in school. He wasn't nearly as shy as I was and therefore did pretty well with the girls. I hated it when Doug didn't come home from school because that meant I had to double up on farm chores. *Someday it will be my turn*, I kept telling myself.

Dad was good to me, letting me get by with doing the housework while I was in school and not spending too much time with the farm duties. Washing clothes by hand, washing dishes, sweeping floors, and other, what I referred to as "girl jobs," could really get to be a drag. Except for cooking: I liked to dabble in the pots and pans and it seemed to make Dad happy that I liked to prepare some different meals once in awhile. I even tried to bake bread, but that wasn't too successful, unless you liked hard flat bread. Dad never complained.

Doug left home immediately after graduation. He and John Hopkins found work at some chicken farm up north by Hackensack, about thirty miles away, so Doug lived on the chicken farm all summer. He earned a small amount of money which he saved to help with college. In the fall, he and John enrolled at the Bemidji State Teachers College. He came home just long enough to pack some things in a box and he was gone again. The lucky stiff was "off the farm" for good. Would I have to wait another four years?

Doug and John wanted to go to school in Bemidji because they offered a pilot training program at the college and that was right up their alley. War was being talked about and the two airplane nuts would be Air Force pilots, fighting off any invaders. When Doug did his solo flight in Bemidji he sent me a big smiling picture of himself standing by his Piper Cub. Again I was very proud of my big brother, maybe a little resentful because I didn't see how I would ever have the same opportunity, but nevertheless was very proud of him.

In the meantime, shortly after Mother moved out, our neighbors, Frank, Emma and Blanche, also moved away, and guess where they moved. It may have been just a coincidence that they moved about the same time Mother did, and maybe it was just another coincidence that they moved to a little farm outside of Pine River where Mother worked. I was too naive to make a connection of these events, but now that I think about it, I'm sure that Frank and Mom got their little affair going again without any worries about big Ed and his big club.

No mention was ever made about this by anyone, and like a lot of affairs, I suppose they eventually just melted down and blew away.

After Doug had been in school for a while, Mother left her job in Pine River and moved to Bemidji where he was. She got a job at a large restaurant there, where she could make more money, and I think she spent everything she made for Doug's college and his pilot training. I felt more alone than ever now: no more trips to Pine River for a movie and no more malted milks. Bemidji was just too far away and so a postcard or a letter once in awhile was the only connection with Mom and my brother.

As someone once said, "Cheer up, things could be worse." So I cheered up, and sure enough, things got worse.

Dad had made friends with a character—a very slick character—named Ray Johnson. Dad had a way of hooking up with some of the strangest people. Ray was not the first and he certainly would not be the last.

Ray was married to one of the Broady daughters, of which there were three: Thelma, Ray's wife, Maxine and Vera. Vera was Mom's best friend until Mom died, but I don't know what happened to the other two. They were very sharp, good-looking girls and the talk of the neighborhood, but they all made very bad choices in marriage. How does it happen that the scumbag guys always latch on to the good-looking girls?

Ray Johnson was the typical scumbag. He never held a job but was clever with wood and made furniture out of worm-eaten little pine trees. The worms would eat the wood just under the bark and when you stripped the bark off it left an interesting pattern of little groves in the wood. After it all got fit together into a chair or bench or something and varnished, it did impress a few people, Dad being one of them. I always thought there were still worms in the wood that would crawl on you if you got near the stuff.

Ray had frequent conversations with Dad about how they would make a dynamic woodworking team together. Dad would be the rough-in carpenter, which he was indeed, a very rough carpenter, and Ray would do the finish work.

One day Ray got wind from someone that they were paying big wages for carpenters in California, where there were government projects to build military bases, defense plants, hospitals, houses, and such. Dad's great ambition in life was to be a carpenter, certainly not a farmer, and Ray convinced Dad he was the greatest carpenter since Joseph. Like most everything else Ray Johnson talked about, I was sure it was about as solid as a bunch of eggs under Dad's big feet.

Then one late summer day Dad announced to me, "Ray and I are going to drive to California and get work as carpenters while they're still paying the big wages."

Wait a minute now. What's wrong with this picture? First Mom abandons the nest and leaves home, then my brother sprouts wings and flies off, and now Dad says he is going to leave too. Is the object of this game just to get away from Floyd?

With a knot in my stomach growing faster than a dog eating a meatball, I asked, "What is supposed to happen to me?"

"Well," Dad said, "I suppose you can go to Bemidji with your mother and go to school there." This wasn't exactly what you would call a custody arrangement worked out between Ed and Rena over the last dependent still around. It was sort of like a custody battle in reverse: "Let's make the other parent take care of the kid."

School was starting in about three days and I knew better than to think he had made any of these arrangements with Mother in advance. There would be a snowstorm in Hell before he would ever talk to her again.

"But Dad," I said, "I don't want to go to Bemidji. Everything is starting to work out okay for me here and I want to keep on going to school in Backus." I added, "Maybe there's a family in Backus I could live with while you're gone." I already had someone in mind.

Again it was obvious that a great deal of thought and advance preparation was put into "What to do about Floyd."

Dad said, "Maybe we can work something out so you can stay with the people that are coming here to live while Ray and I are gone."

I didn't like the sound of what I was hearing up to this point. "Someone is coming here to live in our house? Who are these people anyway and when is this supposed to take place?"

"They're moving in tomorrow, and..."

"Tomorrow!"

"Yeah, Ray and I are planning to leave on Sunday." Sunday was the day after tomorrow.

"What's the name of these people moving in?" I asked.

No doubt they were referred to Dad by reliable Ray with the highest recommendations, but Dad wasn't even sure how to pronounce their last name and didn't know their first names. He had never met them before and knew nothing about them other than Ray's raving recommendations.

Dad said, "I think their name is Krankanovich or something like that."

I never did find out how to pronounce their name, nor did I ever want to. Later on when I asked Bonnie, the wife, what nationality her husband was, she said it was Ukrainian. I had never heard of "Ukrainian" so I looked it up in school and learned that it referred to a part of Russia. *That fits*, I thought. *He's got the personality of a Russian who just lost the revolution.*

Anyway, the next day Krankovich and his wife Bonnie pulled into the yard with their old car loaded down with boxes of their belongings, everything they owned. They had no furniture, just some pots and pans, some dishes, some bedding, and clothes.

Dad finally got around to confront them with this new problem. "The boy here wants to stay with you and go to school in Backus."

Wait a minute Dad, I didn't say I wanted to stay with them. I just said I wanted to continue school in Backus.

Old man Kranko looks at me and thinks, *Yeah, that'll be fine. He's a skinny kid, but I bet I can get a lot of work out of him here on the farm this winter.*

"Can your boy milk cows?" Mr. Krank asked.

"Oh you bet," Dad replied. "He's a good milker. He can do just about anything on the farm."

Geez Dad, you didn't have to make it sound as if I was the working glue holding this dumb place together. I should be the one bailing out, not you.

"That sounds just fine. I'm sure we can provide a good home for the boy while he goes to school."

"My name is Floyd." I didn't like the idea of being called "The Boy."

Along with this recent addition, "The Boy," to their lease arrangement, the deal was that the Krankoviches would live here for a year, take care of the livestock and the farm and they would collect one-half of the cream check each week. "The Contract" between the two parties was some sort of a verbal agreement, I'm sure, maybe a handshake, maybe not.

Sure enough, come Sunday morning Dad and Slick Johnson, the California-or-bust boys, took off in Ray's old jalopy car. Once again there were no hugs or kisses, just a simple "good-bye" and, "I'll write when we get settled." Once again I felt like a piece of stinking shit from the manure wagon, but I'll be damned if I was going to cry.

I tried to look at it in a positive way. *I'm sure I won't have to cook and do laundry anymore, laundry I hated, and having a woman around the house once again wouldn't be all bad.* I wasn't prepared for the rest.

Bonnie turned out to be a very sweet lady, a very kind, good-looking blonde girl, much younger than the Russian. How in the world do these nice, good-looking women get stuck with such losers? He can only be described as one mean ugly SOB.

Bonnie, however, was not a well person. There was something wrong with her other than just making the mistake of marrying the triple-A-hole Russian. She was going to the doctor frequently but they couldn't determine what was wrong with her. Finally one doctor said she was not getting enough citrus fruit in her diet. So the genius Kranko brought home a huge crate of oranges and said, "Floyd, you keep your stinking hands out of these oranges. They are all for the wife. Do you hear?" He forced Bonnie to eat oranges three times a day, but she would sneak one in my school lunch pail once in awhile.

The daily routine of my responsibilities was quickly established, which was to get up very early in the morning to milk my share of cows and the same at night. In addition, I separated the milk morning and night, fed the pigs, and pumped water for the cows and horses. I didn't mind this except the Krank was on my butt constantly to get more work out of me.

I got a cigar box to keep one-half of the cream check in each week—actually they paid you in cash—along with my own accounting sheet to show the total amount of the cream receipt and that divided in half to show the tenant's portion and our portion. I didn't trust the Russkie so I kept a very detailed record and hid the cigar box where the cash and everything was kept. The cream money only amounted to twelve or fourteen dollars per week, so one-half of that for each party only amounted to six or seven. How they were able to live on that I am not sure, but there certainly were no luxuries besides the oranges for Bonnie.

One very cold winter night I was out trying to husk some corn for the pigs. The corn crop was very poor that year, so the stalks had just been cut off at the ground and stacked up by the barn. I had to go through the stack and find some little cobs and husk them out for the pigs. Well, I got very cold and went into the house to warm my hands where the Krank immediately jumped all over me. "What are you doing in the house? You're supposed to be out there feeding the pigs."

I said, "I'm just getting my hands warm."

Bonnie also came to my defense and said, "Yes, he was just warming his hands. Look at all the holes in his gloves."

"With all that money you've got socked away in that cigar box," Mr. K countered, "you could go buy yourself six pair of gloves."

How did he know about my cigar box? Guess I'd better find another hiding place. It was obvious the SOB was jealous about all the money I was stashing away, but getting my butt chewed just for getting my hands warm when it was twenty below was the last straw.

The next day I took a little money and bought myself a pair of wool mittens, but I even felt guilty about that. It was the only time I ever took a dime out of the cigar box for my own use. Otherwise every penny was accounted for when my dad came home. There was no spending money for anything at school, but once in awhile my friend Specs would buy me a coke or something. He seemed to always have money.

I was doing well in school and I tried to get all my homework done at school or on the bus coming home, because after getting up at five or six in the morning to milk cows and do other work, and then doing the same at night until eight or nine, there wasn't much time for anything else. The batteries were also dead on the radio so I couldn't listen to my favorite programs anyway. Perhaps that was a good thing, for if I had been listening to "True Detective Stories," I may have figured out a way to clobber the Krank.

There were indeed times, especially after the holey glove incident, when I thought I may have made a big mistake electing to stay on the farm rather than go up to Bemidji to go to school. But then again, I'm not sure if that option was even available to me.

It was some time before I wrote Mom to tell her what was happening at home because I didn't want her to get all shook up. She wasn't. Dad, of course, had not communicated with either Mom or Doug before he left. Mom did eventually send me some money for a bus ticket to Bemidji for three or four days over Christmas. I was happy about this because I could get away from the farm, see my brother again, and maybe get a malted milk or something at Mom's restaurant. Actually what she gave me the night I got there was something new she had just learned to make and was proud of: chow mein. I ate it but I didn't like it. In fact it made me sick and I threw up in the restaurant. I made a big mess of things and more or less messed up my entire Christmas weekend. There was no offer made for me to stay on and go to school in Bemidji.

Dad finally wrote me a card to let me know that he and Slick were in Albuquerque, New Mexico. Seems that their car broke down and they couldn't make it all the way to California, but they had landed a job there helping to build an Indian hospital. So Dad was finally fulfilling his dream of being a carpenter. I desperately wanted to write back to him to see if he couldn't come home and use one of his big clubs on old Krank, but I couldn't because they didn't have a permanent place to stay and no mailing address. He said they would be moving on anyway and he would write later.

A number of times I was ready to give up and run away, but I didn't really know how to do this, plus I was too chicken. I did ask another friend who lived in Backus, where I had stayed overnight once, if I could come and live with his family. He said I could and then everything changed.

Out of the clear blue, one day early in February, Dad showed up at the house. This was totally unexpected, but I was overjoyed to see him because maybe he could get the Russian off my back or maybe we could even kick him out. No such luck.

"What are you doing back here and what happened to your friend Ray?" I asked. Dad had taken the bus all the way from Albuquerque and someone gave him a ride out to the farm from Backus.

Dad said, "The work was completed on the hospital and there wasn't anything else around there. Ray wanted to go on to California, but I was getting a little tired of him so I decided to come home." We never saw or heard of Slick Johnson again.

I was very proud to turn over the cigar box full of money to Dad. Every penny was there, with each cream check accounted for with the exception of the $1.50 I'd spent for a pair of mittens. It was more money than he was able to bring back after working and living in Albuquerque for five months.

Dad simply moved into the house as if it was his privilege to do so, and come night time, he made up his bed on the little cot in the living room and went to sleep. After the second night of this, old Krank had had enough and told Dad he had to get out.

"You snore so loud it rattles the windows and Bonnie and I are not getting any sleep."

I could certainly vouch for that. The bedrooms had no doors and once he got wound up, Dad's snoring would echo throughout the house like a bulldozer trying to move a fifty-ton rock. But it's one of those things you get used to after a while.

That night, when I came home from school Dad was all worked up and red-faced. The Russian bear had just had it out with the stubborn German bull. Dad couldn't understand how he could be kicked out of his own house, but there was an agreement, flimsy as it was, that allowed Bonnie and the Krank to live there for a full year. This agreement included me living in the house but not Dad.

"We're going to move." Dad said.

"Does that mean I'm going to move too?" I asked. Dad didn't have to answer because he already had the hammer and was taking my bed apart. On the one hand I was very pleased about this because I would be getting away from the SOB slave driver, but I was concerned that we would be moving someplace where I wouldn't be able to continue school in Backus.

"Where are we moving?" I asked.

"We'll move into the chicken coop."

Dad kind of mumbled that remark, and even though I heard him very clearly, I said, "What did you say?"

"I said we would move out into the chicken coop. That SOB may be able to kick me out of my house, but by God he can't make me move off my property."

"But Dad, the coop is full of chicken shit."

"We'll clean it out." he said.

I knew what cleaning it out meant. First, shoveling off the top layer of chicken shit with a scoop shovel, then scraping the rough floorboards with a garden hoe to loosen the frozen and dried-up stuff, then finally sweeping it out with a broom. There was no way we could scrub it as cold as it was, which meant a lot of the chicken poop would still be there. And once we got the barrel stove fired up there was no doubt about who was living there before we moved in. It smelled worse than the backhouse on a warm summer day. Someone told me once that a chicken is the dirtiest animal on a farm. I can now assure you this is true.

I was feeling a little sick to my stomach, but then Dad said, "And you won't have to do any more chores on the farm."

"Really?"

"That's right. The bastard agreed to take care of the livestock on the farm before he knew you were going to stay here, so by God he'd better live up to his agreement. So from now on I don't want you to do a damn bit of work for him any longer."

"You mean I don't have to milk cows in the morning anymore before I go to school?"

"Not a damn one." he said.

Well that was good news. If I can be relieved of taking all the crap from Mr. K, I guess I can put up with a little chicken crap for a few days.

I immediately prayed that no one would ever *ever* hear about our moving into the chicken coop, because I would be too embarrassed and humiliated to ever face life again. That was the worst part of this whole God-awful mess. If anyone ever found out at school that I was living in a chicken coop, I would run away for sure.

I considered scrubbing down the place after we moved in, but it would have been a most difficult task and there is no way I could have gotten all the chicken shit smell out anyway. It had deeply penetrated the rough floorboards and two-by-fours. We couldn't possibly be there more than a few days before we made other arrangements. Little did I know it was going to be nearly four months.

The chicken coop was very small, about eight feet by eleven. It had one low window about a foot off the floor and only about four feet high, so that you had to stoop down just to look out. It was made this way so that if there was any sun shining from the south it would come in on the floor where the chicks were for additional warmth.

There was one small door in the corner opposite the side where the bed was and that was it. If there ever had been an unexpected fire during the night...well, I don't want to think about that. My bed, the one I was now sharing with my dad, was squeezed in between the stove and the wall. Since there was no insulation between the two-by-fours and the exterior siding wall you froze on one side of the bed and got barbecued on the other.

There was no ceiling in the building, just a couple of two-by-fours about five feet off the floor used as stringers to keep the roof from caving in from the weight of the snow. Dad cracked his head on the low-hanging boards so many times that he kept his heavy wool cap on inside or out.

I slept on the side of the cold wall because Dad had to get up and relieve himself during the night and also throw wood on the fire, so he slept on the side by the stove. I was able to keep warm, but with the chicken shit smell and Dad not taking a bath for weeks on end, it was a bit suffocating. But like the snoring, you can get used to some things after a while. I was fortunate enough to take a shower at school after gym class every chance I could.

I wasn't milking cows any longer but I was back doing laundry again, which consisted of a pail of water heated on top of the barrel stove, a bar of soap, and a washboard. Wire was strung up inside the coop to dry the clothes and I insisted on getting the flat irons and ironing board out of the house so I could at least make sure my clothes were clean and meticulously ironed before I went to school. No one must ever suspect that I was living in a chicken coop, and I continued to pray each night that the smell of chicken shit would not come through on my clothes.

Cooking was not easy, but we had a few dishes from the house, some pots and pans and a black iron griddle on which we made pancakes nearly every morning. The top of the barrel stove, which was actually the side of the barrel, had been flattened so that once you got the stove hot enough, it could be used for cooking just like a kitchen stove.

Water for cooking, washing and drinking was taken out of the pump in the barn that was ordinarily used just to water the livestock, because Dad would not let me go into the house any longer, even to get water. How we survived this might be considered a miracle of the medical world, because the barn pump and well was simply a pipe in the ground about six or seven feet down, and it is highly unlikely that the cow pee and shit above all got completely filtered out through the sand before it reached the water level below.

Then one day about the end of April, old Krank told Dad he and Bonnie would like to leave. He didn't want to stay the full year as originally planned unless Dad insisted. For once Dad decided not to be stubborn and said "Okay," or maybe "Good riddance." I figure one of two things must have made up Krank's mind: either he thought it was too much work with me not helping him every morning and night, or they—no, just Bonnie—may have felt sorry for us living in the chicken coop. I doubt that old K had any sympathetic feelings about that or anything else, but maybe Bonnie persuaded him.

Anyway they left the next day and Dad and I moved back into the house again. Wow! My own bed again, a kitchen stove, a pump in the house, a kitchen sink, and more than two feet of space to move around in and space above your head. What luxuries! And more important than was the fact that I wouldn't have to lie if anyone found out and asked me if I was actually living in a chicken coop.

That night as I lay in bed, I said to myself, "I am never going to let this happen to me again. I must take charge of my life. I must do the very best I can in school and in two more years I will graduate. What I will do then I don't know, but one thing is for sure, I want to get away from this life and get to hell off the farm."

THE LIVE-IN CHICKEN COOP

THE HAND WARMERS

Language has created the word loneliness

to express the pain of being alone,

and the word solitude to express the glory of being alone.

Chapter 9

Although it was your strong desire to finish school at Backus, you left before you graduated. What happened?

OF ALL THE THINGS that were screwed up in my home life, I tried to keep them a secret from the kids at school. Apparently I did pretty well, or else they didn't really care, because I didn't get a lot of teasing or ridicule from my peers, as often can be the case. All things considered, I guess you would have to say I was doing an adequate job in school. But then one day early in the school year, the school principal, old man Allen "Baldie" Larson, called me into his office and gave me a real butt-chewing because I wasn't doing as well as I should with my school work.

"What do you mean?" I asked. "Don't you know that I'm making the honor roll?"

He said "Yes, but the teachers tell me you should be on the A honor roll."

Well that ungrateful SOB. I'll show him, I thought. And from that point on I missed the A honor roll only once the rest of the year.

My big brother also motivated me to do well in school. He said he found out after he got in college that it would have been so much easier for him if he had worked harder in high school. I also had hopes of going to college, being a pilot or something like that when I got out of high school, as soon as I could get away from the God-awful farm, so that encouraged me to do well.

My buddy Specs Logan had moved away, but I was now in a groove of competing with the girls in the class so I kept on going. I was also using every opportunity I could to combat that phobia of public speaking I still had. I got to be the president of my class, which was no big deal, but I was also elected president of the student council, which usually was only given to a senior. That was a big deal. I also had the lead in the school play and that turned out very well. I was cruising.

Does all that sound like I am bragging? Yes, I guess it does. I didn't want it to sound that way, but I was very proud of what I had accomplished, or what I had overcome might be a better way to put it, during my junior year of high school. It was my very best year. Especially after spending the first half of my sophomore year with that horrible Russian and the second half of the year living out in the chicken coop, and I'm not even sure which part was worse. I was finally free.

Oh Lord it's hard to be humble when you're perfect in every way.
Can't wait to took in the mirror cause I get better looking every day.

I had been able to keep the chicken coop thing a secret and anybody who cared knew that my mother had left home and I was bacheloring it with my dad. That was no longer something I was ashamed of. I was just having fun in school and everything seemed to fall into place. But then something happened to change all of that.

As the German sergeant once said to his platoon on the front lines, "Today is your lucky day, for you all shall have a change of undervear. Hans, you change with Fritz, and Fritz you change with Hans..."

Life is full of changes. But before we get into that, I want to go back to three separate and unrelated events that I remember very vividly during our bachelor life, which had an emotional affect on me personally and perhaps had something to do with my exodus from the Backus area. Grandpa always said sad things come in threes. If there was a death in the neighborhood it would be followed soon by two more deaths. This was supposed to be true of any kind of undesirable event in life. It is surprising how often this seemed to be the case.

The first of these events was the fire that burned our beautiful house to the ground on the big farm where we used to live. True, it was no longer our house, but as a kid I never fully accepted that. I still referred to it as my other house because that is where life began for me and where I spent many hours going up and down the stairs, playing in the big rooms and actually feeling very proud and lucky about where I lived.

Mother had only been gone a short time when the Pauls moved out of the big house, for reasons which I later speculated gave Frank the opportunity to move closer to Mom. The bank, now the owners of the big farm, rented it to whoever they could as they sure as heck couldn't sell it.

The new tenant following the Pauls was a Finnish couple named Ole and Essie Mykkonen. Ole was a creepy looking, tobacco-chewing, bearded guy of about forty-five. Essie, however, was much younger, petite, very pretty, and about the sexiest female I had ever seen at this stage of my life. And she knew it.

Once again, it never ceases to amaze me how these beautiful young women like Essie can get stuck with such creepy characters such as old Ole. In the summertime she never wore anything but very brief shorts and a halter, I mean seven days a week morning till night, and she was as brown as a Snickers candy bar, my favorite.

On top of it all Essie flirted with any male with pants on, tantalizing them with her suggestive walk and talk every chance she could. How far she went with any of them, I can only speculate, but there seemed to be all kinds of men going in and out of that farm driveway day and night. Old Ole didn't seem to care, he was just very proud of his beautiful wife. Essie flirted with my dad and my brother too, but she was just very nice to me. In addition to being a swinging beauty she was very ambitious and a good cook. So my reasons for hanging around her were simply to get some good cookies or a good meal once in a while. Maybe the other men also liked her cookies. I discovered later in life that there were other things better than cookies.

One of Essie's ambitious ideas was to raise chickens like a lot of people in the country were trying to do at that time. But, since she didn't have a suitable chicken coop, she cordoned off two rooms in the big house, over half of the downstairs area, and let the little chicks get started there. Her logic was that as long as they had to heat this big house with the wood stove in the living room, they might as well let the little chickens have a warm place to live at the same time. Here these beautiful varnished floors, wood work, and wallpaper were being crapped on by a couple hundred little chickens.

All the ladies in the neighborhood that heard about this thought it was just awful, but then again, anything sexy little Essie Mykkonen did, the ladies thought was just awful. Rather ironic now that I think about it, the chickens had this beautiful big house to call their home, and a year or so down the road, I would have a shitty chicken coop to call my home.

One Sunday, one of Dad's bachelor friends, Harold Bishop, came to visit us. Could it be that we had some of these single men visiting us just so they might get a glimpse of sexy Essie in the next house down the road? Whatever the reason, Harold hung around until it got late and Dad said, "You might as well stay overnight." He slept on the little homemade couch in the living room.

During the night Harold got up to relieve himself, came back in the house, and woke up Dad. "Ed, what is that funny light on the top of your neighbor's house?"

Dad got up and looked and said, "It must be the moon coming up."

"Well, no," said Harold, "I think the moon is supposed to be over there," pointing in a different direction from the light.

They looked at it for a while and Dad finally said, "My gosh, that must be a fire." He ran to the telephone to call the Mykkonens.

After about three attempts at ringing their code, whatever it was, old Ole finally came to the phone. He sleepily said, "I don't know anything about any fire," and then, "Well maybe I do smell a little smoke. Holy shit!" He quickly hung up.

Dad then rang the fire alarm code on the telephone which was six short rings. He did it twice and then announced on the telephone, "The Mykkonen house on the old Wachs farm is on fire."

Whoever heard this was supposed to keep sending the call out and then come and assist in putting out the fire. Nobody came. Either they didn't hear the telephone, didn't understand my dad's excited message, or didn't care to get out on this winter night. Dad, Harold, and Doug all put their clothes on and ran to the burning neighbors roof. It was now about three in the morning. They all worked feverishly carrying pails of water up into the attic and throwing it on the fire. They soon realized it was a futile effort.

We were close to a half-mile away so I stayed home and watched through the window until I couldn't take it any longer. I put my clothes on and got to the blazing house just as the fire peaked. Everyone was just standing around watching it burn and making sure that no sparks or burning debris were landing on the other buildings. Except Doug, he was throwing rocks at the big beautiful bay windows with the etched glass. I thought this was a terrible thing to do until I realized they were all going to be destroyed anyway.

Oh yes, Essie was out rounding up the chickens they managed to chase out of the house before they got fried. They were now completely feathered out but still not fully grown, so they spent the balance of the winter in the barn until they could be sold.

I was terribly broken up by this event. I desperately wanted to cry and didn't care who saw me. After all, this house was part of the happier days of my young life and it was now being destroyed. It seemed as if this was just one more thing in a series of events that was coming unglued and nobody was able to do anything about it. What was going to be next? I was very scared and very depressed.

The second catastrophic event occurred almost exactly twelve months later. The Armistice Day blizzard of 1940 had a profound effect on my life, as it did on many people from Minnesota at that time. There may never have been a worse storm in recorded history that created hardship for more people or one that did more to emphasize the need for better weather warning systems among meteorologists. Thousands of people were stranded in cars, in houses, in shelters of any kind for days waiting to be discovered and rescued.

In one house along the highway near St. Cloud there is a story about sixty-five people who sought refuge from the storm and stayed for four days. They ate all the food in the house, which the family stored for their winter needs and they literally trashed the house. When the storm was over and they could leave, they all walked away without paying the family a dime for their services or damage to the property. That was not "Minnesota nice."

In our case, Douglas was home from college for the weekend. On the morning of November 11, Dad was preparing to take him back to Backus so he could catch the Greyhound bus up to Bemidji. There was no snow on the ground; in fact it was a very pleasant sunny morning for this time of year. Ordinarily Dad would have had the tire chains out in preparation for the first snow of November, but it was such a nice day. I remember him saying, "There's no need to take the chains for just this trip to Backus." I don't remember why, but fortunately I didn't go with them and stayed home alone.

Almost immediately after they left the weather became strange. I don't remember if our radio was working then or not, but at that time it would have been unusual to have any kind of weather forecast of a pending storm announced on the radio. Dad made it to Backus, saw Doug off on the bus about two o'clock and started home, but the roads were filling up with snow and drifting shut. He got no closer than about three or four miles and had to abandon the car. He started out on foot.

The snow and the wind were blowing so hard you could not see more than two feet in front of your face, and it was already so deep and piled up in the roads that you could not identify where the road was supposed to be. The wind was less severe in the brush and trees, so Dad left the road and started out across the country. There he became disoriented several times and didn't know where he was. Unless you have ever experienced a storm like this, it is hard to describe the total hopeless feeling. He said he knew he had to walk in a westerly direction and the wind of such a storm always blew from the west, so he just walked heading into the wind.

On three different occasions Dad said he was so tired he laid down in the snow and wanted to go to sleep. I understand this is a typical reaction in this kind of a situation, and it is the reason why people freeze to death. But just before he fell completely asleep, Dad said the thought of me home alone forced him to get up and try again.

Finally he stumbled onto a fence that he thought was the one he had built between his farm and the neighbors'. It wasn't the same fence, but he followed it until he ran across the telephone lines by a road. They eventually led him to the road that went by our house. At about ten o'clock that night, after being out on foot for nearly six hours in the worst storm of the century, Dad crashed through the door and collapsed on the kitchen floor.

He was grateful to be home and I certainly was as well, but then Dad immediately got mad at me. Why? Because I had let the fire go out in the barrel stove, our source of heat. The house was already getting very cold, but I was scared to keep the fire going because of the way the wind was blowing. I thought I might burn the house down. Perhaps I was so scared that I wasn't thinking very clearly.

So before Dad could thaw out he first had to get a fire started and finally we were warm and safe. I don't blame Dad for getting mad at me. But now the cows still had to be milked. About twelve o'clock that night we were able to sit down and have something to eat, which was our only meal since breakfast. I think Dad, and I as well, made up our minds at this moment, although we didn't talk about it, that this was no way to live and we desperately needed to get out of this Minnesota wintertime prison.

The third major event, again occurring almost exactly twelve months later, probably helped to make all this possible. The date was December 7, 1941. It was a date that will change the course of history and it would definitely change the lives of millions of people. It was a date that most of us, old enough to remember, will know exactly what we were doing when it happened. It is just like it was in later years when Jack Kennedy was shot. You will always remember exactly what you were doing when the news was announced that our president had been assassinated.

It was a Sunday afternoon and I was in the house trying to pick up something on the radio even though the batteries were too weak to make anything worth listening to. Then an announcer interrupted the program to say that the Japanese were bombing Pearl Harbor in Hawaii. I listened intently, then there was another announcement that President Roosevelt had declared war on Japan.

I rushed out to the barn to tell Dad, but he wouldn't believe it until I got him to come into the house and listen to the radio. We were finally at war, and to a kid of fourteen it was kind of thrilling, not realizing that my brother and I would eventually be a part of it. My part was very small, but I'm very certain the enemy decided to surrender as soon as they heard that I had enlisted in the Navy.

From December 7 on it was the focus of every red-blooded American to do whatever they could to help the cause of our country and defeat the enemy. It wasn't a case of fear for what the enemy might do to us in our forty-eight states, it was a case of just being damned angry that they could surprise us with such a dastardly attack. If you couldn't enlist in the service, you bought war bonds or you worked in a defense industry.

Dad wanted to do whatever he could because he never made it as a soldier in the first world war, plus the fact that his German-born parents, at the time of the first world war, were ridiculed as foreigners and were accused of being supportive of the enemy. He wanted to reverse this feeling and get a job in some war-related capacity, but I think I was somewhat of an albatross around his neck. After his trip out West, which failed in so many ways, he had made up his mind that he was going to stay on the farm with me until I finished school at Backus.

The war made you do things you otherwise may not have had the courage to do. If there was something you wanted or dreamed about but put off for various reasons, you didn't procrastinate any longer because there may not be a tomorrow. This made it kind of an exciting time. Things were happening.

Nearly three years of college plus some flight training was all my brother Doug needed to be accepted in the Army Air Corps, which later became the US Air Force. Early in 1943, he and his buddy, John Hopkins, went to the Twin Cities to enlist. They were both accepted, but in Doug's case it took a little longer to be sworn in, so he got a job working in a meat-packing plant in South St. Paul while he waited to be called.

I desperately wanted to see my brother before he went off to war. He didn't even come home when he left Bemidji to enlist. After school was out in the spring and after a lot of begging, Dad finally gave me the money for a one-way bus ticket to St. Paul, which was all of about three dollars, as I recall. I knew that I could borrow enough money from my brother to come home.

I certainly didn't realize it when Dad took me to Backus to board the bus that day in early June that I would never again set foot on the farm. I would like to take credit for this absolutely brilliant move on my part even though I had no idea what I was doing or what was about to happen. Mother, five years earlier, had made her escape and fulfilled a portion of her dream at least, by becoming a cook in a restaurant. Doug was able to leave the farm and fulfill his dream of going to college and becoming a pilot. Even Dad was able to leave the farm, at least for a brief period, and satisfy a bit of his dream of being a carpenter. Now, finally, Floyd, although he didn't know it, was going to have his prayers answered and a big portion of his dream satisfied. He was off the farm.

I had no place to stay when I got to St. Paul, as Doug only got room and board. So I just sort of dropped in on my Uncle Charlie and Aunt Martha, living in the Midway district of St. Paul. In spite of the differences my aunt and uncle may have had with Mother and Dad, they were always very good to us kids. They always gave us a place to stay and all the good food that went with it. They had a relatively small house, and with three adult children, Dorothy, Mildred, and Calvin, all living at home, there wasn't a lot of room for guests. In comparison with my country abode, of course, I thought it was a fabulous mansion, with lots of fine furniture, carpets, drapes, appliances, running water, a gas stove, electric lights, and the most wonderful creation of all time: a flush toilet. All you had to do was pull a chain and everything just swirled out of sight. What a palace!

As it turned out, Calvin, who was just out of high school, had enlisted in the Navy and was called up a couple of days before I got there, so I was able to sleep in his room. Little did I know at this point, what was planned to be a day or two trip to visit my brother turned out to be a much longer stay.

My two older cousins, Dorothy and Mildred, were very good to me and I'm sure they felt sorry for this pathetic, immature 16-year-old who was about as uncitified as any country bumpkin could be. Fact is, these girls were two sheltered prima donnas and about as unworldly as you can get, but I thought they were neat people who could teach me a lot.

One day Mildred looked at me and said, "Floydie." (they still called me Floydie and I hated it) "when was the last time you went to see a dentist?"

"Dentist? I don't recall ever going to a dentist. Maybe when I was six or seven years old, I don't know."

"It looks to me like you are long overdue," she said. "While you are here why don't I see if I can get my dentist to look at you?"

I learned quickly that you did not object too much about what Mildred wanted you to do, so more or less to please her, I agreed to see her Dr. Ozzar.

When Dr. Ozzar got me in his chair and opened my mouth, he must have seen a vision or something because his only words were "Oh, my God." Maybe his vision was lots of dollar bills resulting from what he thought he could get out of me. After about twenty minutes of probing, he came up with an enormous amount of work that had to be done. It sounded like every tooth in my head was about to fall out.

That was probably closer to the truth than I wanted to admit.

Dr. Ozzar said, "About the best I can do is maybe one appointment a week which will allow us to finish up before you have to go back to school."

I said, "No way. This is impossible. I'm only going to be here a few days, plus I don't have any money to pay you."

Perhaps the money part, more than anything, caused him to say, "I'm sorry." But he added, "You desperately need to have your teeth taken care before they all fall out."

I walked out wondering how I was going to accomplish this though I didn't really believe my teeth were in danger of falling out. They just ached now and then.

I talked this over with my Aunt Martha and cousin Mildred. To them this was a major crisis. After a half-hour lecture on how awful it was that I wasn't taking care of my teeth, they realized that I wasn't able to do much about it except brush my teeth regularly. They immediately started me on a twice-a-day routine. Now I was sure my teeth would fall out—from all that brushing.

Aunt Martha said I could stay there the rest of the summer and maybe I could get a job to pay for my teeth.

A job! Holy cow!

All of a sudden too much was happening too fast. Mildred said, "Calvin used to work at Montgomery Wards part-time and I'll bet they would hire you, even if you are only sixteen."

I said, "I'll have to write to my dad and I don't think he will give me permission to stay."

I was wrong. Dad wrote back right away and shocked me by saying, "Stay as long as they will let you." *What gives here? Does he want to get rid of me or what?* Well, yes he did, sort of.

It never occurred to me at the time, but after Mother left and my brother found a way to escape, neither of my parents seemed too concerned about providing a home or having me as a dependent. They displayed jealousy if I got any kind of attention from one or the other, and made me feel guilty if I didn't carefully divide up any affection I might have had for either one. No doubt I was sort of an albatross that prevented them from freely getting on with their life, particularly my dad. So I was reluctant to leave Dad alone on the farm, but it was apparently exactly what he wanted.

Dad had gotten involved with another one of his strange acquaintances, this time a bachelor drifter from Pennsylvania. Although I was not aware of it, he had met Ed Whipper some time before I made my trip to the Twin Cities.

Whipper, a rugged-looking geezer, reminded me of the kind of people we used to refer to in northern Minnesota as "jackpine savages." A jackpine savage was a guy who worked in the woods, stayed wherever he could get food and bed down for a while, and was happy as long as he could get his hands on some cheap wine or whiskey now and then. If anyone ever suggested it might be a good idea if he took a bath or shaved the hair off his face, he would probably move on to the next place. Ed Whipper was a lot like that, and the day I left he moved into my bed. He sort of became my replacement.

The two Eds got along fine, or should I say the three Eds. Can you believe, Ed Whipper and Ed Wachs both got a job at this little sawmill back in the woods close to our house, and were the only two employees of another Ed, Ed Mitchell. It must have been very confusing.

Whipper had a relative back in Pennsylvania, a sister-in-law I believe, who was divorced and had a young son. Whipper thought she would make a good match for his new friend, Ed Wachs. He was right. Somehow he got them to write letters to each other back and forth and was smart enough to suggest that they not send pictures of each other right away. "Love is blind" was definitely better in this case.

I had no idea Dad was getting involved with another woman. When I wrote to him to get his permission to stay in St. Paul a little longer, his immediate agreement had a lot to do with this mail order courtship. For some reason Dad wanted to keep this a secret from Doug and me and he also wanted to make a quick trip to Pennsylvania to meet this new-found love. My absence made all of this more convenient.

He made the trip and plans to get married were started almost immediately even though Dad and Mother still hadn't gotten around to getting a legal divorce. Dad finally got busy on that score as well.

I now proceeded to make my cousin's dentist very happy by scheduling a series of ten or twelve appointments. Then I also worked up enough courage to go to Montgomery Wards, not too far away in the Midway district, and apply for a job.

It was easier than I thought it would be, except their application had about five spaces to list the places you had worked before, dates started and left, reasons for leaving, salary, and so forth. What should I do? I had never worked for anyone before; should I lie or leave it blank? Well, I thought I would lie just a little. I put down Ed Mitchell, the sawmill guy, as my most recent employer; salary, minimal. Then the employer previous to that was another Ed, Ed Wachs; salary, practically nothing.

In spite of all this I was hired, and never questioned about my application. Wards did, however, send a verification of previous employment letter to Ed Mitchell. Mitchell sent me a copy of the letter he wrote back to Wards saying he was puzzled about the inquiry because Floyd had never worked for him but his father did. Then he went on with glowing remarks about what a fine young man I was and they would be very fortunate to have me as an employee. Again, no one from Wards ever questioned me about this. I was working. Wow! My first job.

Soon after I got to my aunt and uncle's house, a wedding was being planned for Dorothy, Uncle Charlie's daughter and Aunt Martha's adopted daughter, to marry her soldier boyfriend Bud Starr. At that time everybody was getting married as fast as they could it seemed because there was such little time, and who knows what would happen in the war. They might never see each other again. Just living together in a motel for the few days they were home on leave from the service was totally out of the question at that time. They had to make their bedroom love-making a legal event.

Douglas was able to come to Dorothy's wedding as he still had not been called to duty. This is where he first met the love of his life, Lois Mae Nord, a friend of a friend of somebody's, who was at the house to help serve and clean up after the wedding. Doug called Lois the next day and for the days or weeks he had before going to flight training, he dated Lois furiously, but apparently their courtship didn't reach the point where a marriage was absolutely necessary. Lois had a very strict mother who didn't particularly care for this guy who worked in a meat-packing plant and who would sometimes show up for a date directly from work smelling like the rear end of a hog.

Cousin Calvin also came home from the service on leave later that summer and decided he wanted to marry his high school sweetheart. After all, they were both eighteen years old. All of Calvin's friends were away in the service, so I had to be his best man. This was quite a step up from where I had been. I was more nervous than the virgin bride.

One day there was a phone call for me at my aunt and uncle's house. It was my mother. She was in St. Paul and said she was leaving Bemidji and coming to St. Paul to live with her Aunt Emma. Up to this point I don't think she had ever met her Aunt Emma before, they had just corresponded by mail. Now all of a sudden she was moving in with her. Doug was finally called into the service and, of course, would not be going back to Bemidji. Mother no longer had anything to keep her in Bemidji and since jobs were very plentiful with better salaries in the Twin Cities, she got her aunt to take her in.

Mother wanted me to move in with her and her aunt. I wasn't in favor of this at all at first and told her I would have to think about it because I still wanted to go back and finish school at Backus. I don't know this for a fact, but I think my Aunt Martha may have written to my mother in Bemidji and suggested it was about time she started doing a better job taking care of her number-two son. Martha was the type that would do that.

I didn't have to think about this decision long, because the very next day I got a letter from Dad saying he was going to Pennsylvania to marry his new-found mate, Mayme. He thought he would stay out there and get a job at the big diesel engine plant in Grove City, Pennsylvania. He was going to close up the farm but if I wanted to, I could still come back and finish school and he would make arrangements for me to live with someone in Backus.

Based on past experience, I wasn't too confident about Dad's "living arrangements" for me, so I gave up on the plan of going back to Backus to finish school. This really hurt because I had just finished a very good year and I was really looking forward to being a senior with a good chance of being the class valedictorian and all that that might have meant in college scholarships and so forth.

With my options now rather limited, I reluctantly agreed to move in with my mother and her aunt, who I hadn't met, in this little two-room upstairs apartment on Woodridge Avenue in the Rice Street district of St. Paul.

On the other hand, let's look at it from the positive side: I had a job, and Wards even told me I could work part-time while going to school if I wanted to; I had some money in my pocket for the first time in my life; and I wouldn't have to do cooking or laundry.

I liked the city, the streetcars, and being able to pick a movie from a dozen or more theaters that wasn't always a Gene Autry or Hopalong Cassidy movie.

The most important part was that I wasn't going back to the farm again. I was finally off the farm and never would return, not even for a visit.

Upon completing this chapter of the book, I now realize for the first time that old Floyd's life actually has only three chapters, and after the first sixteen years of life, I have just finished the first chapter.

The second part of "Floyd Off The Farm" covers only about a ten-year period and it is devoted almost entirely to getting the Farm Off Floyd. Yes, an awful lot of greenish-brown stuff from the cow barn gutter and the chicken coop still clung to me (maybe some of it still does), but I desperately wanted to scrape it off. It doesn't come off easy.

The third chapter is by far the better part of my life. More than likely this is because it's where I meet a wonderful girl who took a chance by accepting this country yokel with some brown stuff still showing, who was willing to devote her life to getting me cleaned up. This is where I once again agree, no one has ever been as fortunate as me, to have someone come into their life, who would stand by me as I struggled with my career, banging my head against the cement walls of Sears Roebuck and Co. Without Jeanne I know I wouldn't have made it.

As I look back on the first one hundred pages, I am concerned that perhaps I have painted a rather grotesque picture of my parents. Oh, I agree they may not be the role models I would recommend for Parenting Class 101, but they don't deserve the grimy image I'm afraid you, as a reader, might perceive. Above all, I want to be honest, and I believe I have been, but in doing so it seems that some of their good qualities may have gotten blurred in the fog of frustration, in mine as well as theirs.

The last thing I want to do is to have anyone look at this tale and think I am looking for sympathy for me and my brother Doug during our younger years. Thousands and millions of children all over the world were much worse off than we were. We did not suffer, we were not physically abused, we did not lose faith. We may even have had it better than a lot of our peers of that time.

I will always come to the defense of my father and mother. They were obviously disadvantaged in many ways. They didn't have a lot of experience, that is, good, loving experiences to draw from, and they floundered in life learning mainly by what Mother Nature provided. If they made errors along the way, I can accept that because I really believe they did the best they knew how with only slightly selfish motives.

There wasn't a lot of affection displayed in the family: no spontaneous hugs, kisses, kidding, inflections; the little things that are so darned important. I believe the feeling was there, but because they didn't know how to show it, they thought best not to do anything. My mother and father would rather kiss a cockroach than show any affection towards each other, so they had trouble involving themselves in a more affectionate approach with their children as well.

More than anything I want my children, my grandchildren and generations of children to follow, to know that life is good and beautiful and most people are caring. But it's kind of up to you. If you want it that way, you have to work at it. It is so important to show others that you care and be sure you're involved with the right people who also care. Perhaps in this regard my father and mother could have done a better job, but they're not alone. We all can do a better job.

The Little Sparrow from Northern Minnesota

Once upon a time there was a little sparrow who lived in northern Minnesota where he had to make the long flight south every fall, then back north again in the spring where he liked to spend his summers. This was very tiring and one year he decided to stay up north for the winter. Along about December it got very cold and it didn't take him long to realize that he had made a grave mistake. He had better head south.

The weather was now getting colder and when he got up in the air to fly south, ice started forming on his wings. Soon they were frozen solid to the point where he could no longer fly. The little sparrow plummeted to the ground. He thought this was the end but fortunately he was over a barnyard and landed in a pile of fresh warm cow shit. Soon his wings began to thaw and he was getting warm all over. He was so happy that his life was not really over, that he began to sing.

Lo and behold, out in the same barnyard was a big farm cat who heard the singing. The cat discovered the singing was coming from this pile of cow shit so she ran over to it, reached inside with her paw and fished out the little sparrow. You guessed it, the cat promptly ate the bird.

End of story.

But there is a moral to this story.

If you should ever fall into a pile of shit, it isn't necessarily all bad, and if you should happen to be in a pile of shit and someone gets you out, it isn't necessarily all good. But if you should ever find yourself all warm and happy in a pile of shit, for God's sake keep your mouth shut.

Chapter 10

Moving off the farm, your dad remarrying, your brother going off to war, moving to the big city, transferring to a new school, uniting with your mother again, all happening at the same time, sounds like a plateful. Were you sort of starting life all over again?

THIS WHOLE SEQUENCE of events, like it or not, was probably the best thing that could happen to me at that time. I was finally growing up, and I had to wade through it all very quickly. From this naive, immature, shy sixteen-year-old kid (which I hate to admit was more like twelve), it seemed like an awfully long way to go to be able to survive in this fast-moving life.

On Sunday, the day before school was to begin, I packed all my belongings in an old suitcase my aunt loaned me and found my way by streetcar to the address on Woodridge Avenue, in the Rice Street district where my mother and her aunt were now living. It was a small two-story house with an entrance that allowed you to go directly to the upstairs quarters, probably very adequate for one person, very tight for two people, but more like a sardine can for three. The Rice Street area was considered the worst section of St. Paul at the time and I don't think it has improved a great deal since then.

Aunt Emma was the younger sister of my mother's mother: she was not a great deal older than my mother. She was a very kind, benevolent lady, and to my knowledge had never been married. The idea of having her niece move in with her, which she assumed would likely be only temporary, seemed to fit her charitable nature.

She had always been concerned about the three daughters of her sister who had been left in an orphanage.

Prior to my mother moving in with her aunt, they had corresponded but I don't think they had ever met face-to-face, and I know they hadn't talked about a sixteen-year-old boy moving in at the same time. I was a little more baggage than the nice aunt had planned on. Fortunately my mother had immediately lined up a job at a government defense plant where she would be working the night shift. This allowed the two women to use the same bed because they were seldom there at the same time. Mother worked long hours and overtime on weekends, so the three of us might be together for an evening meal, but that was about it. That's no doubt the reason we all got along quite well.

I hated to move out of my aunt and uncle's house where I had my cousin's room all to myself, but I was freeloading there, which I wasn't very proud of. Now I was moving to a dinky little upstairs apartment. But what the heck, there was indoor plumbing again, a bath tub, an electric stove, electric lights, and even a washer and dryer: When you have gone this long without any of these luxuries, moving into the Playboy Penthouse could not have been much better. (I'm kidding, I'm kidding.)

When I arrived at the mini-penthouse Mother was there and she introduced me to Aunt Emma. "Hello Floydie," Aunt Emma said. "Your mother has been telling me all about you and what a nice boy you are."

What would you expect a mother to say, I thought. *On the other hand, how would she know since it has been over four years since we last lived together.* "Would you mind calling me anything but Floydie?" I asked.

"Sure Floydie, what shall I call you?"

I looked around and sweet Aunt Emma said, "We'll make up a bed for you here on the living room couch, and you'll have to hang your clothes in my closet or maybe we can put a line up over the washer and dryer."

"That's okay, I can just leave them in the suitcase."

My biggest concern was, "Where do I go to school?"

My mother didn't know, but Aunt Emma said, "I think there is a high school about six blocks north of us."

The next morning which was the first day of the new school year, I walked the six blocks or so north and found this enormous building with spacious playgrounds, and football and baseball fields. This must be it. I thought Backus was a big school when I first got there but this made Backus look like a backhouse. Classes were already in session but I walked in and found somebody to give me directions to the front office.

I walked in and said, "I'm a new kid and I'd like to go to school."

"Well that's amazing," the smart lady said, "you're in the right place. What's your name? Spell that please."

After a lot of scurrying around and checking in different files the lady came back and said, "I cannot find where you have been registered."

"Well that's quite understandable," I said. "I haven't registered. I just moved here yesterday."

"Oh dear, we can't let you start school until we have all your records from where you went to school last year. You must do this, do that, and so on and so forth."

She would be the perfect employee for some government agency where their performance is graded on how difficult they can make it for accomplishing anything in an orderly efficient manner. Each new form she stuck in front of me I argued with her, but each time it appeared I was getting closer to being expelled before I even got started.

Finally a man came out of an office, obviously her boss, and said, "What's going on here?" After some three-way conversation the man put together a list of classes for me and suggested, "Follow this schedule for now and we'll adjust it later if need be." This man would never make it as a government employee.

The first class on the list was in room 214. "Where is that?" I asked.

"Susie," the man turned to another girl in the office, "take this boy up to 214 and show him a map of the building so he can find his other classes." I liked this man, who turned out to be the assistant principal.

Susie got me to room 214 and more or less pushed me in. *Holy cow—there must be thirty-five or forty kids in here!* Instantly all seventy or eighty eyes (I think they all had two) zeroed in on me, destroying all the attention the teacher had been getting in his lecture up to now. More questions by the teacher, again all in front of this sea of eyes, and finally he said, "Take a seat in the back there on the left side." When your name begins with *W* you get accustomed to being in the back of the room. Back to his lecture, where no one seemed to be paying any attention now.

Almost immediately a kid in front of me turned around and said, "Hey, where you from?"

I said, "Backus."

"Backus? I've never heard of it. Is that in Minnesota?"

I explained how small the town was, where it was and that there were only eighteen kids in the entire senior class. And then he asked, "Where are you living now?"

"On Woodridge Street, near the NSP plant."

"Really, that's only a couple blocks from where I live." The bell rang and he said, "Where's your next class?"

I said, "Room 309 but I have no idea where that is."

"I'll take you there, but I won't be in that class so just wait there and when class is over I'll come and get you and take you to your next class."

What a guy. "Hey, what's your name?"

"Larry Schwartzbauer," he said. He talked fast and I got the Larry part, but had no idea what his last name was except that it began with *S*, which is why he was sitting close to me in room 214.

Larry was definitely an outgoing individual who was extremely sociable with a positive personality. He was from a devout Catholic family and seemed to have a passion for doing things for people who needed help. Boy, he sure recognized where his help was needed when he saw me.

Larry found me when school was over and said he would walk home with me, except we must go by the way of Rice Street so he could show me all the spots where the guys hang out. Wow! This was really a change of pace for this farm boy. He said, "I'll come by your house about 8:30 tomorrow morning and pick you up." I got home thinking that this day went really well.

He was on time the next morning waiting on the corner by our house. That afternoon we walked home together again and Larry said he wanted to see where I lived. I knew Aunt Emma would not be home but I wasn't sure if Mother had gone to work yet. I took a chance and invited him to our upstairs pad. No one was home. It took Larry about five seconds to scan the place, and then he spotted it. "My God, you've got a telephone."

Larry didn't have a telephone at his house. His family had very basic means, but a lot of people in the area where we lived were quite poor and decided they could get along without a telephone. As soon as he saw the phone, Larry sprawled out across Aunt Emma's bed and started dialing numbers. *Gosh, I hope Aunt Emma doesn't come home now.*

Larry was calling girls. He called one after another and fed them an unbelievable line, telling them how much he loved them, how beautiful they were, how he laid awake at night thinking about them, how he longed to have them in his arms. I couldn't believe it, but the amazing part was that he had all the telephone numbers of these girls in his head, a dozen or more, even though he didn't have a telephone of his own.

After nearly an hour of the steamy telephone calls, with the telephone wires starting to melt the rubber covering, Aunt Emma came home from work. Damn. She quietly walked in and went immediately to the bedroom where Larry was still very comfortably on his back handing out this endless line of mush. Her mouth dropped open. I was ready to run but Larry concluded his conversation with girl number twelve or fourteen, jumped up, grabbed Aunt Emma's hand and said, "Hi, my dear sweet aunt." He gave her a big hug, a peck on the cheek and then proceeded to give her a line about how young she looked, how beautiful and all the other BS just like he had been doing with the seventeen-year-old girls. Aunt Emma's mouth still hung open.

I meekly said, "I'm sorry about all this Aunt Emma." I tried to think of something to say like, Larry is poor and he doesn't have a telephone at home, but Larry just kept on with his jazz.

Finally, as I was pushing Larry out the door, he said, "Thank you, my dear. Floyd is sure lucky to have a nice aunt like you."

As he left Aunt Emma turned to me and said, "What a nice friend you have made at school already. I really like him. Tell your friend he can use my telephone any time he wants to." He didn't need further encouragement. From that day on Larry and I were the best of friends, and fifty-plus years later we still are. I can give Aunt Emma's telephone most of the credit for this.

Even though this encounter was a plus, I was a little dubious if this was the kind of a guy I should have as a friend. But then when I met Larry's best friend, George, I had even more serious doubts. George Muntean, from one of the long-time ethnic families of the neighborhood, mostly Romanian, was much like Larry, very outgoing and extremely friendly, except that he seemed to take his friendship with girls a step further. He was quite popular, not because he was an athlete, but he was the only male on the cheerleading squad, which made him very visible.

George immediately told me which girls in school he had made love with, and which ones I should leave alone because they wouldn't put out. "Just ask me about any babe and I'll tell you if she will go all the way or not." So I asked him about Betty Komlosan, a very cute girl that lived just a few doors from me. "Oh she's a doll all right, but you can't touch her, unless you just want to hold hands and maybe get a good night kiss." That would be plenty for me.

I was stunned, but I wasn't about to admit he was talking to this virgin of all virgin farm boys who had never dated a girl yet, or even kissed a girl, not even a peck on the cheek. I believed George's line for a long time, but later I learned that maybe George expanded on his love-making conquests just a bit beyond reality. "Putting out" and "going all the way" didn't necessarily mean precisely what I thought it did.

Larry, George, and I were together as often as possible although I still worked at Wards after school as much as I could, which would last only until Christmas, when I got laid off. George worked at his family's store on Rice Street, Muntean's Department Store. Larry did not have a regular job. Why these two picked me up as their friend I will never figure out, other than that they must have considered it a challenge to educate this poor slob from northern Minnesota.

We did nothing very special, just hung out at the joints on Rice Street for a hamburger and a coke now and then or at Schwankel's Drug Store where some high school girls worked. I had a small paycheck while I was still at Wards so I didn't mind buying once in a while, and when George was around, he always seemed to have a little money. Larry always wanted to go to the YMCA hi-hop dances and drag me along. He was a terrific dancer, a jitterbug. He tried to teach me but after a number of attempts he just gave up. I was okay until I had to dance with a girl.

Larry also had an uncle that was an usher at the St. Paul Sports Arena where the Saints played hockey. Any time we wanted to go to a hockey game, we just had to arrange for a specific time when we would give him some kind of signal at one of the back alley emergency exits and he would let us sneak in. I saw more professional hockey games while in high school than I have since, and never paid a dime for one game. After the hockey game we would go to a Greek Coney Island place on St. Peter Street and inhale three or four Coney Islands. They were only a dime apiece, but the main attraction was the owner's daughters who worked there. One of them was about as cute as anything I had ever dreamed of. Larry tried every trick in his vast knowledge of wooing women and she would not have anything to do with him. She was even more shy than I, which appealed to me and for the same reason I may have appealed to her a little. Later on, when I finally had enough nerve to ask her out, I did date her, but it was a total loss. She definitely would not put out, whatever that meant.

At times we lived on the edge of breaking the law, like throwing snowballs to break streetlights or derailing the overhead trolley on the streetcars so that the driver had to get out and put it back on track again. There were no drugs at that time, at least none that we knew about. Larry did not smoke or drink, and still doesn't. George did both but it never caused a problem. I just liked a beer now and then and never did have a desire to try smoking.

During my introduction into this big city school, which had the reputation of having more former students serving time in Minnesota jails than any other school in the state, I was beginning to grow up but I had a long ways to go.

Meanwhile, my big brother was down in Texas learning to be a B-24 pilot. He quickly received his commission as a second lieutenant in the Army Air Corps, and boy, was I proud of him. He came back to Minnesota on a quick leave once, but spent nearly all of his time with his sweetheart Lois Mae. They sort of solidified their plans for her to join him wherever he was before he had to go overseas.

Doug no more than got back to Texas when he called Mother to say he was being sent to San Francisco and from there he would likely be going to the South Pacific. He asked Mother if she would travel with Lois Mae on the train to Frisco before he left because Lois Mae's mother would not let her travel alone. Mother got leave from her job, plans were made, and then for some reason they wanted me to go along, to carry the suitcases I suppose. Although I would be out of school for a few days, this sounded like a very exciting trip, and since I had already been laid off from Wards, I agreed to go along, even though it took all the money I had saved from the job.

Doug had made reservations for us at the big Mark Hopkins Hotel in San Francisco, but for whatever reason, the telegram he sent to Lois Mae or Mother about these reservations did not reach us. There were a lot of problems with communication at this time because of the extreme measures necessary to maintain secrecy in troop movements and other military matters. So we boarded the train to San Francisco without any idea where we would find Doug and he did not know that we had not received his reservation message.

After three days of train travel in coach chairs, standing up or sitting on the floor half the way because of the excessive amount of people traveling at this time, we finally arrived in Frisco and checked into the cheapest hotel we could find, certainly not the Mark Hopkins. The next day we made a lot of phone calls, but couldn't find out anything. We could have been talking to Doug's CO, but for security reasons he would not acknowledge a thing.

The following morning we went back to the ferry station on the bay, where most all train travelers have to go through to get to Frisco, and there, purely by accident, by the fate of the angel looking after us, we bumped into Doug among this huge mass of people at the ferry station.

Mother and I soon realized that we were excess baggage on this journey as far as Lois and Doug were concerned, so we turned around and went home while Lois Mae stayed on a while longer. Before she went home, it only took a couple more days at the Mark Hopkins and she had a ring on her finger. The ironic conclusion to all this is that Doug never did leave for overseas from San Francisco, but was transferred to Virginia. Do you suppose he knew all the time that he really wasn't going overseas then and only used this as an excuse to get Lois Mae to join him for a few days? No—I might do that, but I don't think Doug would.

Prior to going to San Francisco, Larry Schwartzbauer told me, "Everyone is making plans for the senior prom coming up after you get back, and you are going too."

I tried to beg off with, "I don't have a girlfriend and I don't know of anyone who would go with me."

"Nonsense. Leave it to me, I'll get someone to go with you." Before the day was over Larry cornered me and said, "There's a girl at Schwankel's Drug Store who I think really has a crush on you and she will go to the prom with you, I guarantee it. But she won't go unless you come in and ask her personally."

He wouldn't let me get out of it. I knew who he was talking about and she was a chubby little blond, not much to look at but I had to start someplace. I eventually got up the nerve to go into the drugstore and ask her, when no one else was around, and she graciously accepted. I had trouble dancing, even the slow ones and couldn't wait until the evening was over. I took my date home and actually kissed her on the lips, very quickly. We never went out again but I had broken the ice. Now I couldn't wait to kiss somebody that I had picked out and I had some feelings for. It took a while but before the year was over I scored a few kisses and was starting to feel like a normal teenager, sixteen going on seventeen.

At Washington High School there were several classes available to me which was different because there was just one set curriculum at Backus. I chose classes that might help me in the service if by chance I could get into the Army Air Corps like my brother. Unfortunately I made a couple of bad choices such as taking second algebra without having had first algebra. It was tough at first but I still ended up tutoring one of the football players in my class who later in life became a Federal District Judge—the Honorable Judge John Connelly. He must have had brains someplace. Maybe he just had to get rid of his jockstrap.

English, of course, is not one of those subjects where you have a choice, sad to say, and that almost became my high school demise. This English class, taught by Ms. Zender, was completely different from anything I was familiar with. The class, a full nine months of it, was entirely about the old masters such as Shakespeare, Chaucer, and others who bored me to death. Ms. Zender would just let her passion ooze out when she talked about these old farts. She was in love with them, which is about the only thing she could ever find to have a love affair with. The books were even written in the old English style, which made no sense to me at all, on top of which they were very difficult to read.

Well, I decided I could fake it through class and never opened a book. The first period I got a C. *Well, that's not too bad.* The next period was a D, which I had never had before. *Damn, this teacher is not only nuts, she is also going to be tough.* I still thought I could get by with good behavior and a little brown-nosing. This got me an F. I was devastated.

I was even more devastated after my conference with Ms. Zender and her threat of flunking me. She said, "No one in my class graduates from this school with a flunk in English." This is getting serious. I now decided to open my books and try to figure out what these creeps are talking about. I worked my way back to a marginal C the next period and then another F, but never got better than a D the remaining two periods.

I learned that my friends, Larry and George, were not doing much better than I was in another class, also with Ms. Zender. The lovable Ms. Zender then told each of us that everything now rides on how well we do in next week's final exam.

Larry said, "Don't worry, my friend Sara McDonough is in Zender's class also and she is taking the exam the day before we do. She's smart and I'll get her to copy down the answers for us." Larry could sweet-talk a girl into almost anything.

That night before our exam, Larry, George, and I, plus another boy who was also in trouble, all went to Sara's house and worked most of the night memorizing everything about the exam Sara was able to copy down or remember. She even looked up the correct answer to some things she knew she had missed. What a doll.

On the day before our final exam, Larry, George, and I were all scheduled in the same room together even though we didn't have our classes together. Who was the first one to finish and turn his exam papers in to Ms. Zender? George Muntean. Who was the second one? Larry Schwartzbauer. I wish they hadn't done that. I at least waited until the entire allotted time was up to turn in the exam, even though I was through earlier. Classes were now over and we only had to sweat out three more days until the graduation ceremonies, which took place downtown in the St. Paul Auditorium.

Everything went well except for this nervous guilty feeling I was carrying around, but I was greatly relieved to see my name in print on the graduation program, including Larry and George, among all the other Washington graduates. In fact, there was an asterisk by my name, along with about twenty-five or thirty other students, not because there was some question about these students being legitimate graduates, but because they supposedly graduated with honors, maybe the upper ten or fifteen percent of the class. Now I really felt guilty, but maybe not quite guilty enough to confess.

When the diplomas were passed out on the stage, we only received the fancy cover with nothing inside. This scared me, but then I learned that I simply had to go to the table marked "T through Z" to get my actual diploma. And who would be standing at that table to give me my diploma? Ms. Zender. I really didn't want to see her again, and she couldn't just hand me the diploma and let me run: she had to ask me about the final exam. "I am just dumfounded on how well you did on your final exam. How did you do it?" No, she would never say she was proud of me.

"I have to confess, I was up until after three in the morning studying for this test."

"And what is amazing," she said, "Larry and George even did better than you did. They had just about the two highest scores in the class."

"Well, we all studied together." I desperately wanted to cut this conversation short and I said, "I really have to go now, my mother is waiting for me." My mother was not even there.

I'm not especially proud of what I got away with, but I did graduate. Glory be!

God gives us our relatives…

…Thank God we can choose our friends.

Chapter 11

Most of your classmates would be older than you and the boys had either enlisted in one of the services or were drafted right out of high school. You had just turned seventeen and could not be drafted yet, but did you pursue other plans for military duty?

IT WAS A VERY emotional period for young men now coming out of high school. Without question you knew that your immediate future was going to be in one of the military branches of service, unless, of course, you were classified as 4-F, meaning that you were not physically or mentally qualified. The war was at its very peak in 1944 and no other exemption from military service was even considered for an eighteen-year-old male.

The fact that you might be thrust into military combat in some exotic part of the world was exciting and adventurous, and gave you the feeling of being patriotic, maybe even a bit heroic just by being a member of the U.S. fighting forces. You were no longer just a bungling teenager: you were finally being treated with some respect.

However, your emotions also took you into the areas of worry, uncertainty, and downright fear of the future. Reports of casualties were coming in every day and it was not unusual to know someone or hear of someone in your neighborhood that was killed or wounded or maybe missing in action. Households displayed banners in their windows that were white with a red and blue border. In the center were one or more large blue stars, representing a father, a husband, or son from that household that was in the military service. If that person was killed in the war, then the blue star was turned to gold. People driving or walking down a street couldn't help but watch for these banners and be proud of the many families that had members in the service, sometimes displaying two, three, or four stars, but you were also very sad if the banner displayed a gold star. That family member would not be coming home.

Prior to graduation, my first objective regarding military life was to try and get into the Army Air Corps like my big brother, even though I was not as passionate about flying as he was. By the spring of 1944, however, the Air Corps had about all the young men they needed. Even the air support personnel positions were taken, usually by pilot trainees that flunked out of flight school.

Next, I went to the Navy to see if they had anything open connected with flying. The recruiters gave me a song and dance and tried to talk me into signing up for their officer candidate school, which was filled, but they would put me on their waiting list. Before doing anything though, anyone under the age of eighteen had to have permission from both parents to enlist. I knew this would be difficult. One thing was certain: if I was going to avoid the draft I would have to enlist somewhere about two months before my eighteenth birthday.

On the day of my graduation I got a call at home from my Aunt Martha. "Did you know your father was in town?"

"No, I didn't. What's he doing here?" I was worried he wanted to come to my graduation, probably with his dirty old overalls on and cow shit on his boots.

"He's at Midway Hospital," Aunt Martha said, "having an operation for his hernia. He wants you to come and see him."

"His hernia? He's had that for years and has been too stubborn to do anything about it. Why does he have to have it operated on now? Anyway, I can't see him today. Tell him I'll come over tomorrow."

The next day I went to see him in the hospital and learned for the first time that he and Mayme were now married and living in Grove City, Pennsylvania, where he was planning to work for this huge diesel engine plant, Cooper Bessemer, building engines for ships and making big money. It sounded very exciting. He said that Mayme convinced him he should take care of his hernia or they may not hire him at the plant.

Dad had also gotten his teeth fixed (most of them were just pulled I think). He was shaving every day, he had bought some different clothes, and he was even brushing his teeth, something he had never done all the years I knew him. I asked him about all this and he smiled and said, "Mayme wouldn't marry me until I did these things."

Holy cow, what kind of a women was this Mayme that had such powers over this bull-headed old man? Mom could never get him to come in out of the rain unless he wanted to.

Dad said, "Mayme and I want you to come out to Pennsylvania and live with us."

"But Dad, I want to enlist in the Navy. They tell me that I might be able to go to their officer candidate school and that way I can also avoid the draft. However, I need your approval."

"No, you don't want to do that. You can't be drafted for another nine months and the war might be over by then. If you come out to Pennsylvania we can get you a job at this diesel engine plant and they're paying as much as nine or ten dollars an hour."

That kind of money I didn't believe was ever possible, so it was a bit intriguing. I had not had any money coming in since Christmas and I spent all the money I had saved on the trip to California. There was a girl from school that I now had nerve enough to ask out, but without enough money to go to a movie or buy an ice cream sundae, I didn't even want to see her.

Dad went on to say, "Mayme has a son, he's a little younger than you, but he's a good kid and you and he can have a good time together." That was another concern. What was I going to do here in St. Paul when all my friends were going into the Army right out of high school?

"I'll be out of the hospital in three or four days and as soon as I get back to Pennsylvania, we're going out to Norfolk, Virginia, to see Douglas and Lois. You can go with us."

That was the clincher. It sounded exciting to be taking a trip to the other side of the U.S. since I had already been to the West Coast. Besides, it would be good to see my brother once again before he went overseas.

Doug was transferred to Norfolk soon after we saw him in San Francisco and he was once more waiting for his overseas assignment. Lois Mae joined him there and they were married almost immediately.

I said, "I'll have to go home and check with Mom."

I thought Mother would put up some resistance, but she didn't seem to object much at all, in fact she practically encouraged it. Mother was unhappy with her job working nights and she had been talking about joining the WACs (Women's Army Corps). This made it easier for her now that she had fulfilled her responsibility of giving me a place to live while I finished school. Just like that, I was on my way to Pennsylvania, another bad decision on my part.

Our bus trip to Grove City was very hot, long, and tiring, and when we got there the picture was a lot more cloudy than the way Dad had painted it. First of all, they lived on a farm. I didn't know that. And then I found out that Dad, Mayme and her son were living in a house, not a very big house, with three of her brothers, two of which were bachelors and the other was married with a newborn baby that cried all night. They needed another body in the house like they needed another space heater on this 95-degree June day. I didn't know all this either, but I suppose it was my fault for not asking the right questions. Did I mention that there were also two dogs and any number of cats?

Henry (Hen for short) was the oldest of the brothers and I believe the owner of the house and farm. Bill, the other bachelor brother, was also older and a very strange, cynical individual. He had lots of money but didn't trust banks, so he had it stashed away in hiding places, which he thought was a lot safer. One time he took me out behind a barn where there was an old car chassis. He reached down behind the back seat and pulled out a roll of money with a rubber band around it that was at least four inches across. On the outside of the roll was a hundred-dollar bill, but he didn't open it up to show me the rest of it. I really warmed up to this guy, but the rubber band stayed very tight around that roll.

Shorty (I don't know if he had another name or not) was the youngest of the Dorsch family. He was young enough to be drafted, but since he was not, I assumed he was 4-F with a disability of some kind. I bet I can guess what it was. His wife was very fat and shorter than he was, and, being the other in-law female in this crowded house, did not get along with Mayme at all.

Mayme's son, also named Bill, was much younger than I expected, still in grade school, so we didn't have a lot in common. He also talked fast with a Pennsylvania mountain accent and I could hardly understand him. Nothing had been done about providing a bed for me, the ninth person in this household, but Mayme said young Bill wanted to sleep out on the porch and I could join him there. This was his idea of a great time. Okay, I'll go along with that, but I didn't know that our bed would be an old discarded mattress that smelled of dog pee and we would be on a ground-level porch with no screens around it.

The next morning around 5:00 a.m. there were a million flies zeroing in on us like we were two dead bodies of tender meat. *What in God's name am I doing here?*

The next day Dad, Mayme, Bill, and I boarded the bus for Norfolk, Virginia, to see Doug and Lois and I was assured I would have a place to sleep inside the house when we got back. It would be an old, beat-up davenport in the living room made up into a bed.

It was good to see my brother, who was now a B-24 pilot with a fancy uniform, but we only stayed a couple days because both Dad and I wanted to get back and start working.

The next day when we got back, I went to the Cooper Bessemer plant to apply for a job. They were ready to hire me, but when I took my physical I didn't pass because they said I had high blood pressure. This was not a total surprise, because it showed up as a concern when I tried out for sports in Backus, but they just ignored it. The nurse at the plant gave me some pills and told me to come back in about two weeks and take the physical again.

Mayme suggested I work for Shorty, who was sort of running the farm, and Mayme's brothers sort of did what she wanted. There was supposed to be some kind of salary involved but I don't recall ever receiving anything. Here I thought I had broken away from life on the farm, but I'll be damned if I wasn't back in the cow shit business and all that goes with it.

It was a very hot spring in Pennsylvania and there I was out in the fields stacking hay and cultivating corn along with all the other sweaty jobs that go with farming. I was almost glad when I got a nosebleed, which was at least once or twice a day, partly due, I suppose, to my high blood pressure. Then I could sit in the shade and put some cool water on my head.

I was finally hired by Cooper Bessemer but I found out the pay was not nearly as good as Dad had built it up to be. Besides, the only opening they had was a three-to-eleven night shift, six days a week. That meant I got home after midnight and had no social life whatsoever. Now I really wanted to get into the Navy quickly.

I was able to ride to work with another guy who worked the same shift, but I still wanted my own car. One of Mayme's brothers sold me his old Model A Ford, a beat-up old jalopy, but at least it was my car. I wish I still had it today as they are now collector's items. When I went into the service, Dad was going to keep it for me, but I never saw it again.

Dad and Mayme also made arrangements to move in with one of her other brothers and his wife, Howard and Sherena Dorsch, who lived about a mile away. The four of us were to have the upstairs, not very big and no separate bedrooms, but still a better arrangement than the other Dorsch household. Howard and Sherena, with a cute little three-year-old daughter, were the most normal of the entire clan, not without many of the Pennsylvania hillbilly characteristics, but we got along fine. Things were looking up.

I still kept bugging Dad to sign the parental consent form. He finally agreed. Now the next problem was to locate my mother. She had completed her basic training and was being assigned to a base someplace in Missouri, but I didn't have her new address and couldn't get in touch with her.

After about three weeks of harassing the mailman every day, I finally got a letter with her new address. She had no hesitation about giving her consent, but it still took another ten days before everything was in place and the Navy would consider my application.

Since I had started this whole process with the Navy recruiter back in St. Paul, I wanted to go back there to complete the enlistment, which I did right after Christmas. I quit my job at Cooper Bessemer, and after buying my car, which I left with my dad, I had just about enough money to buy my bus ticket back home. I still thought of St. Paul as my home, even though there weren't any more permanent ties there than there was anyplace else.

Once again, good old Aunt Martha and Uncle Charlie allowed me to move back in and wait for the Navy to call me. Once again I was off the farm, and once again I swore to myself that this would be the last time I would get trapped into doing something that was not completely of my own choosing. The Navy was all my own choice and I was going to try not to get killed, even though I couldn't swim.

My enlistment was accepted in the middle of February, but it wasn't until March 10, four days after my eighteenth birthday, that I was called to report to the Federal Building in Minneapolis to be sworn in with a bunch of other recruits, at about six-thirty in the morning. This was also a special day because Lois Mae, now living at home back in Minneapolis after Doug had finally been sent to the South Pacific, was giving birth to a son. I was going to be an uncle.

At about four-thirty in the morning we received word that Lois had given birth to their son, Richard, so I quickly got up and made a trip to the hospital to see Lois and the baby. By six o'clock I left the hospital and made it to the Federal Building to be sworn in. We were marched across the street to the Milwaukee Depot and by seven-thirty I was boarding the train heading off to war, or as it turned out, the non-war service life for the next fourteen months.

Lois Mae's brother, Dick, also went to the hospital that early morning to see his sister and nephew, although I had already left before Dick got there. Lois told her brother that I didn't have anyone to see me off at the train station and suggested he might want to run over there and see me before I left. Dick was a couple years older than me, but he would never be able to go into the service because he was involved in a terrible accident when he was younger and suffered with severely broken-up legs.

I didn't know Dick real well at this point, but he was a very happy-go-lucky individual in spite of being stripped of almost all of the normal use of his legs. Later on, he became one of my best friends to correspond with while I was in the Navy, and a very good friend when I got out.

At the train station I was watching all the other guys kissing and hugging their sweethearts, mothers and sisters, and since I had no one to see me off, I went onboard the train and watched from the window, feeling just a bit down. Then I spotted Dick looking all over for me. He was carrying a small package to give to me, which he had spent his last fifty cents to buy, but insisted that I not open it until the train had pulled out. Rolled up in the package was the latest issue of *Esquire Magazine*, a very popular men's magazine of its day (similar to the later *Playboy* magazine), with all the nudity, rare jokes and sexy cartoons. Once I started showing this around, I was the most popular guy onboard the train and it made the trip to Chicago a lot more pleasant.

One more step in the process of growing up was under way. I was now going off to fight a war—well, not really. My theater of war was not the beaches of Iwo Jima or some other remote Pacific island, but merely the beaches of Lake Michigan.

What we anticipate seldom occurs…

…What we least expect generally happens.

Chapter 12

Most people in the military service during World War II considered it a rather grim experience, particularly if they were among the ranks of the lower enlisted men. Was this true in your case?

IT WAS QUITE the contrary. Oh, there were some critical moments of concern at first, but again I was very lucky and on the whole I would say my military days were the very best days of my entire teenage life.

The train ride from Minneapolis to the Great Lakes Naval Training Station outside of Chicago took about ten hours. We were able to eat lunch in the dining car, compliments of the Navy, but we were given a box lunch and bedded down for the night, still in our civilian clothes, in a big barracks filled with bunk beds. We were awakened at six in the morning and marched to the mess hall for our first exposure to Navy chow.

The breakfast chow line consisted of huge quantities of whatever you wanted such as very hard fried eggs all broken up and dumped into a big pot, French toast, also dumped into a big pot and even less appetizing than the eggs, greasy bacon, oatmeal, cereal, and baked beans. Yes, Navy beans were on the breakfast menu every Wednesday and Saturday morning. They were supposed to give you the protein and energy you needed for the week. I don't know about that, but it sure gave everyone a lot of firepower. Now, is that where Navy beans got their name in the first place, or did the Navy start serving them just because they were called Navy beans? Who knows. Anyway, the sign at the beginning of the line said, "Take all you want, but you must eat what you take." So I was cautious and took a bowl of gummy oatmeal and milk and gagged it all down.

After breakfast we surrendered our civilian clothes and spent most of the entire day completely in the nude, getting shots, getting poked here and there, peeing in bottles, bending over and saying "aah," and getting what I suppose was a general physical. It was a gruesome as well as a humorous sight to see a couple hundred men running around with nothing on but a worried look on their faces, many of whom may previously have been shy about taking their clothes off even in front of their brothers. And then there were others who liked to flaunt it, a lot of different shapes, sizes, and colors. One young man with a white, petrified face, backed his butt up to the doc to get his needle, which he was told was a foot long and square, and as soon as he was stuck he started to urinate all over the place. A very funny sight for everyone but the kid and the doctor.

We ended up being fitted for an entirely new Navy wardrobe: Navy dress blues, dress whites, two sets of work jeans and shirts, two pair of shoes, a winter coat, a work jacket, underwear, blankets and two fart sacks. What's a fart sack? It's a sheet-like sack for your mattress that you slept on and let the Navy beans explode. The blanket was the muffler. Everything was dumped in one of the fart sacks and you were assigned to a company and barracks.

The next day was devoted to teaching you how to dress, how to make your bed so tight a quarter would bounce off it, and how to roll and fold your clothes so that everything you were issued (I mean everything) would fit into a sea bag about four feet tall and just a little bigger than a basketball around. It was incredibly efficient and very. practical, especially for shipboard duty. The trick was to be able to roll all your dress blues and whites with all the creases in the right places so that after they were packed inside your sea bag they would be perfectly pressed when you took them out and needed to wear them. In theory this really worked, but the best I could do was to look like I had been run over by a steam roller when I got dressed.

The clothes were designed, I think, so they would show dirt quickly, requiring you to be constantly washing them, by hand of course, in order to look presentable. Your shoes, even your work shoes, had to be polished so that you could see your face reflected in the leather. I learned that the pants were bell bottoms so you could take them off quickly even if you were in water, and we were told that the thirteen buttons in the front of your pants represented something patriotic like the thirteen original colonies. I never believed that. I think they were there to give you, or the girl you were about to make out with, a chance to have a change of heart while you were getting the damned things unbuttoned.

The Navy's overall routine, and especially boot camp, was a pain in the ass sometimes, but I liked it. Boot camp was all about being orderly so that you would accept command without even thinking. I liked the fact that everything was so very clean, neat and uncluttered, all the things I had not experienced on the farm. It was no problem for me to conform to this lifestyle and be very proud to be a part of it.

With a great deal of emphasis placed on cleanliness, you were constantly taking showers and washing clothes in your free time, but I never considered this a negative. I liked it because if you didn't keep yourself clean, the whole company was punished for it, and you could find yourself hauled into the shower by your shipmates and be given what was called a "GI shower." This meant you were held down and scrubbed with a stiff bristled floor brush until your skin was beet red. I saw this once and made sure it would never happen to me. With 140 guys all sleeping in the same room, it is understandable why body cleanliness was an absolute necessity, but there also would be an oddball or two who must get the message the hard way.

After we were in boot camp about a week, we had a "captain's inspection," which could happen at any time without warning. Your bed had to be made perfectly with the fart sack and pillow spotlessly clean. All your clothes had to be laid out in specific order, all clean and properly rolled. Anything that was not shipshape meant extra work duty or drill time, again not just for you but for the entire company. As a result, not only your company commander but all your shipmates were on your ass if you didn't keep everything in perfect order.

On this particular day we were given twenty minutes to get dressed and ready for the captain. Exactly twenty minutes later, in walks this tall man with all his gold braid and silver eagles shining brightly, while we are all standing at stiff attention by our stations, with our clothes laid out in front of us. He walked up and down the isles of men and bunks, occasionally pointing out something to the company commander or asking the orderly to make a note, but when he got to my station he lifted up the pillow on my bunk. Why he lifted up the pillow on my bunk I have no idea, because he didn't do it to anyone else. There under my pillow was a condom. I almost shit my pants.

"Who's bunk is this?" the captain asked.

"Mine sir, Seaman Wachs, serial number _____." (I knew my serial number then but I can no longer recite it.)

The captain said, "Master of arms, march this man over to my office and hold him there until I get back." Now I knew for sure I was going to shit my pants.

When the captain got back to his office I was sent to the office of another officer who had a little lower rank, but just as much gold braid and as many service ribbons. There he questioned me for about a half hour, inquiring about my sexual habits, my preferences between boys and girls, and so on. When he got around to question me about the condom, he didn't believe me when I told him I wasn't sure what it was because I had never seen one before.

He went on to explain about Section 8 of the Manual on Naval Regulations (I believe that is the proper section) where it covers reasons for discharge other than honorable or medical. In other words if you were a homosexual, you would be discharged. He used the word "queer." I knew what that was. Finally the officer was convinced that anyone as naive as I was probably was not guilty of hiding a condom under their pillow. I was sent back to my barracks. However, the entire company was put on probation with extra work, extra drill time, and fewer privileges until someone confessed to the prank.

Everyone in the company at this point turned detective and began grilling one another. Because of our extra work and fewer privileges, we were identified as the screw-up company to everyone else in the regiment, so we wanted the problem put behind us as soon as possible. Two days later someone actually confessed to the incident and he was immediately transferred out of our company, probably for his own safety.

We all learned a lot from that experience, mostly that you could no longer do things as an individual. You were now part of a team and you had to do everything good or bad as a unit. It really created dependency and discipline that could not be achieved otherwise.

Boot camp at this time of year at the GLNTS (Great Lakes Naval Training Station) presented a lot of problems because of the weather. It was often very cold or rainy, but if the sun came out it got hot. The typical bureaucratic action on the part of the Navy was that they insisted everyone on the base be dressed exactly the same at all times. You might start out the day wearing your heavy P jacket because it was cold outside. Then it might start to rain, but you couldn't put your rubberized poncho on until there was a uniform change order from the base headquarters. By the time this order came down you may be already soaked to the skin, but you still had to put on your rubberized poncho over your P jacket and you kept right on drilling. Then maybe the sun would come out and the temperature would go up about 30 degrees. You still kept on marching, and sweating. By the time they got around to tell you to strip down to your jeans and shirt, the sun was going down and it was turning cool again, but your body was still soggy from the earlier rain and sweat.

Perhaps all this had something to do with the fact that one day I got sick and begged for permission to go to "sick bay." Sick bay was the Navy's answer to a neighborhood medical clinic, with no doctors, some male nurses and a few medical specialists. Their diagnosis was that I just had a cold and I should get back to my company and quit complaining. The next day it was the same routine with the weather and the appropriate uniform, but I was now getting sicker. Not wanting to be a complainer, I tried to tough it out and then I started vomiting during a close order drill exercise. This really upset the company commander and he ordered me to go back to sick bay.

When I got there the nurse or the doctor or whatever he was said, "Pull up your shirt and let me see your belly." He poked his finger into my belly and stepped back. The diagnosis was different this time. "Hey swabbie, you have a beautiful case of scarlet fever. Your belly is a very ripe strawberry. Stay right in this room and don't talk to anyone while I get a vehicle to take you to the hospital."

Later, I learned that out of our company of 140 men, 111 already had scarlet fever when they were kids. The remaining twenty-nine were almost certain to get it. By the time I got to the hospital my temperature was 105 and for the next two days it never dropped below 106.

When I was too weak to climb up into my upper bunk, they moved me from a ward of about sixty men to a ward of about twenty-five. One of the patients there told me that four men out of that ward had already died from scarlet fever, which did wonders for my spirits even if he may not have known what he was talking about. One of the nurses asked me (they at least had female nurses here), "Do you want us to contact your parents?"

I said, "Does this mean I'm going to die?"

If Mother, Dad, and Mayme all converged on me at once, I thought that in itself may be enough to kill me. "No thanks. Let's not call anyone yet."

I don't know how long it was before a real doctor finally came to see me. My fever still hadn't broken in spite of the penicillin and the extra heavy doses of sulfa I was getting. The doctor said to his nurse assistant, "This kid needs the serum. Get it ready right away."

A large syringe of purple fluid was shot in my veins, one in each arm. The nurse told me the serum was in limited supply and very expensive, so they would only give it to someone who was critically ill. Since it had to be made from the blood of someone who had been cured of scarlet fever, I was told that I would have to give a pint of blood before leaving the hospital.

Almost immediately my fever started to break and for two days I did nothing but lay in bed and sweat. I had all the symptoms of total dehydration, but I couldn't keep anything in my stomach, not even water. IV injections of fluid, for some reason, were not used there, or at least I did not see them.

Penicillin was the new cure-all medication of this day and I was being given the maximum dosage: a shot every four hours for ten days straight, or a total of sixty shots. After your butt has been stabbed sixty times, thirty in each cheek, it's hard to find a new piece of skin that hasn't already been drilled. For many guys, may I say, this was a real pain in the ass. The secret was to completely relax your muscles, so the needle would go in freely, but some guys were so tense about getting a needle, they would grip the sides of their bunks for dear life and turn as white as the fart sack. Well, that old needle would just bounce off their butts like throwing darts into a concrete wall.

This problem was further magnified because some of the nurses would come on duty for their midnight shift drunk, I mean really falling-down drunk. Most of the nurses were male, but it seemed like it was only the four or five female nurses whose drinking affected their ability to give a penicillin shot. It was hard to relax under these circumstances, but I saw one nurse bend three or four needles on a guy's butt before she could get one to penetrate, and then she almost fell over into his bed in the process. These were not the kind of girls you would want in your bed, drunk or not.

If you were what they called a "bed patient," you were not allowed to leave your bunk other than go to the bathroom. Once you were well enough, you were labeled an "up patient" and you were immediately required to do work detail from that point on, which included kitchen duties, washing windows, scrubbing floors, laundry, cleaning latrines, and so on. I was very fortunate to be assigned KP duty, kitchen patrol, which was the easiest I think, plus you had access to more food.

After three weeks in the hospital I was scheduled to go back to active duty, but I first had to give my pint of blood. I was scheduled to give blood at ten that morning, but the rule was, you could not have anything to eat before you gave blood. Ten o'clock came and went, which seemed to be quite normal for this place, but it was almost three in the afternoon before they got to me. By this time of course, all the mess halls in the hospital were closed, so now I had missed two meals.

By five o'clock I was transported back to the regiment headquarters and after more delays and more paper work, I was told to pick up my gear and head for my new company barracks about a quarter-mile away. My gear was all bundled up and tied together with my sea bag, which I'm sure weighed at least 120 pounds. It was all I could do to lift it, but I finally got it up on my back and started out across "the grinder" for my barracks. (The grinder was a blacktop area of about four or five city blocks where we did all our marching and various exercises.)

I don't think I made it halfway across before I passed out. When I woke up I was in the back end of an ambulance, going like hell with its sirens wide open, on my way back to the hospital. They all fussed over me at the hospital for a bit until I convinced them the only thing that was wrong with me was that I was starving to death. As soon as they fixed me a tray of food I was fine, but I still had to stay in the hospital another two days.

The next time I was sent back to active duty they were not going to take any chances with me. They transported me right up to the front door of the barracks. I was assigned to a new company made up of guys who had all been discharged from the hospital. They called it the "sickie company," which didn't bother me a bit because we got special treatment: we didn't have to take swimming lessons, overnight marches, hard-core combat drills, and a lot of other silly stuff.

Once again I was a lucky son of a gun because I learned that my original company went on to train as frogmen for the eventual invasion of Japan. Can you imagine me being a frogman in the Navy when I could barely make it across the swimming pool dog paddling? I actually did pass my swimming test, which consisted of jumping off a high tower into a deep pool and then dog paddling or floating around the pool for a period of two minutes. I guess that was an exceptionally good day for me because I haven't been able to do it since.

In the final analysis I suppose I should say, "thank God I got scarlet fever." But then, of course, the atom bomb took Japan out of the war. No one in our company, including me, had to go through the anticipated invasion of Japan, which would have been a horrible slaughter. Except that I wouldn't have been killed by the enemy; I would have drowned as a frogman.

Being assigned to the sickie company meant that I had to spend another five weeks in boot camp. I was desperate to get out, but then another snag turned up.

Our company, the sickly sailors, again got special treatment. We were all to be assigned to stateside Naval bases. In fact, I was even given a choice of three different locations where I could go, something totally unheard of before or since in any branch of the military service. My three choices were Traverse City, Michigan; Olathe, Kansas; or Minneapolis. Traverse City was a small station of about 250 men. Minneapolis, I believe, was even smaller and Olathe was quite large. I didn't really care about going back to my hometown area, so I chose Traverse City. I couldn't have made a better choice.

I was given my orders, my train tickets, my travel allowance and four days to get to Traverse City. This was no problem from Chicago, so I decided to go home to St. Paul for the weekend. The snag in all this was that I had to have my teeth checked and any needed work completed before I could leave the base. When your name begins with "*W*," you are most always on the tail end of any schedule and the best appointment I could get with the Navy dentist was at nine p.m. on the night before I was to leave.

I arrived at the dental clinic well before nine and waited and waited until I was the last patient in the building. Finally the dentist came out of his cubicle, gave me a disgusted look and said, "Go on back to your barracks. It's nearly 9:30 and I'm through for the day."

He was an officer and I was trained to say, "Yes sir" when a command was given, but in this instance I had to plead my case. In about ten seconds I covered my situation of almost dying of scarlet fever, of being on this base for thirteen weeks without seeing beyond the ten-foot fence, of having the opportunity to go home for two days before reporting to my new assignment and all I had to have was his approval that my teeth were okay before I could go.

He must have had a heart somewhere under his white jacket and reluctantly said, "Get in here and get up in that chair." It was now just a little past 9:30 by his clock. He was obviously very tired from what was no doubt a twelve-hour day and he said, "This better be quick. Open your mouth."

His next words were, "Oh shit!" I have a way of extracting the most choice remarks from my dentists. He hollered for his dental assistant—"Get your ass in here!"—prepared a syringe of Novocaine, pushed my chair completely back, and jumped on my lap straddling me like you would ride a horse. He knew it would be the only way he could keep me in the chair once I experienced what he was about to do.

He first shot my jaw with the Novocaine for a wisdom tooth that had to come out. He then began drilling two molars that had to be filled and the smoke from the dull drills rolled out of my mouth along with efforts to scream, while I kept reminding myself, *I've got to go through with this if I want to get out of this place.* Finally, after pulling the wisdom tooth and stuffing my mouth with cotton to soak up the blood and muffle the swearing I was directing at him, he said, "Okay sailor, get out of here and have a good trip home."

I said, "Thanks, you SOB," but I don't think he could hear me. Before I left I looked at the clock on the wall and it was just about 9:40, meaning the entire procedure took less than ten minutes. And the Novocaine was just now starting to take effect. I staggered back to my barracks and spent the rest of the night spitting blood and stuffing my mouth with the extra cotton the corpsman had given me. By six in the morning I had my duffel bag packed as well as my mouth and was ready to board the train to St. Paul, still in a great deal of misery, but grateful I was finally through with an experience I will never forget.

At my aunt and uncle's house in St. Paul there was a surprise waiting for me. My mother was on leave from her WAC base, and had arrived there the day before. There was no prearranged plan for us to meet in St. Paul, it was just a coincidence that we both arrived there about the same time. I hadn't seen Mother for a long time, in fact I had not even seen a picture of her in a WAC uniform and I was quite impressed by how good she looked.

Her health apparently wasn't that good, though, and she expected to receive a medical discharge. What the illness was, I'm not sure: some kind of female disorder I believe. Anyway, she was in St. Paul to look for an apartment when she got out of the service. Apparently she was not invited, or did not want, to move in with her Aunt Emma where she had lived before.

After two days in St. Paul, I was back on the train again looking forward to my new life in Traverse City, Michigan, where I must say, I really first started to grow up.

THE NAVY DENTIST

There are two kinds of men who never amount to much...

...Those who cannot do what they are told and those who can do nothing else but what they are told.

Chapter 13

Everyone knows war is hell and most unfair, but it must have been totally devastating to you when you realized your theater of war, beginning in June, would be the summer resort community of Traverse City, Michigan. Tell us about some of your spine-chilling battles and heroic missions.

THE PART THAT was hell was that I was still a kid and not quite ready yet to deal with the quick conversion to manhood and the opportunities that lay before me. (That may not have been the best choice of words.)

Traverse City was a neat little resort town that was the home of a former Coast Guard station, which had since been converted into a small Naval air station. The base only had a compliment of about two hundred and fifty men, but it had everything any military base would normally have including a PX, a mess hall, a sick bay, a brig and, last but not least, a fire station, the unit to which I would be assigned.

What made this place so unique was the fact that it was the ideal place for college girls from Michigan State, the University of Michigan, and other schools to go in the summer and work or just spend their summer vacations. It was some bright sailor's calculation based on some published statistics that there were at least 2.8 single available females in Traverse City in the summer for every man on the base, single or otherwise. No man in the history of military service could ever be so lucky to have a mission to defend his country in a place like Traverse City. I did my best to serve my country well.

After checking in at the air base in Traverse City, I was taken to the fire station, introduced to the other men, given a bunk and a locker, and shown around.

The routine for the firemen was twenty-four hours on duty and twenty-four hours off. Every other weekend you were on duty for forty-eight hours. You could also arrange to have a three- or four-day weekend periodically if you could work out a trade with the other guys.

On the afternoon I arrived, I was on the off-duty shift and other members on the same shift were getting ready to go on liberty. Nobody spent much time hanging around the fire station if you were off duty because if you were there and there happened to be a fire, you could quickly be called into service.

One of the guys (his name was something Osbourn, but he was only known as Ozzie) called me aside. The first thing he said to me was, "How old are you?"

I replied, "I'm eighteen."

"You look older than that. Let me see your ID card." Like he was a Navy SP or something. (That's shore patrol or a Navy cop.) I showed it to him and he went into another room with it.

About twenty minutes later he came back and said, "Here's your ID. You're now twenty-one and you're going out with us tonight."

I looked at the ID and I couldn't believe it. It appeared to be encased in the same plastic it originally came in, but my year of birth was now 1924, not 1927. Whatever he did, it was perfect, as if it had been typed that way originally. I kept this same ID card all the time I was in the Navy and no one ever challenged it.

It was common knowledge that nearly everyone under the age of twenty-one had false IDs, but it seemed there was no real concern about it.

In spite of the fact that a second-class seaman's pay was only fifty-four dollars a month, I believe I consumed more alcoholic beverages during the summer and fall of 1945 than any other time in my life. That may not have been the only thing I did in my young Navy career that I was not too proud of.

All the men at the fire station were older than me, and everyone got along amazingly well. I never did get to know too many of them by their real names because everyone had a nickname and that's what they went by, which for the most part was tied to their nationality. For example, the Polish guy named Modesko, was called the Polak, an English chap named Chamberlain was called the Limey. One was called Dutch, another the Frog and so on. Even the Mexican lad, also from St. Paul, was called the Spic. I'm sure glad there were no African Americans in the group because the fire house gang wouldn't have hesitated to use the "N" word for his nickname. That may have been a problem.

Ozzie, the counterfeit man, asked me, "Where you from?"

I said, "Minnesota" and almost immediately some other guy said, "You must be a Swede."

From that moment on I was known only as "Swede," even though it had nothing to do with the fact that I was half-Swedish.

There was plenty of work to do around the fire station and you always had to be ready to jump on the truck when there was a fire or a fire drill, which occurred at least two or three times a week. I started out as a hose man but was quickly assigned as a second driver on one of the trucks because I had some experience with machinery, could drive a vehicle with a clutch transmission and because I tested well.

The drills were set up by the chief at various locations on the base. You never knew for sure if it was a drill or an actual fire until you had driven to the scene, laid the hose, tied into a hydrant and got the pumps going. The fastest time we ever had on a drill was at the BOQ building: two minutes and twenty seconds from the alarm to water running out of the hose. This was a remarkable time and we constantly tried to beat it, but never could.

We were recognized as a very efficient fire company and were given lots of accolades including some by the Traverse City fathers. When there was a city fire we were also called and most often we were at the scene before the city units got there even though we were farther away. The majority of the real fires were very small and the type that most any drunken sailor could put out with his own personal hose and a full bladder. But we were called to a farmer's place once where the barn was in full blaze. We couldn't save it, but we kept his house from burning by using a large tank full of fruit orchard bug spray and pumped it on the house to cool it down while the barn burned.

There was also a liquor store fire in Petosky, a little town about twenty miles north of Traverse City that we were called on. Since there was no city water system, we could only use the tanks of water carried on the trucks as long as they lasted. This at least kept the restaurant next door from burning, which happened to be owned by the same guy who owned the liquor store. He was so grateful to have his restaurant saved that he allowed us to load up the empty water tanks on the trucks with any unbroken bottles of liquor, wine, and beer. The chief wasn't with us on this run, so we had to be especially creative in finding hiding places for all the stuff when we got back to the base. For a little while at least, going out on liberty and getting smashed was a little cheaper.

I was soon about to discover a new phobia that was much worse than my original fear of speaking in front of a group of people. No, it wasn't the fear of fire. That didn't bother me in the least. It was acrophobia, the fear of heights and going up a ladder, not something too beneficial for someone whose occupation as a fireman.

One day an alarm came in calling us to the base radio tower. All the other guys knew about this drill except me. It meant that we were to climb a hundred-foot tower on a wood ladder attached to the side going straight up to the top. It may not have been exactly one-hundred-feet tall, but after you have gone up the first thirty or forty feet, it makes little difference if it's eighty or ninety or the Sears Tower. The tower was a simple wood frame about five-feet square that had a little larger platform on the top and a narrow walkway around it about halfway up.

There were no guard rails or safety screens around the ladder.

All the guys in the drill scrambled up the ladder and I was the last to go. I managed to make it to the narrow walkway halfway up and decided to take a little rest. There I made the mistake of looking down and could not possibly have gone a step further even if there had been a million dollars waiting for me at the top. In fact, the big question was, how was I going to get down. When the other guys climbed down past me I managed get my knees to stop shaking long enough to make the first step.

Back at the fire station Ozzie asked me, "What happened Swede? You didn't go all the way up the hundred-foot tower?"

"I don't know, Ozzie. I just froze and I couldn't make my legs go any further."

"What did the chief say to you?"

"He hasn't said a word."

"That probably means he's pissed and you can be sure we'll be going on another tower drill soon."

"But I don't think I can make it, Ozzie."

"You've got to, Swede. Otherwise you could get a court martial for disobeying an order."

"Oh shit, what does that mean? Not a firing squad I hope?"

"No, they only shoot you if you disobey an order during combat, but you could go to the brig for two weeks on bread and water, and the chief could have you transferred off the base."

I certainly didn't want that, but I was like Jack Benny, the penny-pinching comedian, when the robber stuck a gun to his head and said, "Give me your money or it's your life."

After a few moments the robber said, "Come on, what will it be?"

Jack Benny said, "I'm thinking about it."

The next few days were the worst of my Navy career: stressed with anxiety, not sleeping, and worrying about what I was going to do when the order came to climb the f-ing hundred-foot tower again. Sure enough, about ten days later, the alarm went off and the dispatcher said, "To the tower men, on the double."

I instinctively jumped on the back of the truck and good old fearless Ozzie was there beside me. "Don't worry Swede, I'm going to help you." I didn't answer him.

We got to the tower and four or five other guys went ahead leaving only Ozzie and me. "Okay Swede, get up there. I'll be right behind you." All the way up he kept on giving me encouragement. We got to the walkway and he wouldn't let me stop; I gritted my teeth and kept on going. It seemed like an endless climb, but we finally made it to the top.

I crawled on to the platform and just sat there. I think my knees were shaking too much for me to stand up anyway. It actually was quite beautiful up there. You could see the entire town of Traverse City below, the rolling green hills to the east, Traverse Bay to the west and way out into the endless waters of Lake Michigan.

Finally the chief hollered the order to come down and once again, good-old Ozzie stayed behind to wait for me. "I can't make it, Ozzie."

"Yes you can, Swede. Going down is a lot easier."

"But I feel like I'm going to pass out and if I fall to the ground I'll go splat like a bug on a windshield."

"If you start to feel faint, Swede, just lock your legs in the ladder rungs and you won't be able to fall even if you pass out. Here let me show you." He went down the ladder a couple of steps, locked his legs in the ladder rungs, took his hands off the ladder and leaned back. "Look, Swede."

I couldn't look at him. Eventually I eased over to the edge of the platform and stuck my leg down to feel the first rung of the ladder. When I was able to make the first step, Ozzie was there hovering all around me and he was right, the going down part wasn't that bad. I swear, if it wasn't for Ozzie, I may never have gotten off that damn tower or maybe they would have hung my dog tags around a rock on the ground where I splattered.

Finally on the ground with my legs like two hunks of Jell-O, the chief said to me, "What's the matter Swede, a little shaky up there?" I wanted to say, "Go f--- yourself, chief." But I just walked away and didn't say anything. I wasn't going to get court-martialed now. I also made up my mind that, now that I had made it up the hundred-foot tower once, I could do it again. I was finally going to grow up and be a man. But I also prayed that the dumb sadistic chief wouldn't make us do that again.

Apparently my prayers were answered because we were never required to do that drill again. It seems that when we were all up fooling around on the f-ing tower, the base commander was watching from his office window. The next day our chief had a larger new rectum carved to fit the rest of his personality. Shortly thereafter he was transferred off the base for good, leaving our firehouse much more a fun-house.

The purpose of the Navy air base was to test new warfare equipment such as pilotless planes, rockets, gliders, and other innovative means of transporting high explosives into enemy targets without risking human life in the process. Some of these included V-2 rockets captured from the Germans, which the base was studying and trying to duplicate. So our fire-fighting tasks involved a lot of these maneuvers. A rocket might set off a brush fire around the base, or a glider might go down where it wasn't supposed to, with maybe someone in it, or maybe not.

We never actually had to rescue anyone out of a burning plane, but we drilled constantly on the procedure should it ever come about. We practiced using the carcass of an old Navy trainer that we would cover with oil and set afire. Dummies were set in position where men would be and it was our job to go into the burning plane and pull them out. We got so good at this that it got boring, so one of our guys volunteered to sit in the burning plane in place of the dummy and then we would rescue a live body, hopefully he would still be a live body. Guess who the volunteer was: my friend, gutsy, crazy Ozzie.

Ozzie was heavier than the dummies, but after a little struggle we pulled him out. Unfortunately there was a little too much burning oil around his feet and it melted the rubber on his boots, giving him some sizable blisters on his feet and shins. The chief complimented us on a fine effort, but at the same time begged us not to tell anyone what had happened or he would have been court-martialed for sure.

Early on while fighting the bloody battles of Traverse City, I became smitten with a little French girl named Jane, who seemed to quickly accept my shy backward ways. She was a real beauty, but I just as quickly became disenchanted when I found out she had been out with half the men on the base, and was hanging out in the town bars even though she still had a year to go yet in high school. I was still too naive and not ready to accept the lifestyle of these fast females that grew up around military bases. But it turned out for the best.

I got to know Jane's cousin, Louise, and she was a lot different. Her mother was very skeptical of boys in bell bottom trousers, especially those that had replaced their thirteen pants buttons with zippers. Louise became my regular friend while in Traverse City once I got on her mom's good side. This I did by getting things out of the PX that civilians couldn't buy in the local stores such as soap, sugar, shortening, nylons and many other things that I could acquire for little and sometimes for nothing.

On our first date, I asked Louise what size nylons her mother wore. When I showed up with the nylons and five pounds of sugar, her mom thought I must be a real sweet guy. I'm sure she thought I was a fairly safe risk for not getting her daughter knocked up. Mothers can be naive, too.

To begin with I was still only allowed to sit on the back porch and listen to records or go to the beach with Louise, but that was okay because I was always short of money. Later on, when I was allowed to take Louise to a movie or some party, I would have to say, "I would really like to see you this weekend, but I am broke."

Louise would say, "Mom said she would give us ten dollars, but she wants to know if you can get her some bath soap."

"I can do that, but I am really flat broke. I don't even have enough money for bus fare."

"That's okay. I can get the car as long as I don't stay out too late." What a deal. It was really a tough war up there on the beaches of Lake Michigan, but somebody had to fight it.

The reason I was always broke was because I was only receiving half my pay, or twenty-seven dollars a month. The balance was taken out and sent home to my mother because of her medical discharge from the WACs. After her discharge she was recognized as my dependent and along with the other half of my pay, she was also given a small pension by the government to live on. But typical of government welfare programs, this would all be taken away from her if she got a job, so she did nothing. The good news: with Mother as a dependent, I was able to get a discharge from the service much earlier than normal, and in spite of my good life, I was ready to take advantage of that.

The duty as a fireman couldn't have been better, especially after the old chief got transferred out. We had special privileges, like always having a vehicle with a radio wherever we went. We were served our meals in the mess hall without standing in line so we could eat quick and get back on duty. We even had the means to prepare our own meals back at the firehouse, like eggs, bacon, toast, and coffee. Our duty days and our liberty days were from noon to noon so you had time to sleep off a hangover before you had to go back to work.

Speaking of hangovers, one day my friend, the Polak, asked me if I had ever been to a Polish wedding. We had a long weekend off together and he had a cousin that was getting married in Flint, Michigan, on the other side of the state. We had to hitchhike and didn't make it in time for the wedding ceremony, but the timing was perfect for the two- or three-day reception that was to follow. His cousin was marrying another swabbie and we were the only other two military people at the wedding. The food, wine, beer, and what-have-you was poured immediately and we were treated like heroes. After about six hours of lapping up this hero-worship stuff; along with the wine and beer, I no longer had a conscious nerve in my body.

I woke up Sunday morning in an upstairs bedroom of a house to the smell of bacon and eggs cooking downstairs. *Where in the hell am I? How did I get here? Who put me to bed, and took my clothes off?* I quietly got up washed my face, and put on my uniform, now smelling a bit like the bottom of a beer barrel, and timidly walked downstairs to meet a very nice Polish family with three beautiful daughters. They were all in a jovial mood. They assured me that I had been a perfect gentleman, and immediately thrust a Bloody Mary in my hands, the first time I'd ever tasted such a drink. They said I had simply passed out, like it was an everyday occurrence. The daughters had to convince their parents that they should take me home, but I never did find out, nor did I ask, who took my clothes off.

Without thinking I asked, "Where is my friend, the Polak?" As soon as I said it, I knew I shouldn't have used the word "Polak," but I didn't know him by any other name.

"We haven't seen your friend, but don't worry about him. He'll no doubt be at the party again this afternoon."

The second party was no different from the first: more food, more barrels and bottles, and sure enough, my friend showed up. Everybody but the bride and groom showed up, all moving a little slower, but ready to eat, drink and be merry like there was no tomorrow. There was a tomorrow and we were invited to stay for a third day of partying but we had to get back to our base. I haven't been to a Polish wedding since. I wonder if they still do that.

When the war ended in the summer of 1945, our base was scheduled to be closed and everyone was starting to ship out. This was a real blow to most of the civilian population because the Navy base, small as it was, was a big part of the economy, especially the bars. And, of course, the girls, some of them maybe now pregnant, were losing touch with their men before they got their hooks into them. The big parades and celebrations over the Japanese surrendering had a bit of a cloud over them, at least for the local girls.

As a fireman, I was among the last of twelve men to stay and secure the base and then finally close it down and turn it over to the city. The city turned it into their municipal airport and I believe it still operates as such. This gave our fire crew even more privileges. For almost a month we were transported into town to the Grand Hotel for all our meals three times a day. Everything on the menu was available to us representing quite a change from the many meals of Australian mutton we were living on before.

On the day of our final departure in late October, crowds of civilians showed up at the train station to say good-bye. They even had the local high school band there playing "Anchors Away." Wow! We were treated like heroes.

I'm sure I wasn't the only guy to have this problem, but I had two girls show up at the train station to see me off and get my commitment to be loyal to them, exchange pictures, promise to write and so forth. In addition to Louise, there was another gal I dated (can't remember her name now) who was a cashier at a local supermarket and, in my opinion, looked like a young Barbara Stanwyck. I did my best to say good-bye to each girl without the other one seeing me. And in the process, I forgot to get my Navy authorization form converted to a train ticket, which could only be done at the Traverse City station. As a consequence I had to dodge the train conductor, hide in the John, lie, use deceptive maneuvers and with a lot of help from my Navy buddies, I went all the way to California without a train ticket. All that female attention I was getting back in Traverse City made it worthwhile, and now I could handle it. California would be totally different.

We arrived in Mojave, California, in late October, which was always the rainy season of the year. It was a mess. The desert, ordinarily a dusty, windy, flat rock, was now a muddy hole. The only ship I ever saw, all the time I was in the Navy, was one built out of solid concrete, stuck in the middle of the desert and used for target practice.

Our new base was formerly a Marine air base, but was now being taken over by the Navy to continue the program of testing unusual and experimental aircraft. As the Marine soldiers shipped out and the Navy sailors moved in there were a lot of fights in the town bars, some of a very serious nature. The hospitals and jails were filling up rapidly. Fortunately most of this was over with by the time I got there.

I was again assigned to the base fire station, this time as a driver on one of the big pump and ladder trucks. It was very quiet duty with no serious fires and very few fire drills all the while I was there. Our schedule of duty and liberty was even better than Traverse City, but unfortunately there was nothing to do. Some of the guys even got civilian jobs driving trucks during their off-duty time.

While there was an abundance of girls at Traverse City, there were only two girls I knew who lived in the little town of Mojave that were even remotely eligible. They were good looking and, of course, would not associate with anyone but the base officers. We poor swabbies had to travel to Bakersfield or L.A. to find any female companionship, and that was very limited and risky.

A few of us had a week's liberty over the Christmas holiday and we went to L.A., Long Beach, San Diego, and Tijuana, Mexico. We toured Hollywood, went to the Red Skelton show, the Edgar Bergen, Charlie McCarthy show and several others, wherever the tickets were free. We were even given tickets to the Rose Bowl game on New Year's day, but it was so hot there that we chose to spend our time on the beach or the air-conditioned bars. Long Beach was not a friendly town to the sailors. It hurt to see signs in the restaurant windows that read "Dogs and Sailors Not Allowed." Any girl who might be willing to talk to you had to be a hooker or even worse.

The day of my scheduled discharge finally came in May, and although they put a lot of pressure on some of us to volunteer for a tour of duty involving the atom bomb testing in the South Pacific, I said no, and no, and no, to everything. Ed Koperskie (Ski), Tony the Wop, and I were the only three guys still together from the Traverse City firehouse, so we decided to have a little party on the Saturday before our Monday morning departure.

Ski was married to a Traverse City girl who came with a newborn baby, so he and his family lived in Quonset hut quarters, an ideal place to have our private party. The party supplies consisted of two cases of beer and a fifth of bourbon, which was enough for the five of us only because Ed's wife, Emma, and their baby did not drink. Emma also baked a cake, which I helped decorate with green-colored frosting. The fact that it was green and the fact that I ate half of it, probably had something to do with fact that I got so sick that I thought I was going to die, and then later I was afraid I wouldn't die. (The beer and bourbon had nothing to do with it, I'm sure.)

On Sunday morning, with Ed, Emma, and Tony being good Catholics and wanting to go to their last Navy Mass, I was left to baby-sit the little Koperskie daughter. As soon as they walked out the door she began her panic crying, but all I had to do was breathe on her and she would go right back to sleep. The poor kid probably became an alcoholic before she was two months old.

On Monday morning, still a bit hung over, we all got on a bus and headed for Paris Island in the Long Beach area, where we were to get our discharge. After filling out another mountain of papers, on which I said NO to everything again, I was given a little emblem to sew on my uniform jumper. It was a golden eagle in a circle, which they called a ruptured duck, but it meant that I was once again a civilian. Glory, Hallelujah, and Amen.

If a man doesn't keep pace with his companions,

Perhaps it is because he hears a different drummer.

Let him step to the music he hears,

However measured or far away.

Chapter 14

Like thousands of other servicemen now being discharged, no doubt you gave a lot of thought to school, work, and other decisions about what you would do after military life. What were your post-Navy plans?

I DIDN'T HAVE a clue about what I was going to do. My only immediate plan was to go visit my brother, whom I had not seen in over two years. I got my final pay, bought a train ticket and headed for Dayton, Ohio, where Doug and Lois were living at the Wright Patterson Air Force Base.

I hoped to get some sage advice from Doug about where I should live and what I should consider doing in the immediate future. After all, I still admired the guy a great deal and trusted his judgment. He had been decorated for his combat service, so he should have some smarts about steering his kid brother in the right direction.

I knew I didn't want to go back to Pennsylvania to live with my dad and Mayme, but I also wasn't sure if I wanted to live with my mother.

My hero brother was of no help. All he would recommend was that I try and go back to school and take advantage of the free college tuition the government offered to any discharged serviceman. That was a given, I already knew I wanted to do that.

While in Dayton I had a good time as the guest of this hot shot Major Wachs, his wife and child. Right away I let him know that I wasn't going to salute him because this ruptured duck on my uniform said that I was a civilian and I didn't have to salute anyone.

Major Doug pulled some strings one day and took me for a ride in a two-seated Air Force trainer. It was one of those low wing prop driven jobs with tandem duel controls under a total glass canopy. We flew all over the state of Ohio. In fact, he even let me fly it, which would have gotten him in serious trouble if anyone found out about it. He had me convinced that I had gotten us totally lost while I was flying it. Needless to say he was shittin' me and we made it back to the base on schedule.

We also went to a major league baseball game in Cincinnati—my first major league game ever and a major thrill.

Lois was always finding some reason to throw a party and my presence was one of those reasons. I tried my best to act like an honored guest in front of all these officers and their wives, but I blew it with my recent drunken sailor upbringing and a few of the basic descriptive adjectives for my vocabulary I had learned in the Navy. I remember telling a group of ladies about one of my fire-fighting experiences and when I got to the exciting part, I was talking fast and I simply said, "That motherf-ing fire got so f-ing hot it burned my __!" I just blurted it out before I realized what I had said and then I ran off to the bathroom to bury my face in a bowl of cold water. I was terribly embarrassed, but it didn't seem to bother Lois and Doug. The ladies just couldn't stop laughing.

The next day Lois took me downtown to Daytons to buy some civilian clothes, which was a lot of fun because it was the first time I can remember ever shopping for anything of my own choosing. By evening, I was on the train on my way back to St. Paul.

Mother acted like she was all bubbly about my coming home and how we were now going to set up housekeeping together in an apartment she had rented for the two of us. Actually it was an apartment for a single person, but she and the landlord agreed to make it a two-person apartment if I did some part-time janitorial work like taking care of the coal furnace in the wintertime. That way the rent would stay the same, which was very little to begin with. I still hadn't made up my mind about living with my mother, but she seemed so excited about it that I couldn't turn her down. The fact is, I didn't have an alternate plan, or the means to go out on my own anyway.

Compared to some of the lavish palaces I had lived in on the farm, this apartment was still a dump. It was an old brownstone house on Ashland Avenue, close to the St. Paul Cathedral, a one-family home a hundred years ago maybe, but now it was the primary residence of about ten separate households. It has since been condemned and torn down, which should have happened at least fifty years earlier. I had a tiny room that was possibly a closet or a pantry at one time. There was just room to squeeze in a single rollaway bed. Mother slept in the living room on a fold-out davenport. The bath was down the hall shared by two other tenants.

On my first night there I was startled by a faint noise from the kitchen. I got up and turned on the kitchen light and watched hundreds of cockroaches scurry to their daytime hiding places. They must have been practicing for the cockroach Olympics or something. They were running relays, sprinting, broad jumping, and they even had a race where one cockroach would ride on the back of another. I had never seen that one before in any of the Olympic games. It was very exciting indeed, but they only practiced at night.

The place was infested with bugs, but no kind of insect repellent seemed to phase them. Mother kept assuring me this was only temporary, and sure enough, about two and a half years later we finally moved.

Upon getting out of the service, I immediately joined the "fifty-two-twenty club." That sounds mighty grand but it was simply a government unemployment subsidy program for discharged servicemen who couldn't find a job. It allowed you to collect twenty dollars per week for a total of fifty-two weeks, or until you found work. Any number of ex-servicemen lived on this as long as they could because it actually meant you received the equivalent of fifty cents an hour, tax-free, which wasn't too far from what you could expect to earn on a minimal labor job.

It drove me nuts to sit around and do nothing, so I went out every day to look for work. I got so good at it that I could do ten to fifteen applications per day if they were in one general area. I didn't get a response from any of them, which may have been because I was honest and indicated that I would be going to school in the fall.

After exhausting most of the possibilities in St. Paul, I decided to take a streetcar to Minneapolis to see what I could do there. In doing so I had to transfer to another streetcar at Chicago Avenue and Lake Street to get to downtown Minneapolis, right on the corner where the big Sears building is located.

"Hey, aren't you Floyd Wachs? What are you doing here?" It was John Hopkins, Doug's high school and college friend from Backus.

"Well I'll be damned, it's Tubby. I certainly didn't expect to meet anyone I knew. Are you out of the Air Force already?" Tubby was the nickname John carried all through high school because it fit his rather round figure.

"I just got out last week," John said. "My dad passed away and I got a dependency discharge to help take care of my mother and my young sister."

"That's the way I got an early discharge from the Navy also, but now I need to find a job."

"Why don't you go over here and apply for a job at Sears? They're a real good company to work for, I hear," John said. "I already have been offered a job, otherwise I would consider going to Sears."

"Geez," I said. "I worked for Wards for a while and I thought they were awful. Besides they don't pay anything."

We kept on talking a bit longer and when I looked up, the streetcar I was waiting for went clanking by. I now had another thirty minutes to wait for the next car. I might just as well run over to Sears and give them my application.

I found the personnel office on the second floor and quickly filled out their application, but where it asked if I was planning to go to school, this time I said "No." This wasn't entirely false, because when I went to the University of Minnesota to explore college possibilities, they told me I had virtually no chance of being admitted in the fall. In fact, it didn't look very promising for the winter quarter either. I turned in my application, but I didn't expect to hear back from Sears either.

The next day I was home when a telephone call came for me. "Hello, this is Edna from Sears and we would like to have you come in tomorrow morning about ten o'clock to take a physical, and if everything is okay we may have a job for you."

I wasn't too excited because I still had some doubts about working for Sears, but this was the only thing I had going. When I got to Sears and completed their five minute physical, I went back to the personnel office for my interview with Edna.

There were three other young guys waiting to be interviewed by Edna, and when your last name begins with W, I knew I would be one of the last ones to be called in. Edna's office only had a six-foot wall around it and being open on top, I could hear everything she was telling the other three applicants.

"We're going to start you out on the fifth floor as an order picker and you will be making sixty cents an hour," Edna said.

The next guy was called in. "We're going to start you out as a light merchandise handler at sixty cents an hour." It was something similar for the third guy and still sixty cents an hour.

I thought to myself, *Sixty cents an hour, shit, after deducting taxes and so forth that will be less than I'm making at the fifty-two-twenty club. If she offers me sixty cents an hour, I'm going to tell her to take this job and shove it.* In fact, I almost bolted out the door before she called me in. "Floyd, we'd like to have you come to work for Sears and start you out in our new warehouse. And we're going to pay you sixty-five cents an hour."

"Wait a minute, did you say sixty-five cents? I couldn't help overhearing what you told those other guys, so why are you going to pay me five cents an hour more?"

"Well you're a well built, strong-looking boy, Floyd, so we want you to be a heavy merchandise handler and that way we can pay you five cents an hour more."

Naturally I was flattered by the "well built, strong boy" stuff and I said, "I'll take it." Little did I know what they meant by a heavy merchandise handler and what they expected for five cents an hour more. I was told to report to work on July third at the Longfellow Warehouse that was under construction at Longfellow and 28th Street. After I left the employment office I thought, what a jerk I am for accepting this job just because they were going to pay me a measly two dollars a week more. But I was committed and I got there at eight in the morning.

My job was unloading a boxcar filled with barbed wire. I was to grab two rolls of barbed wire, one in each hand, carry them out and stack them on a pallet to be hauled away by a forklift to another part of the warehouse. I don't know what they weighed but they must have been at least sixty pounds a roll. It was 98 degrees that day in July and it probably was at least 125 degrees inside the boxcar. After about five or six hours of this I had had it. I was eating salt tablets and drinking gallons of water, but I was getting weaker by the minute.

I finally told my work partner, Charlie Springer, who was sort of a supervisor, that I couldn't take any more and was going to quit. Charlie said, "Well if you have to quit, why don't you try and finish the day and come in and quit on the fifth. That way you will also get paid for the holiday."

"Yeah, that makes sense. I'll get paid for two days, but only work one."

The next working day after the holiday, I came to work for the sole purpose of resigning and getting my two days pay. On my way to the office I ran into the warehouse manager. He said, "You're the new guy that just started the other day aren't you?"

"Yes, I started on the third."

"Well, they now want you for a job over at the main plant on the third floor."

I just about said I was on my way to your office to resign, but instead I said, "I don't have a car. How would I get there?"

He said, "There's a shuttle truck leaving in a few minutes and you can ride over in that." And then he walked away.

I didn't know what to do, but I thought I might as well go and see what this other job was first. The new job turned out to be a breeze in comparison. It was much cooler inside the main building, the work was not as hard and, not that it was important, but there were some girls around.

So I began my career at Sears. How could anyone foresee that nearly forty-one years later I would be retiring from the same building on Lake Street where I first applied for a job, something unheard of today at any company.

I have often thought, how could fate have arranged all those things that seemed to steer me through a series of events that got me on this path at Sears. I am not a fatalist, but why did I choose this day, the 2nd of July, to look for work in Minneapolis, the same day that Sears opened up employment for their new warehouse? How did it happen that when making my streetcar transfer at Chicago and Lake, that I would run into John Hopkins who tried to convince me that Sears, unlike Wards, was a decent place to work? And how did it happen that while talking to Hopkins, I missed my streetcar transfer, giving me thirty minutes in which I ran into Sears to submit my application? And why on this application did I tell them I was not planning to go to school in the fall like I had done at all the other places I applied for work. And how did it happen that I was home the next day to receive the call from Sears, because, had I not been home by the telephone, the lady at Sears would no doubt have just called the next application in the pile and passed me up.

Above all, what was it that nudged me to accept the job when my hourly wage was only five cents an hour more than the ridiculous wage of sixty cents an hour offered to the other guys? Why did my work partner, Charlie Springer, who later became a good friend of mine at Sears, convince me not to quit the day before a holiday, but wait until the day after? On the first day after the fourth, how did it happen that someone had planned a different job for me and I would run into the warehouse manager who relayed that information to me before I had a chance to reach his office to resign and go home? Was all this a plan of destiny? No, I believe it was simply a series of events, just one coincidence after another with everything falling into place. But it turned out to be a good plan.

I pretty much knew from the beginning that I wasn't going to make it at the University of Minnesota, but I didn't want to admit this. I had my mind set to be an architectural engineer, but the U wouldn't give me the time of day on this matter until I had at least two years of SLA college, and because of all the servicemen coming home that had some kind of priority, I was well down on the list for gaining entrance to this college.

In the meantime, I was occupying my time doing some art work, pen and ink sketches actually, which I have always liked to do.

One day I saw an ad in a magazine that displayed a sketch of a girl's face and it read "Draw me and win $1,000." It was just a simple line drawing and I said, "What the heck, I can do that." I submitted my entry and in a couple weeks I got a response back with all kinds of flowery comments about my apparent talent, and while I wasn't the grand prize winner, I was being awarded a $350 scholarship towards a $600 art correspondence course.

The $250 balance due was still more than the correspondence course was worth, but I was naive enough to see it as a great opportunity to explore my art talent. I managed to scrape up the small down-payment they required, and paid the balance over a nine-month period.

Every two weeks there was an assignment in the mail of something to draw along with a little instruction booklet and they would also critique the work sent back from the previous assignment. Their high praise and excellent grades had me believing I was a great illustrator.

Then I heard about a new school of art that was opening up at the Walker Art Center in Minneapolis. I went to see them and learned that the entire tuition, including an allowance for art supplies, would be paid for by the government, another benefit of the GI Bill of Rights. This law also allowed me to work as long as my income did not exceed fifteen dollars a week and then I would be allowed to maintain my free tuition, another wonderful welfare program by the government that penalizes people for working and benefits those who limit the amount of work they do. Fifty years later, our government still continues the same programs that promote laziness in people who really don't need a lot of encouragement.

This subsidy for not working seemed to agree with my mother's lifestyle. She worked at a few odd jobs but collected unemployment whenever she could, which wasn't too difficult.

I had now been working at Sears for about two and a half months, but once again, I had to tender my resignation and sheepishly try to explain to them that I didn't really lie on my application because I didn't know I would be going to art school in the fall. Much to my surprise, Sears was not disturbed at my failure to disclose my school intentions, but in fact, asked me if I would be interested in working part-time. I said I would like to but I could only work about twenty hours a week, otherwise I would lose my GI subsidy. They said that would be okay.

For the next four years, I worked part-time, giving me enough money to live on, but never more than twenty hours a week. If on Saturday afternoon at three o'clock I had completed twenty hours for the week, I just ran to the time clock and punched out, regardless of how busy they might be or how much work I had left undone.

When I first got out of the service, my friend Larry Schwartzbauer was still in the Army so I made contact with Dick Nord. Because he was my sister-in-law's brother, he was almost a relative, but better yet, he was a very good friend.

Dick had very limited mobility in his patched-up legs. He obviously could not serve in the military and also found it very difficult to find employment.

While we were both unemployed, we spent a lot of time together playing chess, bowling, going to baseball or football games whenever we could sneak in the gate or get tickets cheap, or just doing anything that didn't cost much money.

One day Dick suggested we go play golf, and I will never forget this. In spite of his handicap, Dick was determined to do anything anyone else could do. The sad part was, I knew how to swing a club, but I had never been near a golf course in my life and didn't know one golf club from another, or how to use them. I said, "Dick, I don't know the first thing about playing golf."

"Then I will teach you," Dick said with his usual confidence.

"But I don't have any golf clubs."

"I'll let you share mine if you will just carry my bag."

We took a streetcar to the Theodore Wirth golf course on a Saturday morning. Wrong day. But because we were a twosome, we were allowed to tee off in front of some other groups. Dick tees up his ball, takes a swing and whacks it quite well down the middle of the fairway. Shit, this looks easy. I tee up my ball, take a swing, but nothing happens, the ball is still sitting on the tee. What's wrong here? I then take another swing with the identical results. The ball hasn't moved.

Now I'm hearing groans and snickers from all the people standing around watching. Dick is laughing, nothing bothered him, and I'm ready to pee my pants. Let's try it again, another swing and another clear miss. That's strike three. Does that mean I'm out of here? Apparently Dick thought so, because he just walked up, picked up my ball and threw it down the fairway as far as he could.

I probably would have been better off if I had just picked up my ball and gone home. However, as the day went on things improved and after sinking a long putt on one hole, I was hooked. Now if I could just improve each time as much as I did the first time out.

Dick had a beautiful blonde girlfriend named Doris that he had been going with out of high school, whom he eventually married. They both belonged to a temperance lodge, and got me involved in some of their activities, but I still liked beer too much to even think about joining such a group. I dated a couple of the single girls in the group, but right off the bat, because they wouldn't even look at a glass of beer, I knew we didn't have much in common.

At Sears I met Al Johnson, who also joined me in going to art school at Walker. He was a bit more serious about finding the right girl with the right religion and the right set of boobs than I was, but he didn't have anyone steady, so we began hanging out together after work and after school. He would also drink beer.

The first day at art school was a real shocker. After getting officially registered, filling out the government forms to get my free tuition and getting all my supplies together, I finally got settled into my first class, an anatomy illustration class. In front of the room was a platform with a stool on it. Soon there was a girl in a robe sitting on the stool. The instructor told her to disrobe and off came the only thing she had on. She was completely naked, and we were expected to make some kind of drawing of what we saw.

I had no idea this is what art school was about. I had a hard time holding my pencil, let alone trying to put something on paper that might resemble a nude female.

I soon got over the first shock as there were many more days of a similar routine to follow. Most of the models were very skinny (so you could see their bone structure) and about as sexy as a stock of corn. Everyone except Candy. Candy had a cover girl face plus a body with all the curves in the right places, enough to make *Esquire* or *Playboy* blush. All the other guys who didn't take this class, including Al Johnson, were all very envious and were constantly trying to sneak into our classroom for a peek. Our fat old instructor, Art Kerrick, enjoyed this class as much as the students. He had Candy pose in some of the most unbelievable sexy positions. Most of the guys had to sit down to draw her.

I never could figure out why all the girl models had to be completely nude. If we had a male model, he always had to wear a bikini bathing suit. All the girls in the class said this wasn't fair, but that was before men listened to what women thought was fair.

All during the time Mother and I lived on Ashland Avenue, Mother was also entertaining a boyfriend, a big-hearted Swede named Carl Larson. He was a mechanic for Northwest Air Lines, not an airplane mechanic but a vehicle mechanic, so he was very knowledgeable about automobiles. He had a 1929 Pontiac, a very long, four door job with big wood spoke wheels. It purred like a kitten because Carl treated it like a pet, giving it whatever it wanted whenever it wanted it. The car did tricks in return, like barking for food, chasing other cars, and it even tried to roll over once.

When I started working for Sears, Carl knew that I needed a car badly so I was delighted when he offered to sell his 1929 Pontiac to me, on a very low monthly payment plan. That was the kind of guy Carl was; a very caring, easy going, lovable person who probably gave Mother some of the happiest moments of her life.

Unfortunately Carl had a problem—no, not just one problem. He had two problems: Carl was already married and, according to him, his wife refused to grant him a divorce. That may or may not have been the case, but it didn't seem that he was working too hard to make the divorce happen. He said he really wanted to marry Rena but circumstances wouldn't allow it and Mother certainly wanted to marry him. My personal feeling was that the "no divorce" shackle may have been an excuse, because he didn't want to be tied down to another woman again. It didn't seem to bother their relationship that much.

Carl's second problem was that he was a "dyed in the wool" alcoholic. He simply could not go from his job on payday, or any other time when he had some money in his pocket, to his apartment without stopping off at a local bar and getting totally stoned out of his mind. He could somehow always remember our phone number and several times Mother and I had to scrape him off a bar stool and load him into the back seat of the Pontiac, which was now my Pontiac. Sometimes he would spend the rest of the night in the same back seat position. Perhaps it was his way of staying close to his old car.

One Friday night he wanted to go for a drive with Mother and asked me if he could borrow his old car. He suggested I ride along. Since it did not appear that he had been drinking too much, I agreed.

We were in Minneapolis at Minnehaha and about 32nd Street when we were plowed into by a little old lady in her new car. I have no idea who was at fault as I was in the back seat and not paying attention. Carl claims he stopped at the stop sign and she went through it. My perception is, they both ran the stop sign. In any event she was going fast enough that when she hit the right rear wheel it spun us around and the Pontiac rolled over on the passenger side. The fire trucks, police, and ambulance all arrived on the scene in very short order.

All three of us had to squeeze out through the front window because the door was jammed or it was too heavy to force open.

A police officer soon walked up and asked, "Who was driving this vehicle?"

Mother said, "He was," and pointed at me.

I opened my mouth and was going to say, "It wasn't me." But before I could say anything, the policeman said, "Let me see your driver's license, young man." I got my driver's license out and looked around for Carl. He was gone. He had simply vanished in the night.

The policeman did his thing with my license and then he said, "We better get a bandage on your arm." Mother and I both had cuts on our arms, but nothing serious. I wanted to straighten out the matter with the police as to who was driving the car, but I still couldn't locate Carl anywhere, so I just kept quiet.

The medical people with the ambulance were occupied with the little old lady who was banged up pretty bad, so Mother and I, after getting bandages on our arms, were told to get into the back seat of the police car and the policeman would take us to the hospital. In the meantime, the policeman got six or seven men, including some firemen and spectators, to lift the car up on its wheels and push it off to the side by the curb.

Sitting in the police car I asked Mother, "Why did you tell the cop I was driving? And where in the heck did Carl go?"

Mother said, "Just be quiet."

I was too dumfounded to protest, so the accident report was never changed. I was listed as the driver of car number two.

After getting treated at the hospital, Mother and I took a streetcar back to the scene of the accident. I expected to see old Carl sitting on the curb some place but he still was not around. For some reason Mother had taken the keys out of the car and kept them. So I got in, started the old Pontiac and drove it home as if nothing had happened. The car had a couple new wrinkles in the rear fender, two broken windows and a scratch or two here and there where the right side hit the street, otherwise the old tank acted like it was just a normal day on the streets. With today's autos it would have been totaled for sure.

When we arrived back at the apartment, there sat old Carl in the kitchen having a beer. "What happened to you?" I asked.

"Vell, I yost got the hell out of there," he replied in his Swedish accent. He then went on to explain that he had recently received a DWI ticket and if he was again involved in another accident, whether he was drinking or not, he may lose his license. That in turn may cause him some problems on his job. Mother already knew all about this but didn't bother to tell me, or I probably wouldn't have let him drive my car in the first place.

The next morning I called my insurance agent to tell him I was involved in an accident. After getting all the necessary information and conditioning me to the fact that this may affect my insurance premium, he said he would send someone over to look at my car.

About an hour later there was a man at our door. He said, "I saw your car down on the street, and it looks like you were pretty lucky you were not banged up more than you are. Have you received medical attention?"

He proceeded to ask a few more questions and then asked Mother to sign a form, purely routine, since I was only nineteen years old. Mother signed it without reading it or without the man explaining what she was signing. The man left.

About an hour later there was another man at the door. He said. "My name is so-and-so and I'm here from your insurance company to inspect your car, the one you called about this morning that was in the accident."

"But someone from the insurance company was just here," Mother said.

"No, I don't think so. I am the only man from your insurance company. Did you sign anything?"

"Yes we did. It's right here." Mother gave the form to the man. The insurance adjuster looked it over and gave it back to Mother.

"I'm afraid you just hired yourself an attorney."

"What do you mean? We don't need any attorneys." He went on to explain about ambulance chaser lawyers and how they operate. The information about the accident was in the morning paper and there were a couple of lawyers in town that do a business on chasing these cases down. The insurance man said, "It normally shouldn't cost you anything but the accident claim will no doubt be grossly exaggerated and the insurance companies will have to work out a settlement to avoid a costly lawsuit. Your attorney will get two-thirds of whatever you agree to settle for." Gross wasn't the word for it.

A few days later we received in the mail a copy of the summons against the poor little old lady with claims amounting to over twenty-thousand dollars—maybe a half million in today's money. I was flabbergasted. It contained a full page of claims of various illnesses for either Mother or myself caused by the accident: back problems, headaches, dizziness, mental disorders, you name it, none of which were true.

The next day I raced downtown to confront the attorney in his dirty little old office. I said, "What is this? My only expense was about thirty-five dollars to replace a couple of broken windows and the wrinkled fender. A few scratches doesn't hurt that old car."

Mr. Shyster, Attorney-at-law said, "Don't worry about all this stuff. It's just routine. It will never get to court and we'll settle for a lot less. It won't cost you or the other party anything."

It took about ten weeks, but there finally was a settlement, a settlement of $750. How could they arrive at a settlement of $750 from a twenty-thousand-dollar claim? I never could understand that. My portion of the $750 was $250 and the attorney's was $500, something else I couldn't understand. But I sure as heck was learning.

For a long time my opinion of the law profession was pretty low, but I eventually became involved with them quite extensively at work and now some of my good friends are lawyers. I now have a son-in-law, also an attorney, and one of the most super people I have ever met. I don't know if the profession has changed in the last fifty years, but my attitude has definitely mellowed.

During this time of going to art school and working my twenty to twenty-five hours at Sears, Mother decided she wanted to fulfill her lifelong dream of owning her own restaurant. I thought she was nuts but if you are stubborn enough and you can find some bank that is dumb enough to loan you a little money, you can do just about anything. After a few weeks of running down a few ads in the newspaper a deal was consummated. Rena's Cafe would soon be a going business.

The restaurant was located on University Avenue at about Prior in the Midway district, not a bad location because there were quite a few business places located in the area. It was a small place that would hold about thirty customers if it was full, which it never was, but the volume wasn't all that bad. Mother was a decent cook of the comfort food variety: roast beef, roast pork, meat loaf, chicken, turkey, hot beef or pork sandwiches, and of course the damned chow mein she learned how to make while in Bemidji.

The best volume seemed to be late hours, so she attempted to run the place around the clock. I was supposed to just handle the book work, do the payroll and pay the bills. This was good experience and kind of fun for a while, for about two months that is. It would soon become evident that more payroll was needed or the hours opened had to be reduced, but once Mother was locked on to something it was like a radar-guided missile: once it was launched you couldn't call it back. The hours would not be reduced and the needed help in the late evening hours would come from Floyd and Carl, who had to be taught how to peel a potato. That was very inexpensive payroll.

I would now go to school from nine until about three, run to Sears and work my three or four hours and then rush to the restaurant and work as long as I could stay awake. At least I could get something to eat. This routine lasted almost a year before Carl and I put our heads together and said, "screw this." We finally convinced Mother that she was losing money, using some creative accounting on my part, and the restaurant was put up for sale.

Here again my social life went all to hell and I was trying to be good to one of my parents, as if there was a reason for me to feel guilty about the mess each of them was in. The one good thing that came out of all this was that I convinced Mother that the location where we were living on Ashland Avenue was too far away from the restaurant for her to be taking the streetcar and for me to get back and forth to work, to school and then to Rena's Cafe. We finally moved out of the cockroach-infested apartment on Ashland to a less infested apartment on Snelling Avenue.

After three years of art school, which included summer sessions, my commercial art instructor, Bill Whelan, invited me to his house one day after school, a big old mansion in the Kenwood area within walking distance to Walker.

Bill said, "I haven't mentioned this to anyone but LeSure," (he was the school director). "I plan on resigning my teaching position at the end of this year and I'm going to get back into freelance commercial art work again."

Bill had been in business as a freelance artist before taking the teaching job. He had lots of contacts with big agencies in both Minneapolis and St. Paul but had been out of the mainstream now for nearly four years. He was getting a little too old and shaky to do some of the fine detailed work necessary in this field.

He said, "I was wondering if you would be interested in joining me in my business?"

I was flattered and for a minute I thought he had rocks in his head. "Are you sure? There is still a lot I don't know about commercial art."

"That's no problem, I will teach you. I know you can handle the detailed work better then I can. My hands seem to be getting more unsteady as I get older. But I still have lots of contacts, enough to keep us both busy. There won't be a lot of money coming in right away, but as soon as we hook up with a few clients, you could be doing great."

What a lucky break, I thought. "You know I have to earn my own living, so if I can continue to work at Sears while we're getting started I would really appreciate the opportunity."

"Good, we'll work out of my house until we can afford to rent office space. You'll just have to drive back and forth." That was a problem that should have opened my eyes a bit more. Whalen did not drive, in fact didn't even own a car. So all the running we did around the city to the printing companies, the agencies and potential clients was in my old Pontiac.

I think Whalen thought I was actually more capable of doing finished art work than I really was, but we still got along fine together. He certainly did have the contacts in the business and made a point of getting me out to meet them all—people like Paul Foss and Harvey MacKay. (I believe his first name was Harvey, just like his son, the prominent business leader and sports entrepreneur here in Minneapolis today.) They were all in the printing business but often needed freelance artists.

I met the top people at Brown and Bigelow and the guy who originated the Hamm's Beer ads at the Campbell-Mithun agency with the bear and "The Land of Sky Blue Water." I believe his name was Ben Larson. We seemed to be doing more PR work than art work, and I was not earning any money, but I understood this was what one had to do.

I eventually realized that Bill was coming down the other side of the mountain and not much work was going to be coming his way. I was supposed to be the new young talent who could recapture his old business again. It didn't work out that way, although we did line up one good client, Blue Cross and Blue Shield of Minnesota. This was boring stuff, though, because it was just forms and brochure work.

One day Bill called me at home all choked up with emotion. He told me he was in trouble and had to leave the country. He wouldn't explain to me what kind of trouble he was in, only that it had nothing to do with me or our business. I'm guessing it had something to do with his wife, who was a beautiful movie-star-quality gal and much younger than her husband. She did not leave the country with him.

Bill said I could continue on with the business on my own if I wanted to and gave me a couple of names to contact if I chose to do so. I didn't feel I was equipped to handle the business on my own, so I simply gave it up. I didn't expect to ever see Bill Whalen again.

My mother and I had moved to a more high-class dump, precisely where the freeway, I-94 now runs under Snelling Avenue. There was no effort to save this building when the freeway went through. This dump didn't have as many cockroaches to begin with but I think we brought some seeds with us when we moved.

My bedroom was the glassed-in porch in the front of the building. It had no heat and no shades on the windows. I froze in the winter and got a sunburn in the summer if I slept late in the morning. Fortunately the streetcar barns were right across the street so with all the noise they made there was little chance of sleeping in anyway.

The old Pontiac continued to be a factor in my growing up years. One day I bought a can of paint and a brush and turned the original oxidized rust color into a midnight blue. It was pretty for about two weeks, but then it snowed and as the snow melted it dripped blue water. In spite of its looks it was a comfortable and reliable vehicle and it didn't seem to stop girls from going out with me if they thought I might be a marriage prospect. Marriage, however, was the furthermost thing from my mind.

To some of the students and other high-minded people at the Walker Art Institute, my car was looked at as a piece of art, particularly its abstract fender and as the body turned different colors when the blue water dripped off in the rain. Not too surprising considering some of the things they labeled art at Walker.

None of this bothered me. I was proud of the big tub and the attention it attracted, until its twenty years of age started to catch up with it and little things started to go wrong. But I learned a great deal about being a mechanic.

One girl I dated lived on a hill next to the St. Paul Town and Country Club and I would park in front of her house and let the radio play while I tried out some of my necking techniques. Never was too successful, but it was enough to run the battery down and then I couldn't get it started. I would have to push the big tank to the edge of the hill and as it started to roll, I would quickly jump in and throw it in gear. It started every time. But then I would have to drive it home without turning the lights on, using all the back streets where there was no traffic, so that the battery would charge up and I could get it started the next morning. The girl (I forget her name now) would say the only reason I went out with her was because she lived on a hill. Yes, that was one of her better points.

My second car was a 1946 Chevrolet, one of the very first post-war models, that was five years old when I bought it. I was simply trying to improve my image, but I regretted my decision almost immediately.

The Chevy was not a good one and on a trip back from Winona, I blew the engine in Lake City, and never drove it again. The next week I took the bus to my Sears job in Winona and stopped at a car dealer next to the bus station. It happened to be a Plymouth dealer. When the salesman said he would have a wrecker pick up my car in Lake City and give me X number of dollars for it on a new Plymouth, I said you have got a deal. The whole conversation took about five minutes and I became the proud owner of a 1952 Plymouth, my first new car, the most unimaginative, non-sporty, least sexy car ever built.

It was early 1951 when my business partner, Bill Whalen, made his escape from society. Up to that point I hadn't told Sears that I had finished school and was doing some work as a freelance artist. I just continued to work part-time as if I was still in school. But when Whalen jumped ship, I told them I was quitting as I needed a full-time job and I needed more money.

When I got the Sears profit-sharing story and all the additional money I would have just by working a couple more months, I fell for the bait, although at that stage of my life, my long-range plans consisted of what I was going to do Friday night. So I paid little attention to the Sears profit sharing plan. All I knew was that one of the deductions to my putrid little paycheck each week was five percent of my salary that went into profit sharing, which amounted to a couple of beers or a gallon of gas. But then the gal in the personnel office showed me my record for the past four and a half years and what it would amount to if I just worked another two or three months. Wow! That would be a lot of beer and a lot of gas, too.

So I withdrew my resignation notice and begged them to give me more hours of work whenever they could. Most of the time it was close to forty hours a week and I may have been all the way up to about eighty-five cents an hour by this time. I needed a better job.

About ten days before my five years of service date, I made another trip to the personnel office to be sure I could get all that profit sharing they were telling me about. "But you understand, Floyd," the lady said, "once you withdraw from profit sharing you cannot get back in again. Most people never withdraw it until they leave the company."

"Then I want to resign," I said.

At this point the assistant personnel manager, Evelyn Gray, popped out of her office and said, "Floyd, I understand you are out of school now." I had never met Mrs. Gray before, but it was obvious she knew something about me.

"Yes, I've been out of school for about six months now."

"What do you plan to do now?" she asked.

"Well I'd like to get a job as a commercial artist, but there is not a lot available right now."

"How would you like to consider our management trainee program?"

"That's nice of you to consider me, but you know, Mrs. Gray, my school was an art school and I don't have a regular college degree." I knew that the other trainees were all college graduates, with probably degrees in business administration.

Mrs. Gray said. "I know that, but what we do is give you a battery of tests and if you do well on them we can waive the college requirements. We give the same tests to the college graduates but I think you can do as well as most of them. Why don't you give it a try?"

I think someone must have been putting some pressure on this lady to get a bunch of management trainees lured into the system quickly. *What the heck, I have nothing to lose. Why not go for it?*

"Okay, when do I get started?"

For the next two days I was up to my armpits in one test after another and my eyeballs were hanging out of my sockets. I didn't think I would have a snowball's chance in hell, and I was planning to resign anyway, so I must have been relaxed enough to do reasonably well.

Two weeks later Evelyn Gray called me and said, "Floyd, next Monday come to work with a suit on. You did really good on your tests and you are now a management trainee."

Holy Shamoly! I'm going to be one of those ninety day wonders, as we used to call the young Navy officers fresh out of college that were given a commission in ninety days. But I don't even own a suit.

I borrowed some money from Carl and went with my friend Larry over to his uncle's house, where he had several racks of suits hanging in his garage. Larry said, "There are no labels in these suits and don't ask where they came from, but they're about a third of what you will pay in a store at regular price, as long as you've got the cash. My mom will sew cuffs on the pants for you if you want her to."

I bought two suits and still had money left over. "Larry, let's go to the hockey game tonight. My treat." Of course I counted on the fact that Larry's uncle, the same one that sold me the suits, would let us sneak in the back door again. So with some money still in hand, we went to our favorite downtown hang out, the famous Coney Island Restaurant on St. Peter Street, where the cute daughter that didn't put out worked and where the little wieners in a bun with chili sauce were still only ten cents. We each had about six of them.

Everything cometh to he who waiteth,

So long as he who waiteth,

Worketh like hell while he waiteth.

Chapter 15

You are now twenty-three years old and apparently starting out with a management career at Sears. Isn't it unusual for trainees to remain in the same location where they are recruited? Did you have to move and what about your education as an artist?

I WAS UNCOMFORTABLE going to work in a suit and I no doubt looked the part. Never before had I ever done anything where I was required to dress up, so with my no-label suits and borrowed pre-war ties, I'm sure I looked like an idiot, but I would eventually get the hang of it.

A number of job-related incidents should be told to illustrate why I progressed so well in my early days at Sears. It may sound in places like I am boasting or that I was really good at what I was doing. I assure you, I wasn't. I was in the right place at the right time and nothing more. That's how stars are born and that's how any number of executives made it at Sears.

I started out working in a troubleshooting department which got you into every corner of the business. You acted as sort of a spy on other managers; if you found them not following company policy, you could get them in trouble. Naturally I was trying to do my job the best I could, so it was easy to get my nose in things that rubbed some people the wrong way.

My boss, Harold Specht, was a good guy, but didn't always bail me out when I got in over my head. But this was good training. I learned to be more diplomatic and I learned that when some people didn't always follow company policy to the letter, it was often for the company's good. It was always very easy to find managers who didn't follow company policy, made mistakes, or simply used poor judgment.

I started to learn when to blow the whistle and when not to.

Harold actually requested that I be assigned to his department, so he tells me, because he remembered something that took place about a year earlier. It involved an incident that I had nearly forgotten about, though apparently he had not.

While going to school I had been working part-time at the Longfellow warehouse, getting my twenty hours a week in the easiest way I could. My job was to fill catalog orders that customers would buy at the main plant and then pick up at the warehouse. This included items like plumbing, heating, linoleum, tile, roofing and yes, some of the fencing that I previously unloaded from a boxcar on July 3, 1946, my first and almost last day on the job at Sears.

It was one hot summer night when Don Erickson, two other guys and myself were filling these catalog orders while the customers waited in a rather small room by the warehouse entrance. The four of us were on our own without a supervisor. There must have been a sale on or something because we were swamped with business this particular evening and there were a number of customers standing around waiting.

One customer was more than a little bit annoyed by all of this. He started shouting along with a bit of cursing, perhaps expecting to find one of us guys sleeping behind the partition around the little waiting room. Actually we were busting our tails, hustling to get everyone's order filled so we could get out of there and go home.

Over on the other side of the waiting room another gentleman, somewhat larger than the little loud-mouthed individual, said in a calm voice, "Maybe if we could have it a little more quiet around here these boys could get their work done."

The little loud-mouth walked over towards the taller man and said, "By chance are you referring to me?"

"Could be," the bigger man said.

I was behind the partition assembling a plumbing order for a customer and heard what was going on and even saw some of it through a crack in the wall, but I was too busy to worry about it.

The smaller man replied, "I suppose because you're bigger you think you can say anything you damn please."

"No, I just think you should be patient."

"Well I don't have to and what are you going to do about it?" The smaller man walked up to the bigger man about six inches from his face and said, "I dare you to hit me. Come on, I dare you to hit me."

The next thing I heard was a loud "whop" like when you blow up a paper bag and clap it in your hands. Instead it was a very large open hand across the face of the guy who couldn't keep his mouth shut.

I rushed into the waiting room and saw the red face of a small, Jewish-looking man with one side of his face redder than the other. He grabbed for a telephone sitting on a desk and said, "I'm going to call the cops."

At about the same time, Don Erickson, who had been out of listening range, walked into the waiting room. He had heard some shouting but didn't know exactly what was going on. Erickson grabbed the phone out of the man's hand and said, "Sorry mister, you cannot use this phone."

What he should have said (but didn't) was, "This telephone is here only for internal use in the warehouse and cannot be used to call anyone outside this building, including the police." He didn't have time to say all that.

"Young man, are you refusing to let me use this telephone?" the frantic little guy screamed.

"I'm saying you cannot call anyone on this phone," Erickson replied in his typical authoritative manner. "If you want to use a public phone there is one about three blocks from here at Lake and Cedar." Don was a take-charge sort of guy.

"What is your name young man?"

"My name is Don Erickson. What's yours?" The little man did not reply but turned and walked out the door. The other people in the waiting room applauded.

My instincts told me we may not have heard the end of this so I quickly copied down the names of the people remaining in the waiting room, thinking we may need some witnesses. Indeed we had not heard the end of it.

It turned out that the beady-eyed little man was a high official with the Teamsters Union, a union that was trying desperately to organize Sears employees, without much success. At the same time Sears was bending over backwards to be nice to the union because we still had to depend on the truckers and a tot of other Teamster workers outside of Sears to keep business functioning.

The next morning the fit hit the shan. The small man's lawyer, same nationality, was on the telephone to the Sears general manager, Lou Regan, screaming the same way as his client did. He demanded, among other things, that Don Erickson be fired immediately, and Sears obliged. Don didn't seem to care too much because he only had a couple of months before he graduated from college, and I have a feeling that Sears told him when he was out of school, that he should come back and they would make him a management trainee, which they did. Don went on to become an outstanding executive at many locations with Sears and ultimately came back to Minneapolis to be the general manager and finally closed the catalog plant for good before he retired.

Just about every ranking executive in Minneapolis became involved in the face slapping incident, with one common goal in mind: to "save face." Harold Specht, who would eventually become my boss, was put in charge of investigating the entire matter. He had each of us write out a full account of exactly what happened. I was prepared. I got the warehouse secretary to let me dictate the complete story to her, covering witnesses, conversations, and details, and then she typed it for me. It was six pages. I remember Specht asking me if I was going to school to be a lawyer. My statement was like a deposition for a grand jury, he said.

So it may be that this crazy warehouse scuffle gave me my first break as a management trainee about a year later. Harold Specht remembered my name when it appeared on a list of new trainees and asked that I be assigned to his staff.

While working on this job one day, I got a surprise phone call. "Who is this?" I asked.

"Someone who wants to buy you lunch if you can sneak away from Sears for an hour or two. Does the name Bill Whalen ring a bell?"

"My God, whatever happened to you and where have you been?"

"I'll tell you when you get here. I'm at a small hotel in the Loring Park area, but I don't want anyone else to know that I'm in town, so I'll have some lunch sent in."

I found the little hotel (can't remember the name of it now) and I was surprised how well Bill looked, because he used to be constantly in need of a hair cut and generally looked a little seedy. We had some catching-up conversation but he still would not tell me the reason why he vanished so abruptly about eight months ago and I didn't push him. He said he was now living in Montreal, Canada.

Finally he asked, "Do you remember the guy you did some art work for while you were in school at Walker?"

"Yes, I can't think of his name now, but I remember he was a good friend of yours. I did some illustrations of some machine parts for him that he was selling out of a catalog. It also took me about six months to get paid by the SOB."

"Well, his name is Albert Pick, and that SOB, as you call him, is now a very wealthy man. Sit down let me tell you the story about him."

Bill went on. "You recall he had that little machine shop in St. Cloud. Well, it burned down and he lost just about everything. All he had left was his old pick up truck and a few personal belongings. So he packed up his pickup and headed out West to prospect for uranium in the Utah and Nevada mountains. Well he hit a big one, I understand it was one of the richest uranium discoveries in all of North

America, although he almost lost his life in the process. It seems that he must have drank some river water that was poisonous or something. Anyway he became very ill, got disoriented and couldn't find his way out of the mountains. He was almost dead when some other prospectors found him, but he was still able to stake his claim on the rich uranium deposits. Hollywood is even thinking of making a movie about him. Pick then moved to Canada and started a motel chain called the Albert Pick Motels.

"I have never heard of them," I said.

"Well, he's just getting started. He's putting them up mostly in the East, but he is also building one in St. Cloud."

Later in my travels at Sears, I remember the Albert Pick in St. Cloud and I used to also stay at one in South Bend.

"Pick has hired me as his public relations and advertising manager, and for that reason among others I am now living in Montreal."

Is this a bunch of bullshit or what? Why is he telling me all this? Bill had been known to expand on the truth once in awhile, but this takes the cake.

"What I want you to do is come and join us as the art director for the company and that's why I'm here in town today."

Here it comes now. "You know Floyd, I'm getting a little shaky at my age. I still have the creative ability, but I need you to carry it out for the newspaper ads, the magazines, the brochures, the signs, and so forth. Pick just got a new airplane for the company and he told me and his pilot to fly up here and pick you up if you're the guy I want for the job. There's others I could have hired I suppose, but you're single and not tied down and I assume you don't have any art business going here. Besides, you know we work well together."

Holy shit! I was dumfounded. How do I know if this is for real. "You are really here on a company plane?"

"Hell yes. It's a beauty. If you've got time we can drive out to the airport and look it over."

"I've got to think about this Bill. Can I call you later on?"

"Sure, we're flying back in the morning. Hell, we'll even take you along right away unless you have to give some notice to Sears or something."

After lunch and some more sweet talk, I left with my head in a fog. I didn't know how to go about checking out his story, but there was a little bird or some crazy intuition that said to me, "There is something that doesn't completely add up here." I called Bill that night and said I was flattered beyond words, but I just couldn't do it.

Maybe if there had been some cash laid out on the lunch table or a contract with some big bucks in it, I might have made a different decision. There certainly wasn't much holding me here. I had just started my trainee job at Sears, but there were no guarantees with that and the money was still peanuts.

Needless to say, I have often wondered what my life would have been like as an artist in Canada. But turning down this job offer helped me make some other decisions that I needed to make. I gave up the idea of being a commercial artist and just do art for my own enjoyment. I would also concentrate my energies at Sears and make out of it the best career I could. I think I made the right decisions. I never heard from or saw Bill Whalen again.

Shortly thereafter, I was beckoned to go to the regional sales office at Sears for a temporary assignment on a different job. I was told that I would be going to Winona, Minnesota, where I would oversee a catalog store relocation. Everything was supposed have been planned beforehand and all I was required to do was to see that the workmen had what they needed to get the new building in shape.

When I got to Winona on Monday morning, surprise, a general strike had been called by all carpenters, painters, plumbers, electricians, every trade that was necessary for our needs in relocating the Sears store. This was not planned. The contractor that had been procured for Sears was a non-union employer, but the workers would not work on a Sears building because the union would throw up a picket line and there may be trouble. Sears management could not accept that, either.

I called the regional sales office and was told to just sit there. Hopefully the strike could be settled in a couple of days, but I was also told that the lease on Sears' present building was up in less than sixty days and it could not be extended under any circumstances. I sat around the balance of the week and came back the following Monday. No change.

The next day I heard there was a union meeting and although I was not invited, I decided to sneak in and see what was going on. I eventually found some union bosses, so I explained my problem.

The local union leader said, "Who's your contractor?" I told him and I also had a copy of the agreement which I showed him. He looked it over and said, "You know, your contractor is one of our biggest problems. If he would let his workers sign up and pay them the wage he is supposed to, we might not be having this strike."

I said, "I had nothing to do with acquiring his services. What can we do?"

"You can tell him to go to hell. Your contract says he was supposed to start on a certain day, which he didn't, and there is no way he can complete the job on time. So in effect he has negated his contract and you can tell him to fly a kite."

"That's not going to get our store moved," I replied.

"That's where we can help you. I can line you up with a union supporting contractor and we will allow him and his workmen to start tomorrow morning. I'll guarantee you he will get the job done before the deadline and I'm willing to bet he'll beat the hell out of your other contractor's price. But I'll need your okay right now."

"Let's do it." That was either one of the dumbest or the smartest quick decisions I ever made for Sears. I don't know which.

The next morning there were a dozen or more workmen going at it strong, ripping out walls and getting the building prepared to install our new fixtures. The original contractor, however, went through the roof.

About ten o'clock the assistant store manager located me and said, "Floyd, we just got a call and was told to locate you immediately. They said you are to get your ass back to Minneapolis as fast as your car will take you and don't stop for lunch."

I first went to the union boss and told him, "The fit has really hit the shan this time. I think I am in big trouble."

"Don't worry about it. You have done the right thing."

"Will you back me up when my boss wants to fire me?" I asked.

"Of course. Do you want me to call your boss right now?"

"No, but stay close to your phone."

When I got to Minneapolis, I was ushered up to the general manager's office. Wow! I had never been in Mr. Regan's office before. All the brass in the building were there and there was one empty chair in the middle of the room. I figured that one was for me. Mr. Regan was on the phone to Chicago, with some attorney at headquarters, I believe. The contractor in Winona did not bother to call Minneapolis, he went straight to the top in Chicago.

It seemed to me that the first concern of this high powered group was not how to get the Winona store moved on schedule, but how they could make this green new recruit the scapegoat in the whole affair. After bouncing me around like a fuzzy tennis ball while they rung their sweaty hands, somebody (I don't know who he was, but he apparently had some clout) said, "It looks to me like Floyd may have done the right thing here and maybe we should go along with it."

Yeah man, I like you, whoever you are.

It took a couple of days, but after the air was cleared our original contractor was told to get lost and we never heard from him again. We got the new store relocation completed on schedule, got everything moved and it was a very successful grand opening, well under budget, I might add, which seemed to be the most important thing to some people. In a space of two or three months, I went from a total unknown to a bloody hero, and for a while carried the label as "That Winona Kid." Once again, being in the right place at the right time proved to be more valuable than brains, education or experience.

I didn't know it at the time, but I was being compared with another individual who was working on a similar new store project in Grand Rapids, Minnesota. The one who completed the job best to everyone's satisfaction, would likely get the assignment on a permanent basis. The Grand Rapids store had different kinds of problems and it turned out to be a bit of a mess. I got the nod as the permanent building coordinator for our region. Needless to say, I was once again reminded to never, never make a decision like I did in Winona without going up the ladder of executives in the region, the territory, or headquarters and getting their approval.

Yeah sure, I thought. *I'd still be sitting in Winona waiting for the union and the contractors to settle their differences, while the powers that be in Minneapolis tried to make up their minds.*

Following the Winona project I was assigned a series of new store locations, or remodeling jobs around the state, places like Fairmont, Faribault, Hastings, Stillwater, Marshall, Hibbing, and Thief River Falls. My area also included Wisconsin, Upper Michigan, Iowa, North and South Dakota, and Montana. Sears gave me a lot of latitude once I learned the manner in which to communicate my problems, that is to always offer a suggestion on how to solve the problem so that if they didn't accept my suggestion, then it became their problem also. What I learned early was that the two most important things to management were to stay within budget and finish the job on schedule. I therefore made this my priority also.

It was a fun job. I was single, and it was not a problem being on the road even if it was over a weekend once in awhile. I was usually in a location long enough that I got acquainted with the local Sears people at least, so I even had some female companionship if need be. With each new store, relocation or remodeling was unique with different problems, mostly because of not receiving all the necessary fixtures on time.

This was particularly true at Brookings, South Dakota, when on the day before the grand opening we still did not have the big vertical Sears sign that was to be erected on the front of the building. We learned that it had been shipped and it would be on a freight car arriving in Brookings about three in the morning. I pleaded with the local sign company to have a crew there so that we could have the sign up before the opening. They were there but unfortunately they could not locate a crane big enough to hoist the heavy sign up.

One of their engineers, however, figured out that a long telephone pole up on the roof of the building with one end sticking out over the front to hold the sign would be sufficient and then they could hoist the sign up with a block and tackle. Everything was fine except the sign was a little heavier than expected. He figured he needed maybe another hundred pounds or so on the other end of the pole to hold it down. "You weigh more than that don't you Floyd?"

Being up on the roof didn't appeal to me, and on top of it all it began to rain like a cow peeing on a flat rock, but I wanted to get the damn sign up before the grand opening about four hours from now. I climbed up on the roof and straddled the big telephone pole like a horse and rider, a very wet horse and rider. Each time the sign crew pulled on the rope I would bob up and down like I was on a big teeter totter. "Hang on, Floyd." I could see myself being catapulted up over the building to the street on the other side. *If I get lifted up more than four feet, I am going to jump off and let the damn sign crash to the ground.* That didn't happen fortunately and when all the big shots from Minneapolis showed up for the grand opening, everything was done including the big neon sign that sparkled brightly in the rain.

"Did you have any problems getting everything done, Floyd?" my boss asked.

"Naw, it was a piece of cake."

At any new store project, everything was usually arranged in advance of my involvement, including the building, the landlord, the lease agreement and maybe even the contractors. But on one assignment I was given the task of negotiating everything from scratch, with the ultimate approval of the home office, of course. The location was Williston, North Dakota, where a sizable oil field had just been discovered. There were no other big cities nearby and Williston was about to become the oil boom town of the Northwest. Sears desperately wanted to open a catalog store there.

The only contact I was given was a local banker in Williston. "Go talk to him and do whatever you have to to get us a building and a new store open as soon as you can." They even said, "Don't worry about a budget."

I arrived in Williston by train at about six in the morning during a February blizzard raging across the wide open spaces of the North Dakota prairie. I was the only person to depart from the train that morning, and there was no one at the station that would be boarding the train. In fact, there was no one at the station, period, out on the edge of town. The agent normally there had locked up the station and went home apparently believing no one would be stupid enough to get off the train in this kind of a blizzard.

I could see that there was a north and south street that crossed the railroad tracks and occasionally through the blowing snow I could see the flicker of a street light, but that was it. I was now experiencing a winter "white out," which blanks out everything ten or fifteen feet away, even the street light on this dark morning.

Which way was the town? I could walk either north or south, they both looked the same. Thank God I chose north. I had the usual businessman's trench coat, gloves, no hat and a pair of ear muffs and after three or four blocks of plowing through the drifting snow, I was a frozen zombie. I finally spotted the faint glow of what I thought was a neon sign along the side of the road, but at this point I am almost delirious and I wasn't sure if it was a real light or one of those beams in your imagination before you black out. I followed it anyway and it turned out to be a little early morning cafe, but to me it was a star from heaven that was put there purposely to save my life.

Many times I have wondered what would have happened to me if I had chosen to walk in the other direction. I suppose Sears would have eventually marked the spot where they found the body of old frozen Floyd and maybe some day they would have erected a plaque there in my memory with an inscription, "This is the last stupid decision that The Winona Kid made for Sears. He walked south when he should have gone north."

There was one girl in the little cafe who was the coffee maker, cook, waitress, maitre d', sweeper, and she could easily have been the bouncer as well. She was glad to see another human being even though she thought I must be nuts. After a half dozen or more cups of coffee and a couple of pit stops, my blood started to circulate again and I got directions to the bank so I could make contact with the one person I came to see.

"It's a shame you had to come all the way out here," the bank president said, "when we don't have a thing to show you. If you had been here ten days earlier perhaps we could have done something, but the last building in town we just leased to a guy who wants to open a card and gift shop."

"Where is it?" I asked. "If he hasn't moved in yet maybe we can buy him out of his lease."

It was an old grocery supermarket building which would have been ideal for a Sears store, just a half block off main street, good parking space, and a loading dock in back. I went to see the gift shop guy but he wasn't about to give up his new venture and its good location, but he did admit it was bigger than what he needed.

I said, "You know that building has two doors opening onto the street. If you would be interested, we could construct a wall down the center of the building and you could have half and Sears would take the other half. Maybe your rent wouldn't be cut in half but it would certainly be reduced, and with a long term lease with Sears, the landlord would also be substantially better off." It got the man thinking.

I went on to say, "Sears will pay for all the construction and we will put a back door in on your side of the building because it only has one now." He was thinking some more.

"Do you think it might be a little favorable for your business to be next door to Sears?" That was the clincher. The landlord also saw all the benefits to this, to have Sears as a tenant, but most of all the increased rent, and before the day was over a deal was struck. Sears had their first store location in Williston and within eight weeks we were open for business.

Once again I was a survivor only because Mother Luck was on my side. As my grandfather would have said, "Sometimes disaster can produce laughter and laughter can produce disaster."

Nearly freezing to death when I arrived in Williston was scary enough, but at a later date, leaving Williston also gave me some scary moments of a different nature. I had been working on the store for three solid weeks without going home, so when the next Friday came around I was more than ready, and in addition, I knew about a good party going on Friday night in Minneapolis. I was desperate to make it home and the train wouldn't get me there until Saturday morning.

I knew there was a flight to Minneapolis out of Bismarck Friday evening—if I could just get to Bismarck. I inquired at the hotel if they knew of any way I could get to Bismarck. "Well are you ever in luck," the clerk said. "There is a new airline service that is just starting today. It flies to Bismarck this afternoon."

"You're kidding me. Where can I get a ticket?"

"Well, the hotel here is handling their ticketing, so I can write you a ticket, but I've only written one other one so I'll have to get the instructions out again."

The airline was called the Wild Goose Airline, which was my first clue that there may be something more here to fear. Then the clerk, having finally figured out how to write the ticket, told me not to go to the main gate terminal to catch the plane, but to go to the hangar at the north end of the airport and wait for the plane there. That was my second clue that there is something wrong with this picture, now adding to my worries.

But I did what I was told and sure enough, at the scheduled hour the Wild Goose showed up and taxied up to the designated hangar. It was a very small two engine job, maybe six or eight seats for passengers. The two engines and cabin hung down from a high wing, with the landing gear coming out of the engine cowling. It looked like the cabin was only about eight inches off the runway and when you landed it felt like you were about eight inches below the runway. A man came out the side of the plane who I originally thought was one scared passenger, but no, he turned out to be the pilot. He looked younger than I was, he had no uniform, there was no copilot, no stewardess, and no passengers. Was I to be the very first?

No, another man hanging around the hangar (Is that why they call it a hangar?) was also considering taking this same goose flight to Bismarck.

The pilot took our bags and threw them in behind the last two seats in the cabin and then invited us to get in. We were both reluctant but the other man was braver than I was, got in first and took the seat opposite the door. I climbed in and, wanting to be sociable, sat in the seat next to him, and right by the door, a big mistake.

After checking the tires, or the oil, or whatever they do, the pilot crawls in, but he has to crawl over my legs, the two or three seats in front of me, and finally up into the cockpit. That didn't bother me so much, except that when he crawled in over my legs, he just casually closed the door behind him as you would a car door and went on over the seats to the front.

In my increasingly petrified state, I was absolutely sure that the door right next to me was not closed tight. Nobody checked it or pushed a lock button, if there was one, and I was not about to touch it. I thought of yelling at the pilot, but he now had his earphones on and was starting the engines, so he couldn't hear me anyway. Clue number three was very apparent. Why am I doing this?

With my seat belt so tight I was blue in the face, and with my head bowed in prayer, we began our takeoff. But the first thing the crazy kamikaze pilot does is put the plane in a very steep bank to the left forcing me to lean against this half closed door. It seemed like an endless 180-degree turn, and I knew the door was going to pop open any minute. I wanted to tighten my seat belt even more, but I was afraid to touch it in case I might accidentally unfasten it. I could see Wild Goose's second passenger flying through the air over the Williston oil fields. What a gusher that would be.

We no more than got settled down when we hit a storm cloud and then there was hail smacking against the plastic windshield. It sounded like a machine gun going off right inside this aluminum tube we were sitting in.

When approaching the Bismarck airport we could easily hear all the communication between air traffic controller and the pilot on his radio, but I didn't like what I heard. The man said, "There is a student in a helicopter practicing takeoffs and landings on the runway and he doesn't have a radio. Make sure he sees you before you land."

"Well what the hell is he doing on my runway if he doesn't have a radio?" the pilot asked.

"There wasn't supposed to be any planes coming in this afternoon but we forgot this was your first scheduled flight," the radio said.

I had heard enough. I covered my eyes and ears and began praying again. The next thing I knew we were bouncing on the runway, one very big bounce, then a lesser one, and after a couple more we were on all three wheels. When we finally stopped, the smartass pilot said he wouldn't charge us any more for the extra landing bumps. I suggested to the pilot that a more appropriate name for his airline would be Wild Goose Bumps. To my knowledge the airline was not in business long enough to have a name change or have an accident that killed anyone.

All during my early days as the coordinator for opening new stores, Sears still had not given me an executive status. Perhaps I was still on trial yet, and as a time-card employee they could lay me off with no hesitation for any reason. Sears however, at that time, for some reason, found it very difficult to release executives.

Since I was responsible for keeping my own records, I decided to read the personnel manual covering non-executive pay. I learned that I could actually be dismissed if I did not accurately report the hours I worked, including the hours worked at night, weekends, or any hours beyond the forty-hour work week.

I also learned that any traveling time for any non-executive, whether it was by car or train had to be included as time worked. Well, on the Williston job, when I left home on Sunday night by train and arrived back two or three weeks later on a Saturday morning, it added up to more like seventy-five or eighty hours a week. So even though my hourly pay was still pretty meager, with the time and a half after forty hours and double time on Sunday, my take home pay was looking pretty good.

Unfortunately, when my boss found out how much money I was making as a time-card employee, he immediately put the wheels in motion to make me an executive at the minimum salary for beginners. Later on, while working on a Montana job, I went to my boss to complain that my earnings had dropped to forty-six cents an hour when considering my travel time and the hours actually worked. His only comment was, "Do you think you're worth it?"

After the Williston store there were five new catalog stores opened across Montana, interesting places like Glendive, Miles City, Bozeman, Livingston and Havre, but then my job started to peter out and I ordinarily may have been laid off. But now, by hook and by crook, I was one of the Sears family of executives.

Possibly we ran out of good markets, or it could have been a budget squeeze, or both. In any event my need in this activity was drying up and I had to be reassigned. And because I was a salaried employee, I would be pushed off to another assignment.

Since I was already working for the field sales organization, they decided they could use me as a "specialist" in some of the new post war merchandise coming out and I could go to some of our catalog stores and put on demonstrations. I spent a couple hours with a buyer to learn about each product, which was a long way from being an expert on anything, but for a North Dakota farmer or a northern Minnesota miner it was probably as good as they were going to get. I was a TV specialist in the winter, a home improvement and carpet specialist in the spring, a home freezer specialist in the summer, a gun specialist in the fall, and between Thanksgiving and Christmas, you guessed it, I was a traveling Santa Claus.

I was very uncomfortable about all of this, because I was not a salesman by any stretch of the imagination. When I was supposed to be the TV expert, it was really weird, because there were so very few TV stations in our territory, mainly just in the Twin Cities. But that didn't seem to bother the local farmers. They were so eager to be the first family in the neighborhood to own a TV, they were easy to sell. They would buy even if the only reception was a bunch of snow on the screen and occasionally there would be an outline of a person's face, and then only when you had a tall antenna on the roof. I would squat down and work the dials and when they recognized something on the screen they would ooh and aah and say, "Got to get one of those picture radios."

The same was true with the home freezer, which was a big new item on the market. My boss wanted me to learn to be a butcher so that I could demonstrate how to take a side of beef or pork and cut it up for freezing in the home freezer. Most of the rural customers were still butchering and preserving their own meat yet, so a home freezer became a most valuable item. I convinced my boss that if I was the butcher there would be blood all over the store, not from the animal carcass, but from me.

Each of these programs were set by first running a full page ad in the local newspaper the day before the event showing my picture and describing me as TV expert, a carpet expert, a gun expert or what have you. Talk about false advertising.

The gun shows were fun even though I hate guns. For a couple months in the fall I had a rented truck loaded with guns, display racks, and related items and drove from store to store. I would arrive at night, set up the display and be ready for all the sport goofballs that came in to prove they knew considerably more about guns than I ever would. That took all of two minutes. But it didn't make much difference, they bought guns anyway.

Being a Santa Claus was the most fun, but it was also one of the hardest jobs I ever had at Sears. Fortunately it only lasted a month. A full page ad in a local paper telling the people on a certain day Santa Claus would be in town, in a community that perhaps never had a Santa Claus before, was a big event and it really brought out the little no-neck monsters. At one store (I believe it was Superior, Wisconsin) I walked from my hotel at about nine in the morning and saw there was a line of kids nearly a half block long standing out in the cold, hanging on to their moms, waiting for the store to open just so they could talk to Santa Claus.

When I got inside I found the store manager and said, "For God's sake let those poor people in. I will get into my Santa suit right away." Well, I recall sitting down in my Santa chair a little before ten o'clock in the morning and not getting up until 9:30 that night when the store closed. The line went back and forth inside the store and they never stopped pouring in. I didn't have the heart to get up and take a break and walk away from those kids that were dying to talk to Santa.

I didn't have to go to the bathroom because with the wool suit, the beard and the pillow on my stomach, the sweat took care of all the moisture in my body.

I did get hungry and sent someone out for a hamburger and a malted milk, but I found out I couldn't get the hamburger through my whiskers while I was talking to the kids so I just drank the malted milk through the straw. The kids got a big kick out of watching me do all this. When the store finally closed, you can be sure, Santa Claus went out and finished off three or four martinis and a healthy T-bone steak, and Sears paid for every bite of it.

After the first of the year, I believe it is now 1952, another budget cut or something put a halt to my job in special promotions, which didn't make me feel too bad. Somehow the catalog credit manager, a salty old Scotsman named Dan MacLaughlin, was persuaded to interview me for an opening he had as a credit field supervisor. Not having a college degree or any accounting experience was enough of an obstacle, so I didn't tell him that I didn't know the difference between a debit and a credit.

The interview lasted all of five minutes, maybe six, and MacLaughlin as much as told me he didn't have much choice in the matter, he was going to have to take me for the job. He was preparing himself for retirement soon so he wasn't fighting things as much as he used to. "Don't worry," he said, "we'll teach you everything you need to know." I thought, this is like teaching a Chinese coolie to be a football sports announcer when he has never seen a football game and can't even speak English. Nevertheless, I was sent on my way to Austin, Minnesota, on Monday morning to report to the credit manager there for my three or four weeks of training.

The credit manager at Austin was a crusty little old Irish gal named Addie. She welcomed me like a school of hungry piranhas in a bath tub. "Who are you and what are you doing here?"

I introduced myself and said, "Mr. MacLaughlin sent me down here to be trained as a credit field supervisor." It was pretty obvious that MacLaughlin had forgotten, or was scared to call Addie and advise her of his desire to have her handle the training of this green numb nuts.

"Oh for Christ sake," Addie said. "Here I am up to my ass in alligators (Addie had a way with words) and they want me to train some young rookie." It was obvious that she was extremely busy and was probably short handed as most of these stores were.

"I'm sorry you were not informed," I said.

"Shit, nobody tells me nothing around here."

"Well, if you just want to give me your operating manual or something, I'll just go off in a corner someplace and read."

"No, you don't learn anything that way. You learn by doing and you're going to be doing." Addie went to her desk drawer and came up with a raft of papers. "This is what we do here. Each of these forms represents a delinquent account, real deadbeats. Some of these people haven't paid a dime in over six months. The balance they owe is listed down here, the merchandise they bought is over here and the last payment they made is shown here."

I learned later that all of these were defaulted accounts meaning they were at least six months past due with no activity and were ready to be charged off to profit and loss as uncollectible as soon as a field man came by that had the authority to do so. There must have been forty or fifty forms. Addie said, "I want you to take these forms and go out and talk to each and every one of them personally. Don't call them on the telephone. You must look them in the eye personally. And don't come back here until you've got either the money or the merchandise." I didn't ask any more questions. I just grabbed the forms and took off.

I believed this business of "Don't come back until you've got either the money or the merchandise," which she emphasized quite strongly, but it was just her way of getting me out of her hair. I don't think she had any hope that there was any blood left in any of these turnips. But I took her literally.

I left and checked into a little bed and breakfast place I saw on the way into town, then went to the chamber of commerce and got city maps. I also went to the post office to get directions to some rural households. I learned it was against postal regulations to give directions to where people lived, though I did get the location of the postal routes. I discovered that people in the country know where all their neighbors live, particularly if they are deadbeats so it wasn't too difficult to get help in finding my way around. Then I went to a restaurant for lunch and planned my strategy. The balance of Monday was a learning experience because I struck out on my first two calls, but on Tuesday and Wednesday I was in the swing of things.

On Wednesday afternoon old MacLaughlin back in the Minneapolis office called Addie and said, "I'm sorry Addie, but I think we forgot to telephone you the other day to tell you we were sending a trainee down to have him receive the benefit of your vast experience and your wonderful training skills. So how is he doing?"

Sweet Addie replied, "Thanks a hell of a lot for telling me Mac, but your protege ain't here. I sent him out to call on a few deadbeats and he never came back. I'm guessing he must have quit and gone home."

"The hell you say. Did you check the hotel?" MacLaughlin asked.

"Yes, and he never even checked in. Chalk it up to a bad choice Mac. This job ain't for everybody you know." Then she added, "What pisses me off, he took off with all my collection forms I had prepared and now I've got to do them all over again."

"Damn. I'm really sorry Addie and I thought this kid might have some promise."

On Thursday morning, after the store opened, I wandered into Addie's office, two and a half days after I left. Addie's mouth dropped open and she said, "Where in the hell have you been?"

"Well you told me not to come back until I talked to all these poor people. Man, they are really hard up. And I'm terribly sorry, but there were three of them that I just couldn't get any money and it looked like they were wearing the merchandise they bought so I couldn't get that."

Then Addie's mouth really dropped open when I started pulling money out of various pockets of my suit. I said, "I also have my car out back loaded down with merchandise so I'll need to know what to do with that. There's a washer and dryer and two TVs that we'll have to send a truck after but the people promised I could get them if I came back today. Two people have moved out of state but I have their new addresses. One of those that I didn't get was in jail. But I went to see him there and he was so glad because I was the only visitor he had had all month. He didn't have any money but he said he would call you when he got out in a couple weeks."

For the first time Addie was speechless. She wanted to kiss me, but I suggested we better just go unload my car. She placed a call to MacLaughlin right away and said, "Hey, your man is still here. He's standing right in front of me, and he's the best damn trainee you guys have ever come up with."

From that point on I got all the attention and benefit of her experience that I needed. I was now confident that I could handle the job and thereafter Addie became one of my favorite people in the business. I would now be a credit executive, although I was still very much in a fog about what that meant.

On my first assignment as a credit field supervisor, I was sent to International Falls. The place was in a mess and at the end of the week I wrote a rather critical lengthy report, which I was expected to cover with the store manager, in this case a motherly type lady at least twice my age. She was a former school teacher and when she read my report and picked out all the misspelled words, errors in punctuation and told me how my report would be much more effective if I would change the sentence structure here and there. She totally ignored the substance of the report and all the problems that were going on in her store.

I think I learned more about my own job from this trip than anyone else did from my presence, but I also got myself a pocket dictionary for my briefcase.

One of my more interesting assignments was presented to me by Mr. MacLaughlin at two o'clock in the morning. He woke me up and said, "Our store in Superior, Wisconsin, is burning down and I want you to drive up there and make sure our credit records are secure."

I arrived in Superior in time to watch the firemen with a cable on a winch trying to drag one of the heavy safes out of the basement of a totally gutted building.

Our credit records were always stored at night in a fireproof safe while any money carried over to the next day was stored in another safe. It was our credit safe that the firemen had located after it had fallen through to the basement, now resting in about three feet of water. Since the safe contained only records, the combination was taped to the safe door so that if there was a burglary, the burglars could open it up and see that it contained no money so there would be no need to cart it off.

That actually happened at one of our other stores. The burglars in their haste accidentally scraped off the combination instructions, which we found on the ground by the back door loading dock. I would have liked to have seen their faces when they struggled to blast open that heavy hummer and found nothing of value. We never saw the safe or records again, but we were able to reconstruct the credit records with only a minimal loss.

This was now going to be my task in Superior, to reconstruct these water-soaked records so we could carry on business as usual. As a matter of fact, Sears was open for business by ten o'clock the morning after the fire. There was a suitable vacant building just across the street from the burned-out store, and the landlord of this building was on the street early in the morning to watch the fire. The store manager and the new landlord negotiated a lease right on the sidewalk. The telephone company began work immediately putting in new telephones and they were even able to restore the same telephone numbers, so that unless the customers knew about the fire from the radio or TV, they would not know that anything had changed.

Superior was a very good credit store, so there was nearly a half million in receivables that had to be salvaged. The ledger cards for individual customer accounts were all hand posted using a ball point pen, so after being soaked in the dirty water the ink was all blurred and unreadable on many records. The typed name and address was still readable, so this much we could reconstruct with little difficulty, once I set up an iron and ironing board to dry them out.

After about two weeks of working with customers who were amazingly cooperative to bring in their receipt books and canceled checks, we came within a dollar and some cents of restoring all of the receivables. Once again I was given credit for doing a great job. I was just lucky to be in the right place at the right time.

Oh Lord, it's hard to be humble when you're perfect in every way.
Can't wait to look in the mirror, cause I get better looking every day.

While working in Superior, I couldn't keep my eyes off a very cute little blonde girl who worked part-time and left the store about 5:30 every evening. I seemed to have a thing about blondes at that time, with all my favorite movie stars being blondes, such as Betty Gable, June Allison, Lana Turner, Jane Powell and so on. This Sears blonde was more the Jane Powell type, I thought. One night I approached her and said, "I see you waiting here each night for someone to pick you up. Would that be your boyfriend?"

"No, my father picks me up when he gets off work."

"Oh really. Well why don't you tell your father that he doesn't have to pick you up. I can give you a ride home."

"He's probably already left work and I wouldn't be able to reach him now," she replied.

"I didn't mean tonight. Just tell him I'll take you home tomorrow night and then he won't have to come by and pick you up."

"Okay," she said. Boy, how lucky. I could hardly wait until the next day to give this gorgeous creature a ride home...and maybe more.

The next day I asked her, "Do you have everything worked out with your father so that I can give you a ride home?"

"It's okay." At 5:30 I met little Jane Powell and walked with her to my car.

"How was work today?" I asked.

"Okay."

"Just okay? Well, would you consider joining me for dinner this evening? There is a restaurant over in Duluth I'd like to try."

"Okay."

"Why don't I run you home first and then I'll go back to my hotel and freshen up before we go out."

"Okay."

"You'll have to give me directions on how to get to your house."

"Just keep on this street out of town."

We drove on and on which seemed like several miles, particularly when her only conversation was "yes" or "okay."

"Are we soon going to be at your house?"

"Yes."

When we finally got to her house, twenty-two miles from where we started, I said, "This is going to make it a little late to drive back to the hotel and then come back to pick you up. Are you sure that's all right?"

"It's okay."

I was hoping she would let me off the hook or suggest something else. No, everything was "okay."

So I drove the twenty-two miles back to my hotel, did a quick fresh up and drove the same twenty-two miles back to her house again.

By the time I got there, it was pitch dark. There was no street light or a front door light on her house so I felt my way in the dark up some steps where there was a screened-in front porch. I rapped on the screen door but there was no response. Apparently they couldn't hear my knock from inside the house so I tried the screen door and it was not locked.

I walked in and found the front door, but just as I was about to knock on the front door, a dog jumped up and locked his jaws around my wrist. It was a Spitz, not real big, but a thousand-pound Bengal Tiger couldn't have scared me more.

Miss Blonde's mother quickly came to the door and rescued me from the dog, or maybe she was rescuing the dog from me. She apologized all over the place and said, "Why don't you take your suit jacket off. Maybe I can sew up that rip."

"No, that's all right. I'll take it to a tailor when I get back to Minneapolis." I didn't even notice at the time that my arm was bleeding quite a bit and my white shirt was soaking up the blood acting like a bandage. I never even thought about the possibility of the dog having rabies or something and I was too embarrassed to ever mention the incident again. Fortunately the dog was okay, he was just hungry for a little human flesh.

We proceeded on to Duluth to the restaurant I had my appetite all set for which turned out to be a bust. The food was almost, but not quite, as dull as my dinner date. When I asked her how her dinner was. Guess what she said: "It was okay."

"You're right," I said. "Okay is being very generous in describing it."

On the way from Duluth back to the blonde bombshell's house, we had to drive right by the Superior hotel where I was staying. For a brief moment I thought about suggesting to my date that she spend the rest of the night with me and save me all this driving. But I was afraid her reply might have been, "Okay." That had all the makings of a bigger letdown.

When you are up to your ass in alligators, it's hard to remember that you came in to drain the swamp…

Chapter 16

Previously you indicated that your life story could be divided into three parts: the first fifteen years as a boy on the farm, the next twelve years or so trying to get the farm off the boy and then finally, your life with Jeanne. You are about to meet Jeanne. Was it love at first sight? Did you realize how much your life would change from this point on?

RIGHT AFTER THE WAR there was a rush of discharged servicemen coming home and there was a rush by the patiently waiting sweethearts to march down the aisles, get married to these lust-hungry heroes and live happily ever after. A few of my friends did exactly that. Larry Schwartzbauer, for example, married his high school girlfriend right away. My friend, Dick Nord, never got into the service, but he thought he had better lay claim to his high school friend and marry her right away also. My brother couldn't wait and married his true love before the war was half over.

My friend, Al Johnson, seemed to be the only one around remaining single, although I am not sure he wanted to be. He was constantly on the lookout for Miss Perfect. Al and I went to art school together where the females were all a little strange, and we also worked at Sears at the same time but didn't see a lot of each other while working.

One time he said, "There sure isn't many good-looking girls here to choose from." As if Sears was supposed to be his provider.

"There's a cute blonde that works up on sixth floor," I said, "but she is about the only one I can think of."

"That would be Elsie Gustaphson," Al replied, "but I understand she is already going steady with another guy and you can't touch her."

"You know, Al, all these girls that Sears hires now have to pass the ugliness test."

"You're kidding. What's that?" he said

"Well, you know all the crazy tests they give everybody before they're hired," I went on. "This test they just give to the girls by having them sit in this empty room with nothing in the room but a clock on the wall. They are told to stare at the clock, and if it keeps on running they are rejected. But if the clock stops, they are hired immediately."

"Boy, you've got that right."

"Then there are a few of these that you can categorize as coyote ugly. You've heard of that haven't you? That's when you wake up in the morning and find this girl sleeping across your arm. But she is so ugly that you are afraid you will wake her by moving your arm, so you just chew your arm off like a coyote in a trap. That's coyote ugly."

With everyone hurrying to ring those wedding bells, there was a bit of pressure on a guy who just turned twenty-seven as to what is wrong with him. Like, "When are you going to stop jumping from one girl to another Floyd, and settle down and get married?"

Do I have to, I thought. I'm having fun. There's plenty of time. I will admit I had a little fear of ending up like my parents who were totally miserable during the best years of their lives only because they were married. I had plenty of chances to get married if I wanted to. In fact I used to feel sorry for some of the girls I dated because that seemed to be what they wanted to do more than anything, and when they got too serious I moved on.

When I started working for Sears on the road, being gone from Monday through Friday and sometimes out over a weekend for two or three weeks, my social life in Minneapolis took a dive. I would rely a great deal on Al to line up some things to do, and if he was going out with a girl, to have her line up another girl for me for a double date.

It was on one such occasion that I met Geri Babbler, a friend of one of Al's girlfriends. She would be my blind date. We got along fine together, but I could tell from the beginning she was not my type. She was already a year older than I was and it seemed she was looking for a guy to marry and bed down with, and not necessarily in that order as long as you accomplished both. I wasn't interested in either one, at least not with her. But she was a convenient date even though she was a little on the pushy side.

One Sunday night when I took Geri home, I asked her about going out the following weekend because I would be out of town all week. She was very apologetic, acting like I might cry if she turned me down, and said, "I'm sorry Floyd, but I don't think we can go out anymore. I'm expecting to be engaged to another guy this week."

"Oh, congratulations." I acted disappointed, short of crying, but was really not. "Who's the lucky bum? Anybody I know?"

"His name is Sam Lund. He is not from here, but I'm sure you would like him."

"Are you kidding? I hate his guts already." (I was kidding.)

Geri went on. "Incidentally, I have a girlfriend who I don't believe is going with anyone steady right now and I think you and she would hit it off very well."

Have you ever seen it fail? Everybody wants to be a matchmaker once their own match is lit.

"She has a great sense of humor and she is a stewardess for Northwest..."

"Wait a minute. Did you say she was a stewardess?" That got my attention. A stewardess meant three things: number one, she had to be reasonably attractive to even be considered for the job; number two, she had to be single, stews were not allowed to be married then; and number three, she would have to have some single girlfriends.

It was this last point that intrigued me the most because this meant maybe I would finally be able to fix my friends up with some good-looking girls like they were always doing for me. I still lived in St. Paul and had very few connections in Minneapolis where Al and the other guys went to school and where I was now hanging out.

Geri said, "I'll give you her phone number and tell her you're going to call."

This was going to be different. I had never called a girl on the telephone that I had never met previously. I was no Larry Schwartzbauer. I had always been introduced first so we could look each other over and then you would have some kind of picture in your mind when you called. I certainly was not going to go out on a double date with Geri and her new man Sam, but on second thought, I suppose I would if it was the only way I was going to meet this stewardess.

"Well all right, what's her name and give me her phone number. Maybe I'll call her, maybe I won't," knowing very well I would.

I didn't even bother to ask Geri anything about this stewardess. How old was she? Didn't matter. Was she a blonde or brunette? Didn't matter, but I was kind of hoping she would be a blonde. How tall was she? How much did she weigh? What kind of figure did she have? None of this mattered too much. After all, it was my primary purpose to get to know some of her single girlfriends and have her fix them up with some of my friends so I could finally return the favors they had been giving me.

Her name was Jeanne Woods, stewardess for Northwest Airlines. That, along with her telephone number, was the absolute extent of knowledge I had about her.

About noon on Saturday two weeks later I made the call. "Hello, is Jeanne Woods there?"

"Yes, but she is sleeping right now. Who's calling?"

I didn't particularly want to leave my name, so I just said I would call again later. But I, Mr. Procrastinator, didn't get around to call her again until Sunday morning. "Hello, I'm calling for Jeanne Woods. Is she there?"

"No, she left a little while ago on a flight."

"Will she be back later today?"

"No, I'm afraid not. She said she would be on a layover. Do you want to leave her a message?"

"No, that's okay. I'll call some other time."

Strike one? No, it was close, but I think we can call that ball one. But what the hell is this "layover" thing? I've never heard of that before.

Now I'm out of town again for another week. But this time, on Friday night I hurry up and make my call. "Hello, is Jeanne Woods there?"

"I'm Jeanne Woods." She sounded very good.

"This is Floyd, Floyd Wachs."

"Who?"

"Floyd Wachs and I believe we have a mutual friend named Geri Babbler. She suggested I call you."

"Oh yes, I think I remember something about that. She mentioned some time ago that there was some guy she knew and she gave out my phone number, which she shouldn't have done."

After a bit of chit-chat, I said, "I would certainly like to meet you, because Geri has told me so many nice things about you." Geri hadn't told me a damn thing. "But we don't have anyone to introduce us, so how about if just the two of us go out on a date to a movie, a dinner, or something?" This was the most aggressive line I had ever put on a girl. I was amazed at myself.

"No, I don't want to do that," Jeanne replied.

"Are you saying you don't want to go out?" I was crushed.

"No, I just don't want to waste a whole evening on a blind date."

I was not only crushed, I was ground up and spit out. *Waste a whole evening? Who does she think she is? You're just a stew with Northwest. You're not flying with the angels. Besides, you don't know what you're missing. There are any number of girls that would give up an entire night's sleep just to "waste" it with me.*

Jeanne went on to say, "What I mean is, I've had some really bad luck with blind dates recently and I would kind of like to get to know the guy before we go out so we don't ruin the entire evening for both of us."

"Okay, so how are you going to find out what a great guy I am, and how I'm about to change your luck on blind dates?" That didn't even get a snicker.

Jeanne suggested, "How about if you meet me at the airport when I come in from a flight and we can have a cup of coffee in the restaurant?"

"All right, then I can give you a ride home afterward?" It was a question.

"We'll see."

Was that strike one? No, I think we can still call that ball two.

"So when is your next flight?" I asked.

"I won't be coming in from a flight until Wednesday."

"Swell, I'll be out of town then. What about this weekend?"

"I'll be in Washington, DC, but I'll be coming in about 6:45 Sunday evening."

I jumped on that. "That's a date. I mean, that will be our coffee break, or whatever. I'll meet you then."

A cup of coffee. Big deal, I don't even drink coffee. Over a cup of coffee I am supposed to impress this Miss Queen of the Airways that I am respectable and safe and good enough to spend a whole precious evening with. I'll be so nervous I'll probably spill the coffee all over her. Come to think of it, I don't even know what she looks like. I'll have to walk up to every stewardess in the airport and check their name tags. No, you're not the right one, let me check the next one.

The week went by and I planned my big event, The Airport Coffee Break. I got out to the airport early and checked the flight schedule for the 6:45 flight from Washington, DC. Where it normally reads "On Time," it said "Delayed."

I went to the Northwest counter and was told, "There is some really bad weather out East and right now we expect the flight to be about two hours late."

I'll wait. What choice do I have. I can practice drinking coffee.

After the two hours went by there was now posted on the flight schedule board an anticipated arrival time of 10:30. Back to reading the discarded newspapers. I don't need any more practice drinking coffee.

At about ten o'clock I went to the Northwest counter again and I was told that the flight was in the air and it would be in around midnight. *Forget it. If I finally do get to find this stewardess with the Miss. Woods name tag, she won't even want to "waste" her time over a cup of coffee. Besides, what kind of an idiot would spend this much time waiting for someone he has never seen before?*

I went home. Was this strike one? Definitely, right down the middle.

The next week I was in Brookings, South Dakota, again and I made no attempt to telephone Miss Woods, Stewardess for Northwest Airlines, until Friday night.

"Hi, this is Floyd calling, the guy who lurks around in airports waiting for lost airplanes to come in."

"Oh, I'm terribly sorry. I never expected to hear from you again. I hope you don't think I stood you up on purpose." She sounded very sincere.

"No big deal," I said. "It was just for a cup of coffee, right? But one thing you're going to find out is that I am very persistent. Can we try this again? And I'm sorry but it has to be a weekend."

"Well, I have a flight to Seattle tomorrow. It's a layover, so I'll be coming in on Sunday evening again. Will that be okay or do you just want to forget the whole thing?"

Are you kidding? I thought. But what the hell was this "layover" business? I still didn't know what that meant and they seemed to be using it quite a bit. "No way," I said. "More than ever I now want to meet you. I will be at the airport and I promise I will stick it out and not go home at eleven o'clock like I did the last time. What time does your flight get in?"

"It's due in at seven Sunday night and I do hope it's on time."

Once again I was out to the airport in plenty of time. I checked the schedule board for the flight from Seattle and I couldn't believe it. This time it doesn't say "Delayed" or "On Time" or "Late," it simply says "Canceled." What a jinx I must be. I went to the ticket counter to find out what happened to the flight from Seattle and was told there was a mechanical problem and that the flight was canceled.

"What happens now?" I inquired.

"Well there are two other flights coming in from Seattle tonight, so if your passenger is lucky they could be on one of these flights."

"I'm not waiting for a passenger. I'm interested in the flight crew."

"Who knows when they will be in. They could layover again tonight and deadhead on some flight tomorrow."

First there is "layover," and now there's another interesting term, "deadhead." I suppose if you layover enough your head could get rather dead after awhile. In any event, I didn't see this one coming. It was a fast ball right over and without question, strike two. So far I hadn't taken my bat off my shoulder. Needless to say, I didn't wait around. I was back on the road again the next week.

The next week I was in town on Thursday but the routine was pretty much the same. "Hello, this is Floyd. Remember me, the airport prowler? The airport security people have a tail on me so I have to make this rather quick." It was getting more difficult to be humorous.

"Once again I am so terribly sorry. I can't believe this is happening. I really am surprised to hear from you this time. I wish there was some way I could have called you to let you know our dumb aircraft was sick." She sounded very considerate and apologetic.

"I know it's not your fault," I said, "but I'm not sure I am not a jinx for your flights. I should be the one apologizing. Did you have to spend another night in Seattle? Is that called a double layover or just a laid up?"

This got a little laugh. "We had a ball," she said. "After sitting around the airport for a couple of hours waiting for our flight to be canceled, the entire crew all decided to go downtown to this new restaurant that we all wanted to try, and since we didn't have to work anymore, we had a couple bottles of wine and had a great time."

That didn't make me feel any better. I had visions of a drunken orgy with pilots and stewardi, or whatever the word is for two or more, laying all over the place. Is that where layover got its name?

Jeanne said, "I don't believe you are a jinx, but I wouldn't want to take the chance and make you go through this again. You have been far more patient than anyone I've ever known and if you still want to, I would be willing to try some other way to meet. And if you don't want to, I will also understand."

"Well the people out at the airport are starting to look at me rather suspiciously for hanging around so much and I would just as soon not waste another evening on a non-date event." *Oh, I wish I hadn't said that.* She made no comment. "Yes, by all means," I went on. "I still want to meet you any way I can, but I would prefer not the airport."

Jeanne agreed. "If you're not busy tomorrow afternoon or evening why don't you come over and we can figure out something to do."

"Great! What time and where do you live?"

"I live at 5313 Chicago Avenue in a double bungalow. How about 6:30? If it's a nice day I would like to get some sun in the afternoon."

Wow! I think I just got a base hit on a two and two pitch. Now if I can just stretch it into extra bases.

"I'll be there."

It was a Friday, a beautiful warm day in May when I walked up the steps at the little double bungalow on Chicago Avenue. The door was already open except there was a screen door. I rapped on the screen door.

"Come on in. The door is open," the voice said from inside.

Finally I am going to meet this stewardess girl who I feel like I already know, except I have no idea what she looks like.

The first thing I saw was a pair of richly tanned bare legs and bare feet stretched out over an ottoman. Moving up into the over-stuffed chair there was this smiling face, not a pretty face, but certainly not unattractive, and more beautiful bronze bare skin of shoulders and arms. Over her mid-section was draped a newspaper as if she had been reading it, but then maybe not.

Where are her clothes? No visible sign of any clothes. My God, she couldn't be. She doesn't have any clothes on! What have I got myself into here?

I had heard some weird stories about stewardesses, or stewardi, but I didn't believe I would ever get this close to one of the weirdest. Wait 'til the guys hear about this one. I didn't know what to do.

"Rather warm day for May isn't it?" I said, as I felt the hot blood rising in the back of my neck.

The newspaper-covered nude in the chair made no move to get up or introduce herself. She simply said, "Why don't you sit down?" And then she giggled a little. I couldn't look at her.

I said, "It must have been a good day to get a tan." At the same time I sneaked a peek at her and she was neatly tucking the newspaper around her hips and bosom to make sure not too much was exposed. She giggled some more. No question about it, at this point she knew that I thought she was lying there in the nude and she decided to make a little game out of it.

There was a little more chit-chat and more giggling, but I have no idea what I said. I was just wondering how I could get the hell out of there and kick myself for all the time I ended up "wasting" on this broad.

Suddenly from the back of the room, another girl appeared, "Hi, I'm Jeanne. You must be Floyd."

"But I thought you were… You're Jeanne? Wow! Am I ever pleased to meet you." My mouth dropped open but I had trouble talking. I was overwhelmed with relief.

Jeanne was a little startled at my reaction but later on I would explain. She then said, "It looks like you have already met my roommate, Mary."

"Well yes," I stuttered. "I guess we have but I haven't finished reading all of the newspaper yet." I didn't know what else to say but I still tried to be cool.

Mary giggled again and got up from her chair. She pulled off the newspaper to disclose that she was dressed in a pink, off-the-shoulder, one-piece bathing suit. Needless to say I was very pleased to see that because I didn't know how I was going to deal with this nude person greeting me.

I'll have to admit: it was definitely not love at first sight with me and Jeanne. In fact, to be perfectly frank, I was not immediately impressed with what I saw, but that was going to change quickly. It was obvious that Jeanne had been out in the sun all day because she was one mass of vibrating brown freckles. Her face had at least ten thousand freckles and each of her arms must have had double that.

(At some point later on I would kid, "If we don't have anything else to do, I could always count your freckles." She quickly read my mind and assured me that skin does not freckle where the sun does not hit it.)

Actually, the freckles did not detract from her appearance as they do on some people. They seemed to be very natural and went well with her personality, which right away came through as being sparkling and fun loving. Most freckled people I thought were red heads, but this girl had black hair cut very short, so that it almost looked like she had a beanie on her head. Maybe this is why for the longest time I thought she was Jewish, not that it would have mattered one way or another.

She was also very slender, almost to the point of being skinny, but that was fine because I had been out with a couple of overweight girls and couldn't wait to say good-night. Being very slender meant she didn't have any prominent bumps on her chest either, but that was okay. I was a leg man not a boob man, but I hadn't gotten a look at her legs yet. I wondered if she was sizing me up with her first impressions also, as I was trying very hard to make a good first impression.

If someone tapped me on the shoulder then and said, "Do you know that this is the girl you are going to spend the rest of your life with?" I would have said "You've got to be kidding, man. I'm not ready to settle down yet."

We left the house and got into my still quite new and freshly polished Plymouth to begin our getting acquainted process. My car was not what you would call a "chick" vehicle to say the least, so no impression or comment was expected here.

We drove to a place called Lilac Lanes on Highway 100 and Excelsior Boulevard, which was a combination bar, restaurant, and bowling alley. I don't know why I chose this place other than it was a rather nice restaurant where you could dine casually or just have a drink if you preferred. It also had booths with big high backs where one could sit down and have some conversation without being disturbed.

When we walked from the car into the restaurant, I touched her hand and she spontaneously took hold of mine and pulled in close to me as we walked. It felt very natural and comfortable. I thought, *Hey, I'll bet she is a snuggler*. It was a good guess.

Later when Jeanne left the booth once to go to the bathroom, I turned around to get a good look at her legs. They were a definite "10," long and slender with curves in all the right places. I learned later that her legs were voted the best in her stewardess class. (I wondered if they also voted on the best tits and ass and so on.)

It was very easy to have conversations with Jeanne. We talked non-stop for hours I think, while I had two or three beers and Jeanne had a Scotch and water and barely touched it. She had a flight later the next day and was very conscientious about the rules of drinking before taking a flight. She said she hated beer. I would have to do something to change that.

We talked about where we were from; the similarities were amazing. We were both from very poor families from small farms in northern Minnesota, and felt very lucky to have been able to escape that environment in favor of the big city. She was pretty much on her own at fifteen or sixteen, as I was, and she finished high school in Minneapolis as I did in St. Paul.

In addition to her fresh and positive personality, Jeanne was incredibly honest. Some people will avoid talking about things that might not put them in a good light. That didn't even cross her mind. She blurted out everything. She was also the type of person who would also walk five blocks to a store where a clerk may have given her a dollar too much change, just to pay it back.

I've only known a few people who were so naturally honest. Such people seem to be very fair, responsible, confident and trustworthy. They can also talk about their own good qualities and achievements without sounding boastful, and they would not hesitate to do the same if the facts were reversed.

We left the restaurant and drove back to the double bungalow on Chicago Avenue. It was still early so Jeanne invited me in, only to find that Mary and her boyfriend were sitting in the living room. It was a small room, so after spending a little time in the kitchen, seeking a little privacy, we decided to go for a ride again. I wanted to make sure her blind date was not a total waste of time, so we drove around Minnehaha Falls and tried out a little necking. She had some definite rules about that sort of thing, but "no kissing on the first date" was not one of them.

I was beginning to like this girl and was generally pleased, I guess, that she had some strict rules. Before I took her home, I asked her if she would be willing to go out with me again Sunday night.

She immediately said, "Sure."

On the next date we went to a movie and doubled up with Al and a nurse friend named Mary, whom he had met on one of our trips up north at Bar Harbor. I didn't think they were all that serious, and I wanted Al to know that I had finally met someone that had a whole bevy of good-looking girlfriends waiting to be fixed up.

Every weekend from that time on, Jeanne and I got together, at least whenever I was in town and she was not on a flight someplace.

She started to bid her flight schedules so that she could be home on weekends. To my knowledge neither one of us dated anyone else from that time on, though we made no commitments to each other about that.

One day I asked Jeanne, "Do you by chance have any girlfriends that you could fix my friend Al up with on a blind date?"

"Oh I think so," Jeanne replied. "As a matter of fact, one of my good friends is not going out with anyone steady right now, and she's very cute."

"Great. Does she have big boobs?" I asked, "I think Al kind of goes for that."

"No, she is a little flat-chested. But is that all that matters?

"Well is she Scandinavian?"

"No, I think she's Irish."

"I hope she's Lutheran. Al seems to be pretty firm about that."

"No. I know she's Catholic," Jeanne said, "But, my God, he doesn't have to marry her."

"Well, let me talk to him and see what he says."

I called Al the next day and said, "I've finally got one of Jeanne's friends that wants to meet you and go out on a double date with us. I haven't met her yet but she sounds like a doll." I wasn't going to lay all the negative things on him right away.

There was a long pause and finally Al said, " Well Floyd, you see, all.... Well Mary and I are.... Well I sort of got engaged last night. I haven't given her a ring yet but I better not go out with anyone else."

"Shit, Al, you have no idea what I have gone through just to meet this stewardess who has got all kinds of good-looking, single girlfriends. Now you have to go and blow the whole damn thing by getting engaged."

"Geez, Floyd. What can I say?"

"Well congratulations, or whatever, but don't tell me I didn't try."

On one trip I made for Sears out to western Montana (I believe we were setting up a new store in Bozeman), I was expected to stay out there for three weeks. That would be tough, not seeing Jeanne for three whole weeks, so I asked her if she couldn't try and get a flight out to Montana someplace and meet me. As long as there were empty seats on the plane I knew she could fly on a pass just about anyplace, and even if there were no empty seats she could con the gate agent into letting her on board and sit in the jump seat, as they called it.

Jeanne said, "I might be able to do that. How would it be if I met you in Billings? I have a girlfriend that lives in Billings and maybe I could stay with her."

"Sounds great. Could you spend the weekend?"

"There's a flight that gets into Billings about nine on Friday night but I have a Monday morning flight the next week, so I'll have to go back Sunday night."

"That's perfect. I'll meet your flight Friday night."

"No, I don't want you to meet me. I don't want anyone to know I'm meeting a boyfriend in Billings and start a lot of gossip with the airline people. I'll just ride to the hotel with the crew and I'll meet you there. They all stay at the Great Northern Hotel."

"Okay, I will get a room there and I'll get a room for you also so you won't have to bother your friend late on Friday night." I had devious thoughts that maybe we wouldn't have to use both rooms, but I at least wanted to leave the impression that I was an honorable man. Let's see, should I get some roses to put in her room, or maybe a bottle of champagne? I'll go to the bar for a beer and think about it.

That Friday night at the Great Northern Hotel in Billings, I sat in the bar and waited, planning my evening with Jeanne, when a bellboy walked through the bar announcing, "Telegram for Floyd Wachs. Telegram for Floyd Wachs."

"Here I am." I grabbed it and tore it open. It read, SORRY OVERSLEPT MISSED MY FLIGHT WILL ARRIVE ON NINE AM FLIGHT TOMORROW. I couldn't believe it. I was devastated, but it was typical of Jeanne's honesty. Anyone else would have come up with a more acceptable excuse, but she actually did take a nap at four in the afternoon, which was not unusual for airline people and their crazy schedules, so she simply overslept and didn't make it to the airport in time to catch her flight.

What a let down. The cost of the extra room didn't bother me, but I didn't know when I would get a better opportunity than this again, not that it would have paid off anyway. I was frustrated and the cold shower didn't help.

The next morning I was sitting in a booth having breakfast when Jeanne walked into the Great Northern Hotel restaurant looking for me. It was difficult to hide my disappointment. In fact I didn't even try, and though she did apologize, she did not totally understand why I should get so upset. She abruptly left, leaving me sitting there, and went to call her girlfriend, Dorothy. After a few minutes she returned and said, "Dorothy is picking me up and were going to spend most of the day shopping. When I get back, if you still want to, maybe we can have dinner together or something."

"Fine." What else could I say, "I'll just hang out around the hotel here." Once again I was back reading the newspapers and magazines in the hotel lobby.

Later that day, after a couple of messages, Jeanne got ahold of me and said, "Dorothy and her boyfriend, Jim, want us to go out with them tonight and do a little Billings bar-hopping. Dorothy has also asked me to spend the night with her." This wasn't exactly what I had in mind but then Jeanne told me she got somebody to take her early Monday morning flight and she wouldn't have to leave until late Sunday night. She assured me we could spend all day Sunday together if I still wanted to. Yes, I did, so I reluctantly agreed to the Saturday night on the town of Billings.

What I wasn't told, because Jeanne didn't know either at the time, was that Dorothy's boyfriend, Jim, had a friend, Joe somebody, the son of some important Montana politician, a senator I believe, who had just received delivery on a big, beautiful new Oldsmobile convertible, and wanted to take Jim and Dorothy for a ride. Jeanne was conveniently invited to join them to make it a foursome. But then Joe was told he would have to stop by the hotel to pick me up. Joe was probably as disturbed about this as I was, realizing that one of us, either Joe or Floyd, was the fifth wheel in this arrangement. But he had this super sex wagon with the other four wheels. Advantage Joe.

I got in the front seat where Jeanne was, which squeezed her over next to Joe. Someone introduced me to Joe, but I immediately decided I wasn't going to care for this guy. He seemed to be too comfortable with Jeanne by his side. Even worse, Jeanne seemed to be enjoying it too much also. Joe took us for a ride to see all the sights of Billings and was busy explaining all the features of his new convertible to Jeanne. I was treated like a glob of cow dung on Joe's pretty cowboy boots, but I was determined not to let him scrape me off.

We went to a couple of bars and had something to eat at one. The waitress gave each of us a guest check and Joe the jerk quickly grabbed Jeanne's to pay for hers. Once again I was invisible. *I really don't like this guy!*

The next place we went to, there was a little band playing some good dance music and there was an area for dancing. The show-off son-of-a-senator grabbed Jeanne right away and off they went dancing. *I'm really getting to hate this guy.* Dorothy and Jim also went out on the dance floor, so I was sitting there by myself dancing with a beer bottle.

The music stopped, but before Jeanne and the jerk got back to the table, the band would start up another tune and he would pull Jeanne back out there again. Jeanne loved to dance and this tall blond boob was probably pretty good.

When Dorothy and Jim came back to the table, I said, "If that SOB doesn't bring her back here pretty soon I'm going to go out there and mop the floor with him."

Dorothy obviously didn't know me very well or she would have known that I am not a fighter. But she was scared that I was about to start a brawl or something so she ran out on the dance floor and grabbed Jeanne aside. She said, "You'd better get back to the table because Floyd is really mad and he wants to come out here and punch Joe's eyes out." Jeanne immediately came back to the table, grabbed my arm and never let go of me. Poor Joe never got another dance.

We soon left that place, and when we got to the car, the big, fancy convertible, Jeanne quickly jumped into the back seat with me right beside her. When they all dropped me off at my hotel, with Joe-the-shmoe watching in the rear view mirror, Jeanne gave me a long, loving kiss good night. It was indeed an erectifying moment.

There, how do you like that you big blond baboon? Now take your cutesie convertible and drive it up your pompous ass.

That night in my hotel room, I made up my mind that I really did like this girl and I didn't ever want to let go of her. Up until this point I had never thought seriously about marrying anyone, but without a doubt I knew Jeanne was the girl I wanted to marry. Love at first sight may be great, but this was so much stronger and so absolute.

The next day I rented a car and picked up Jeanne at her girlfriend's apartment. It was a plain vanilla Chevrolet and not a convertible. I also picked up some sandwiches at a deli and a six-pack of beer. After several intense lessons, Jeanne was starting to get the hang of drinking beer. We had no particular place in mind to go except we both wanted to be together by ourselves.

We ended up going up in the Bear Tooth Mountains at the north entrance to Yellowstone Park. We drank a beer on the way up and had our sandwiches and another beer when we got to the summit. It was breathtakingly beautiful. We were both enjoying our relaxing moment together, when Jeanne asked, "Did you happen to see a place to go potty on our way up?"

"No," I said, "and I really have to go too." The beer, the high altitude, the thin air, all have a very "right now" effect on your bladder. We started down the mountain with all its hairpin curves looking for a port-a-potty or anyplace where we could relieve ourselves. It was straight up rock mountain on one side of the narrow road and straight down rock cliff on the other side. I remember steering, shifting, and braking with my legs squeezed together for twenty-three miles before we even got to the tree line. At the first sign of some bushes on some level ground, I stopped the car and Jeanne ran one direction and I went the other. Five minutes later we both emerged from behind our bushes with a big smile on our faces.

That weekend in Billings was very significant for both of us. While there had not been any commitment of any kind between us up to this point, or had we even thought of any, I believe we both realized it was for real. From that time on, I planned my days in town to be with Jeanne every moment I could, and she worked her flight schedules or traded trips to coincide with my schedule. She was by far the greatest thing that ever happened in my life and I had never been happier. And to think that it came so close to being screwed up by that damn Northwest Airlines.

Prior to meeting Jeanne, I often wondered as I dated a number of different girls (not that many really), that I could have ended up getting married to any one of them, but how would I know when the right one came along. Is there a God of matrimony or some super spirit that comes along and taps you on the shoulder and says, "This is it you dummy. Go for it!" or must you rely on your instincts? After all, this may be the most important decision you will ever have to make in your entire life and why shouldn't you be able to go to someone other than your friends and relatives and get some real absolute assurance.

Unfortunately I am sure many people make this decision without any kind of help and maybe not even the full support of their own instincts. Once again I was especially lucky. I got the tap on the shoulder.

NORTHWEST
5

Norman Vincent Peale taught us how to win friends and influence people. This lesson can be summed up with one word...

INTEGRITY

Chapter 17

You have obviously met the girl you want to marry, and you're certainly old enough at 27, yet another year goes by before the wedding. Why the delay?

JEANNE AND I never talked marriage, because somewhere along the way she had sent up some kind of signal to me that she didn't care when or if she ever got married, she was having so much fun in her job. Being a stewardess was a coveted job at that time, and for this little girl from a pour family with no more than a high school education, it was indeed quite an accomplishment. Why give it up so quickly just to get married? In addition she had some older sisters who already had some problems with the men in their lives, so the picture of being married with maybe a couple of bratty kids coming along didn't seem to be an attractive alternative.

I also stayed away from the marriage idea, not because of the picture my parents had painted about married life, but because I was also enjoying my single independence. On the other hand maybe I was just scared to ask Jeanne to give up what she had and spend the rest of her life with me. Even I could see that wasn't a very good trade. Furthermore, if I did ask her and she turned me down, I would be destroyed.

Of all the good qualities I could identify in Jeanne, she did have a flaw that bothered me just a little: smoking. Not that anyone had any great concern about smoking at that time: the medical problems were only suspected then, so nearly everyone our age smoked. Oh, I tried it, several times I think, when I was in the Navy, to prove that I was a regular guy. I just didn't like it. It bothered my nose to the point where I would try to move away from anyone who was smoking. Jeanne didn't smoke that much and I certainty was not going to let that spoil our relationship, so I wasn't going to talk about it until the right moment came along.

The right time developed one day following our Montana weekend. I had been working in Watertown, South Dakota, and I had spotted a new car at an Oldsmobile dealership that I fell in love with. It was a turquoise and white two-tone job, very popular at that time, with much more sex appeal than my old Plymouth, although not quite up to the level of Joe-the-shmoe's, the Billings boob. But who needs that?

That Friday night when I got home I asked Jeanne to go for a ride with me the next day. We drove to Watertown and it took about ten minutes to finish the deal that I had already started. I said good-bye to the Plymouth and we drove off in the sparkling fresh Oldsmobile with only four miles on the odometer.

Somewhere along highway 212 Jeanne reached in her purse and pulled out a cigarette and I said, "Are you going to replace my new car smell with cigarette smoke?"

"Oh, don't you like cigarette smoke?" she asked.

"I've never smoked," I said. "But I have tried it enough to know that I don't like it and it really stuffs up my nose." Maybe I exaggerated that a bit, but I wanted to make sure she knew I wasn't in favor of her smoking.

"Well, I didn't know," she said, and then in a rather dramatic fashion, she rolled down the car window and dumped out the remaining cigarettes left in the pack. "There, that takes care of that. I've been trying to quit, but at least I won't smoke when I'm around you anymore."

And she never did smoke again, other than a brief time after we had been married for a while, and then our two kids pestered her about it until she finally quit for good. I don't recall that she has ever given us credit for saving her life.

I won't mention all the flaws that Jeanne discovered in me during our early courtship, but I will reveal just one. At the same time, I also discovered that she had a bit of a temper—justifiably so.

Jeanne did not profess to be a culinary expert, but she wanted to impress me a little that she was beyond the stage of boiling water, and planned her first dinner party with me. I was invited to be at her apartment at about four on a Saturday afternoon. Her girlfriend, Geri, and the guy she dumped me for, Sam Lund, were also invited. They had now been married for a short time and this was the first time Jeanne would get together with them since the wedding.

Unfortunately, it was the Saturday that Minnesota was playing Michigan for the Little Brown Jug, a very important football game. I most definitely had to listen to it. It was a close, exciting game, and it lasted a little longer than normal resulting in my arrival at the dinner party at least a half hour late.

Even though she never said a word to me when I arrived, I had this uncanny rocket science ability to tell when somebody was really pissed. No sir, I didn't need to be hit over the head with a ton of bricks, just one would do. The drawers in the kitchen cabinets closed with a bang, utensils made a crashing noise when they hit the table and the heels on her shoes cracked when they hit the tile floor. Yes sir, nobody had to tell me. I knew when there was something wrong.

"Honey, did you listen to the game today?" No answer. Apparently she didn't hear me. "A tremendously exciting game, wasn't it?" Still no answer. I had not yet discovered how tremendously unimportant games of any kind were to her. "I'm sorry it lasted longer then normal, but we won."

Lucky for Minnesota, because I was about to lose. I had never before considered leaving before the end of the game or even listening to it on the car radio on the way to her house. Guys would understand that.

Oh Lord it's hard to be humble when you're perfect in…

No, now is not the time to be singing that.

After Geri and Sam left, the first of very few words Jeanne spoke to me that day were, "Do you by any chance know how to use a telephone?"

It wouldn't be the last time she would ask me that question. The question didn't require an answer, but it did require lots of praise for the wonderful barbecued rib dinner, praise for how well the table looked, praise for how well she looked, and lots of apologies the next day along with a clear demonstration on how well I knew how to use the telephone. Yes, I damned near screwed things up royally, but I did recover, and Jeanne, now fully aware of one of my weaknesses, accepted me back.

That fall in 1954, Al and his nurse friend, Mary, made plans to be married and I was beckoned to be included in the wedding party. Jeanne was also invited. The wedding took place way over on the eastern side of Wisconsin, so it meant spending a couple of nights in a motel, and once again, me and Jeanne had separate rooms. There were a number of other friends from Minneapolis also going to the wedding and staying in the same motel, so even if I had thoughts of some hanky-panky motel room visits—it was always on my mind—it would not have been easy to pull off, not that I had a chance anyway.

Jeanne lived up to her reputation along with her four sisters. The Woods girls were known in their community as the "Wouldn't girls."

We continued on with our weekend-only relationship. Work was going well and Sears was giving me more responsibility. My trips to the Dakotas and Montana were long hours, but Jeanne was involved in the work she enjoyed as well, and even though we missed each other between the weekends, we didn't feel this was an unbearable arrangement.

We coupled up with Al and Mary, now old married folks, for a lot of our social life, and believe me, if we did something that required an overnight stay, they were very disciplined chaperones. I wanted to marry this girl in the worst way, but I was scared to ask her. How could I ask her to give up her great job for some stumblebum like me who may never be around except weekends. I would quit my job if that would help, but then we would both be unemployed. No way to start married life. If I did ask her to marry me and she turns me down, that would be the end. Best leave well enough alone.

Typical of the way I did things, I stumbled on a way of proposing that wasn't so formal or so final and with a little bit of humor. One night after a quiet evening together, I don't know how it came about, but we were having a discussion about children and I said, "I would like for you to be the mother of my children." I don't know where I had heard that before, but it was not original, and it certainly wasn't planned. It just popped out of my mouth and I immediately thought, *I wish I hadn't said that!* I added, "Yes, I think you have all the qualities for being a good mother."

After a pause wondering what I really meant, Jeanne said, "Does this mean you'd like to marry me or something?"

Yes, yes, it did mean that, but I had to be more subtle, "Well, not necessarily. I know you don't want to quit your job, but I still would like to have children with you."

Jeanne replied, "There won't be any baby-making without being married."

"Okay then, I want to marry you, because I am just nuts about you." *There, I said it.*

"Are you serious?" She was startled.

"Yes, very serious. I want to spend the rest of my life with you whether we make babies or not." I don't remember telling her that I loved her at this point, but I probably didn't. That seemed to be a difficult thing to say. I had never in my life told anybody that I loved them, including my mother and father, and I don't recall anyone ever telling me they loved me, including my mother or father.

There was a long pause before Jeanne said, "I'll have to think about that. That's kind of important you know. I mean really important." I was almost glad that she didn't jump up and say, "Yes! Yes! Yes!" But at the same time, I was a little disappointed. What on earth is wrong with her?

"That's okay. Take a couple of hours or even a day or two if you want. I don't need an answer right away."

"I'm afraid I'll need longer than that." Jeanne said. "There's no one I can think of I would rather marry right now, but you know I really wanted to remain single and stay on my job a while longer, do some traveling, pay off my bills and so forth. After all I am only twenty-two. Do you understand?"

"Yes, but I'm five years older. I'll try and understand, but I'll be bugging you for an answer."

"I'll let you know. Give me two weeks, Okay?" And then she added, "Oh, I hope you haven't bought me a ring. I don't want a ring."

Holy cow, I hadn't even thought about an engagement ring. Is that what you're supposed to do when you ask someone to marry you, give them an engagement ring?

There was so much about all this that I didn't understand. Well at least I didn't screw up there.

It was a very long two weeks and I didn't bug her, but I called as often as I could from wherever I was. Neither one of us brought up the subject. I had the end of the two-week period planned right down to the hour when I would do something nice so it would be difficult for her to say no. *I don't think I will take her to a football game.*

Finally, I couldn't wait any longer and I confronted her, "I'm scared to death to ask you if you have come to any decision on this little matter we talked about a couple of weeks ago."

"Oh, what was that?" she replied nonchalantly.

"Oh well, Just forget it. It wasn't anything important."

"No you don't," Jeanne said. "You're not going to get out of this that easy. I'm not really sure, but I think you proposed to me and I do accept. So what do you think of that, big guy?"

"Yeah, really?" I'm as nervous as a mouse in a cat house.

"Yes, really. But could we wait awhile? I mean could we wait as much as a year? I honestly have a lot of debts to pay off and I need to earn some more money."

"I'll pay off your debts," I said.

"No, I won't let you do that, and let's not tell anyone about our plans for a while. Okay?"

"I want you to meet my brother and his family," I said. "And you haven't met my mother yet, either."

"If you want to tell them, that's okay, but I don't want anyone at Northwest to know about it yet." We kept our secret, but very shortly I think Jeanne's friends sensed some kind of change in her and they pinned her down. She could not lie.

Christmas was coming up and my brother Doug and Lois called and invited me to spend the holidays with them in Spokane, Washington, where they were living on a SAC air base. It was then that I told them, "There is this girl that is ready to jump off the high bridge if I don't marry her, so if I do come out there, can I bring her along?"

They were ecstatic about the news, or at least acted that way. Our plan was that Jeanne would get a pass to Spokane, and I would fly on a half-fare pass as her brother. We even got her brother, Wayne, to loan us his driver's license to make it look legal, but it still made Jeanne very nervous. She got even more nervous when we got on board the aircraft and I immediately removed the center arm rest and got a blanket to cover us up, not exactly acting like a brother.

We had a great time in Spokane with my brother and sister-in-law and with all their air force friends. Doug was a first pilot on the B-36 at that time, which I believe may be the largest military plane ever built. They were living the good life and they were one of the few couples that didn't end up in divorce with all this fast good life. Jeanne went back to Minneapolis after Christmas and I stayed on a bit longer and then worked my way home across Montana.

We were apart for about three weeks. Even though I let Jeanne use my car while I was in Montana, she was in a funk when I got back. She was certain that she had not made a good impression on my brother and sister-in-law and all their high powered friends, and because I had such a great admiration of my brother, she convinced herself that I was now backing down on my commitment to marry her. Nothing could have been further from the truth. She made a super impression on everybody, but I was still in a cloud and too dense to realize her concern. Obviously I had a lot to learn about the way a female thinks.

Finally we had a long talk and got things back on track again, but then I started to get worried. We had tentatively set a wedding date for around the end of the year, but I pushed to move it up. I realized now that I could not take a chance on losing her because I knew she would have plenty of other opportunities, one of those damn Northwest Airlines pilots maybe. I had to do something special.

A diamond: I had to get her a ring, even though she did say she didn't want a ring. Her birthday was coming up in the middle of March and I made sure our schedules coincided so we could go out for dinner that night. I had purchased a diamond from a wholesale jeweler where Al had some connections, but it was still more money than I had ever spent on one thing in my entire life. On a car you could make monthly payments, but on this deal I had to plunk down the cash. I also had to make sure the jeweler would take it back if she wouldn't accept it, however, there would be a ten percent penalty.

It was the smartest thing I have ever done. Jeanne tore open her birthday present. I had placed the diamond and the small ring box in a much larger box, and there wasn't any hesitation. It just jumped on her ring finger faster then the diamond glitter could reflect back into her eyes. It's amazing what these little things can do, for we were now solidly and happily in love and there would no longer be any looking back with doubts for either of us. I believe it was Princess Diana who said, "The most dreadful disease in this world is the lack of love." I didn't want to be a participant in the spreading of this disease.

"I thought for sure this was going to be my Christmas present when we were in Spokane," Jeanne said. "That's why I was so blue when I left you and went home."

"But you did say you didn't want a ring."

"I know I said that, but you silly man, don't you know that girls never mean those things." Boy, did I have a lot to learn.

We originally planned to get married around Christmastime, which would give Jeanne the opportunity to satisfy her career as a stew and pay her bills, and for me to get better established at work to make sure I could support us both. I didn't want her to work at all once we got married. I would be twenty-eight years old and I wanted to start a family. That may seem like a long courtship but with both of us traveling as much as we did, for the amount of time we spent with each other, it was a short courtship. However, the more we cemented our wedding plans, the more we were encouraged to get the wedding over with at an earlier date.

At some point Jeanne asked, "Have you made any plans for a honeymoon?"

My long-range plans were like, what are we doing next weekend, and if the wedding was still several months away, what's the hurry? But I still made some smart remark like, "Oh, sure. We can either do a week in South St. Paul or a whole weekend in Gary, Indiana."

Jeanne ignored that and said, "How would you like to go to Hawaii?"

"Hawaii, holy shamoly! But we can't afford that."

"You know I have to resign from the airlines, but I think they still allow you one free pass when you get married and maybe I can also get a half-fare pass for you."

"Really? By all means, do it. But can we afford it once we get there?"

"I'm working on that, too. Let's not go out so much and just concentrate on saving our money. And no, you cannot take my ring back."

It was obvious that we would receive absolutely no help from either of our families on the wedding. We were strictly on our own. Neither one of us had close church affiliations, although we were both Protestant, Jeanne was a Methodist and the only church I ever went to was Lutheran. I said "Do you think I could be a Methodist?"

We ruled out a big church wedding, deciding to keep it small with just our close friends and whatever relatives decide to show up. Jeanne, then heard about a woman that arranged wedding parties in her home located in the high-class Kenwood area of Minneapolis. We went to see her and it was just what we wanted: a big beautiful house, a huge central staircase with a large living room and a family room on each side. It even had a ballroom on the third floor but we didn't use that. The woman almost talked us into having a garden wedding because she had a beautiful backyard and because we had now moved the wedding date up to the latter part of September, but even in early fall it could be snowing, so we kept it inside. Besides it seemed that every new idea suggested was escalating the cost. Why couldn't we just run off and get married?

As it turned out, the 24th of September was a terribly warm day, and I believe every single body we invited (and then some) showed up, including the relatives. They were all very curious about this stewardess that the confirmed bachelor, Floyd, was getting hooked up with, besides the unusual non-church wedding.

One of Jeanne's girlfriends belonged to a church that had a young, upbeat Methodist minister who was most agreeable to conducting the ceremony. He was also an excellent vocalist, so he sang the Lord's Prayer during the service. The big house also had a baby grand piano and a small organ, so we hired a pianist to do the Wedding March along with other music. Champagne-spiked punch, lots of *hors d'oeuvres* and the wedding cake was served afterwards. It was all a rather intimate but casual fun party for everyone, all in one place. The final bill was more than we could afford, but it was worth it.

I cannot remember the name of the motel we stayed at the night of our wedding—what a terrible admission—but the next morning we were off to Hawaii and I remember that very well. There was no direct flight to Hawaii at that time, so we flew to Seattle and stayed with a stewardess friend of Jeanne's one night and continued on the next morning.

We couldn't afford to stay at one of the Waikiki Beach hotels in Honolulu, but Jeanne heard about an apartment that we could rent for ten days, only three blocks off Waikiki. This was fine because it allowed us to do some of our own cooking and save some money, but what we didn't know was that the bedroom was equipped with only two small twin beds, not exactly appropriate for a honeymoon couple.

That could have been a big problem, but old Floyd saved the day by creating a bigger problem, the first of many boo-boos of his married life.

Immediately upon arriving in this land of paradise, we got into our bathing suits and headed for the beach because there was about four hours of good sun left in the day. Well you can guess what happened. I fell asleep on my back in the warm beach sand and the sun turned my Minnesota-pale, bleached skin into a piece of fried meat that was so well done that the sea gulls wouldn't even look at it. Deep watery blisters on my feet, ankles, chins, and thighs are not the best Rx for a romantic honeymoon.

Staying off the beach for a few days got me back in shape allowing us to enjoy the balance of our time there and tour a number of places outside of Waikiki that we may otherwise have missed.

Coming home was another adventure. Because Jeanne was traveling on a non-revenue pass, she got bumped off the flight in Seattle and had to take a later flight back to Minneapolis. Here she was, married less than two weeks and already separated from her husband.

She had some fun playing the part of a jilted newlywed with some air force officers flying from Seattle to Spokane, who were very willing to pick up the pieces left by her no-good husband. The lower level of the Stratocruiser aircraft was ideal for this sort of thing because it was like a flying bar where you can get up and move around, with only a few seats like in a nice little lounge.

The propositioning Air Force officers turned out to be friends of my brother's, whom Jeanne had remembered meeting when we were at Lois and Doug's house in Spokane over the holidays about ten months earlier, but they had not remembered meeting her. Jeanne, naturally had fun telling Doug's wife all about the special treatment she received from the flirting flyboys, and Lois in turn, naturally had fun telling the wives of these officers. More divorce material. This world is just too darn small to allow for any fun.

Prior to the wedding we had gone shopping for a house in a hurry and bought practically the first one we looked at, although it turned out to be ideal for our needs. We closed on it before we were married so we could avoid going into an apartment or moving in with friends temporarily. It was a neat little rambler in Richfield with no basement and about nine-hundred square feet, but it still had three bedrooms. Can you imagine three bedrooms in only nine-hundred square feet?

The interior still looked big because we moved in without one stick of furniture. It had two bunk beds built into one of the bedrooms intended to be a children's room but it was acceptable as our bedroom until we could buy the bedroom set we continued to use for the next thirty-five years. We were given a card table and chairs for a wedding present and that would be the extent of our furniture for the next several months.

But we both thought we had died and gone to heaven. We were so happy to be in our own home, no longer sharing living quarters with unhappy relatives. I had been living with my mother, now despondent after separating from her friend Carl. Jeanne had moved in with her sister Ruby, who was even more despondent and had recently returned to Minneapolis after working a couple of years in Japan. She was twelve years older than Jeanne, not married and very jealous of her younger sister who was unfairly getting married so young and acting very happy.

The house cost a total of ninety-nine hundred dollars. That would not even buy a decent used car today. Once more I was able to make use of a benefit from my military life and got a GI Loan at only four and a half percent interest. The monthly payment, including principal, interest, taxes and insurance, was a little over forty-nine dollars a month. Jeanne said, "Can we afford that without me working?"

"Don't you worry, dear. It will be tough but we'll make it."

Quasimodo

Quasimodo, the hunchback of Notre Dame, was getting a little old and was no longer able to ring the huge bells in the church tower, so he advertised for a bell ringer.

A young man answered the ad but Quasimodo immediately noticed that he didn't have any arms. "How could you possibly ring a bell when you don't have any arms?"

The man said, "I have a very hard head. Everybody in my family has hard heads and I can ring the bell with my head." Since no one else answered the ad, Quasimodo thought he might as well give the man a chance at the job.

The young man climbed up in the tower and rammed his head against the big bell as hard as he could. The bell swung up high and rang beautifully. But as the bell swung back, it hit the hard-headed bell ringer and knocked him off the tower to the street below.

As the man laid there dead on the ground and people gathered around, a priest came out of the church and said, "Does anyone recognize this man?"

A bystander said, "I can't say that I recognize him, but his face rings a bell."

Quasimodo again had to advertise for a bell ringer. The second man answering the ad was the brother of the first man and didn't have any arms either. Quasimodo knew that if he was like his brother he could also ring the bells beautifully, so he told him to go up in the tower and demonstrate. The second man ran hard into the bell and it swung high and it rang perfectly, but again, as the bell swung back, it hit him from behind and knocked him off the tower to the street below.

As the dead man lay there, the people gathered around and this time a policeman asked, "Is there anyone here who might recognize this man?"

A man from the back said, "I don't believe I know him but he sure is a dead ringer for his brother."

Chapter 18

After a lengthy romantic courtship, a trip to Hawaii, moving to a new house, and your continued progress on a decent job at Sears, it sounds like you two were in hog heaven. Is that really the way it was?

FOR SOME REASON, even though we closed on the house before we left on our honeymoon, we couldn't move in immediately when we returned and we had to stay with my mother the first week. Mother had just recently moved into a big house on 26th Street and 10th Avenue in Minneapolis, but no house is big enough for a bride of two weeks to be together with her mother-in-law. Jeanne was left there without a car while I skipped out of town. This was definitely not our plan. In a week's time Jeanne got to know her mother-in-law well enough to know that she never wanted to do that again, but that didn't work out according to plan either.

When we finally did make the official move to 7214 Thomas Avenue, I can't remember if I carried Jeanne across the threshold or not, but I should have because there was nothing else to carry in.

Our new house—or should I say, our nine-year-old house but new to us—came equipped with a kitchen stove, but that is all. Jeanne said, "We simply have to have a refrigerator."

"No problem," I said. "I'll buy one at Sears when I go into the office tomorrow."

The next day I called Jeanne and said, "I was able to get a refrigerator for under a hundred dollars because it had a scratch on one side but it's on the right side which is against the wall and you won't be able to see it."

"Well, okay," Jeanne said. But I could tell by the sound of her voice that she wasn't too happy about setting up housekeeping in her new life quite this way. Giving up her great job was one thing, but I think she expected a little more in return.

On Wednesday the refrigerator from Sears was delivered while I was back on the road again for the week. The two delivery men brought it into the house and one of the men said to Jeanne, "You're going to need a block of wood, like a two-by-four or something, to put under the leg to hold it up."

"What do you mean?" Jeanne snapped back. "My husband isn't dumb enough to buy something like that."

"Well ma'am, I think he did," the delivery man said. "See here, it says right on the bill of lading, 'Damaged on the right side.' That's no doubt why he got such a good deal on it." It was installed, it worked and the delivery man did find a block of wood to stick under the leg to keep it standing up. Jeanne was furious. *My husband really is that dumb!*

After being out on the road all week, the traveling salesman was asked, "What's the first thing you do when you get home?"

"I make love with my wife," the salesman said.

"What's the second thing you do?"

"Put my briefcase down."

That wasn't the case with me this Friday afternoon. It was the first time in our newly married life, but maybe not the last, that Jeanne started to cry when I asked how her week was, her first week home alone. Her crying quickly turned to anger and she said, "How could you be so stupid to buy a refrigerator with only three legs and practically the whole side bashed in?"

I looked at it. "Oh my God, dear, you have to believe me. I didn't buy it in this condition."

"The delivery man said you did."

"Well if you would rather believe the delivery man than me, that's fine, but if you can just wait until Monday, I will straighten it out."

At this point I was sure I could read Jeanne's mind like, "Maybe I can wait until Monday, but if I have to spend the rest of my life with this lame-brain, I wonder if I can still go back to the minister and rescind my vows."

Whatever she thought, I made sure the refrigerator problem was resolved on Monday. Fortunately the dispatcher at Sears knew the refrigerator did not have a bashed in leg, and he finally got the delivery men to admit they dropped it off the back of the truck when they were unloading it at our house. We ended up with a new refrigerator without a scratch anywhere. This time it was not old lame-brain's fault, but I will admit to some other screw-ups in our early years that probably tested the strength of our marriage vows more than this one.

Fortunately, the house, although small, had a lot of charm, and while I went out of town every Monday or Tuesday, Jeanne kept herself occupied putting the place in order with her personal touch. She was good at that. We were definitely luckier than most newlyweds to have a house of our own immediately, and the nice part was that I could afford it on my little Sears salary without Jeanne working.

To begin with, I was very adamant about Jeanne not having to work as she really didn't need to, but I didn't realize that money is not the only reason why both partners should consider working. So I was surprised when I came home one week and found Jeanne ecstatic over the fact that Northwest Airlines had called and offered her an opportunity to come back and work as a stewardess temporarily even though she was now married. Northwest was expanding rapidly at this point and it seems that they could not find enough single girls to fill the jobs.

This was a major departure for the industry and Jeanne, together with five other girls, set a precedent of married stews flying that would later revolutionize the status of married women on all airlines. The biggest obstacle was the passengers, who didn't want to tolerate having some married broad serve them "Coffee, tea or me."

I was happy when Northwest called a halt to the married women departure because occasionally Jeanne was called out on a trip and I was only home on weekends. But the working desire was still there and several different jobs were taken on before the really big job of being a mother took center stage. Parenthood took nearly five years of married life before it happened. I never could understand how some people can get it done in less than a year or maybe even in a couple months or so. Well I was out of town a lot.

Actually we didn't want children right away and for a while we did control the process other than abstaining, or birth control pills. Those little gems were not available yet. But later, after a couple of miscarriages, and with the help of a wonderful ob-gyn doctor, along with a lot of charts and record keeping, which told me to sneak home on Thursday rather than Friday—Sears would understand. We finally got it figured out. Heck, it was a piece of cake.

Soon after we were married, some things were developing at Sears that would eventually affect my career. My boss, Dan MacLaughlin, was preparing to retire after thirty-plus years on the job as the first and only credit manager of the Minneapolis Catalog Region. He wanted to leave Sears as a hero and set some all-time profit performance records in the company by reducing payroll and other necessary expenses beyond reason. Instead he got things screwed up, big time.

All credit operations had been converting to a cycle billing system rather than the hand posting method they had been using up to now. Old Mac didn't see the need to get too involved in this since he was going to be out of there in a few months anyway. His two assistants that worked in the Minneapolis office could have done something about it, but they more or less just sat back and waited for the old man to dig his grave. There was no love lost between them.

One of the assistants, John Powers, was a son-in-law of a big Sears executive and considered himself as the rightful candidate to replace Mac. Actually he was experienced and smart enough for the job, but he was lazy and his politics were not right among other managers. The other assistant was in and out of the hospital as a mental patient and because of this, I believe left the company for good about this time.

The local general manager, Lou Regan, wanted to replace Mac with one of his favorite good old boys, but headquarters in Chicago insisted that a credit man with retail background be transferred in for the job because credit was rapidly becoming a major profit-producing segment of the company. It was typical for a place like Minneapolis to try and make it a family operation and bring everyone up through the ranks to the point where they were almost inbred.

Headquarters sent in Harold Robinson, better known as "Robbie," a heck of a super guy, as Mac's replacement, and it didn't take him very long to recognize that the place was in a chaotic mess. For starters there was a terrible off-schedule condition, many billing irregularities, many customer complaints, poor collection results, and bad employee morale. Robbie got a team of five or six headquarters people to come in and help clean the place up and you can imagine how that sat with local management. The Powers individual (who thought he should have had the job) sat and sulked for a while, and though he should have been fired, Sears transferred him to a small store in Kentucky, which was typical of Sears in dealing with substandard executives.

I was called in from my field supervisory job to assist the headquarters team in their clean-up effort probably because I was the only field executive that lived in the area along with having some basic credit experience. I was put in charge of identifying an accumulation of misapplied or unapplied payments and credits. No one had a count of how many or how much these amounted to. All I know is, the volume filled two large Diebold safes and it was being added to every day. I concentrated on shutting off the source of the stream and once we had that under control, we could begin the clean-up. Now that I was spending my time working in the catalog plant again, I could quickly see that none of the trouble-shooting team, including my new boss, Robbie, knew beans about the catalog business, which was indeed different. So my knowledge in this area, although it was very limited to say the least, became a most valuable asset. I faked it a lot and learned as I went along. I allowed my nose to get a little brown, but what the heck, coming from the farm, I was used to brown, and it was finally starting to pay off.

After about six months we finally got the place running on all cylinders again and Robbie rewarded me with an unscheduled raise in pay. Shortly after that he convinced the powers that be that he needed an assistant manager, so I was given the promotion along with another good pay raise, a total of fifty dollars a month, enough to cover my house payment with one dollar to spare. Holy cow! I was now making more money than I ever dreamed I would. But dreams have a way of catching up with your income, regardless of how much that might be. Robbie put me in charge of all credit field activities, but I didn't have to travel quite as much as I did before which really pleased Jeanne and me. I was now more or less my own boss and I scheduled my own time.

I rushed home to tell Jeanne about my big raise and being given the title of assistant credit manager. She was impressed but not as excited as I thought she should be. There was something else on her mind. She wanted to talk about having children and some of the things we may have to do to make that possible. "Well," I said, "I should be in town a lot more than I have up 'til now. That should help shouldn't it?"

"According to my doctor that's not the problem," Jeanne said. "How would you feel about being tested? The doctor thinks you may be shooting blanks."

"Who me? What makes you think there is something wrong with me?"

"There may not be anything wrong with you, other than your stubbornness." Jeanne went on to explain all the things the doctor told her we may have to do, including my test.

The idea of being tested bothered me, so to avoid that I said, "I think you should quit working. I think that's the problem." This comment was ignored.

Jeanne had just started her fourth or fifth job since we were married. After going back to help out poor little Northwest Airlines, she started a part-time job working for the state unemployment office. That lasted only a short time, but while there she learned that it might be possible for her to collect unemployment against Northwest Airlines, even though no one had been successful in doing that before. This was most gratifying, not that she wanted to collect unemployment, but it would be a way of getting back at Northwest for laying her off.

Actually, the stewardess union was on the brink of going after Northwest for making the single status of a female a requirement of employment, which, of course, was not a requirement of men in the same job. Equal employment rights for women was not a law yet but it was being talked about. In fact the head of the stewardess union wanted Jeanne to be a test case in their grievance against Northwest, but she was afraid it may louse up our trip to Hawaii, so she turned it down. This action was tested and won by the union, but it was some time later before the stewardesses, now called flight attendants, and now married, were allowed to go back flying with continued service, seniority status, and other benefits. Jeanne still wonders if it might have been worth it to be a part of that.

Before the period ended for collecting unemployment, Jeanne went to work for New Holland Machine Company, which had a local branch in Richfield. She hated her boss there. He could have been sued for sexual harassment in today's world, but then again, many of us in a management position at that time would have been in trouble with today's laws. We wanted to take off on a vacation and when her boss would not give her the time off she was happy to quit.

Her next job was Chicago Avenue Transfer, a trucking company, but they went belly-up and had to lay her off after a short stint. American Cyanimid, a pharmaceutical company, was the next job, a very good place to work, but once again, we, or perhaps I should say I, wanted to take a trip out West on vacation, so Jeanne again, had to give that up. I guess I was pretty selfish about wanting to take off on vacation whether Jeanne could leave or not, but I didn't want her to work in the first place and she wasn't all that sure. She also wanted the vacation.

The last job she had was at Honeywell, where she was the secretary to five or six instructors in a training school. This was a fun job that she enjoyed and perhaps that is the reason she got pregnant rather quickly. Each of the instructors wanted to take credit for that event. "After all," they said, "this is what we do all day long, show people how to make things."

Jeanne's doctor advised her to get off her feet and stay in bed as much as possible or she could end up with another miscarriage. Our son, Bill, should be grateful that she heeded his advice and quit another job. After doing what the doctor ordered, the pregnancy went fine and in a few months we were blessed—really blessed.

Being new in the business of baby making, we tried to do all the right things: going to classes covering pre-birth, after birth and baby care, getting the right equipment and preparing the house; but nothing can prepare you for the emotions that are racing up and down your spine when the baby arrives. Jeanne knew when it was time. The doctor said it would be around the 29th of July. So on the morning of the 29th, Jeanne got up about three o'clock, showered, shaved her legs, put on make-up and combed her hair. Then she woke me up. "I think it's time."

Before I even had time to get nervous, we casually drove to the hospital where we spent the next couple hours in the labor room waiting for all the unavoidable labor pains to occur. Jeanne was in misery and I became a basket case before they kicked me out and made me wait in the Father's Room. Finally the doctor showed up to tell me that Jeanne was doing just fine. I made some stupid wisecrack like, "I sure hope it's a girl so she won't have to go through what I'm going through some day."

The doc didn't think it was very funny I guess because he didn't laugh. Maybe he didn't get it. They wouldn't let me go to the delivery room with Jeanne. Maybe this was a hospital rule or maybe it was a doctor's rule that just applied to me. Anyway I was required to wait in the Father's Room with a couple other nervous fathers-to-be.

After about an hour of walking the floor and wringing my hands, a nurse came to the door with a bundle in her arms, "Mr. Wachs?"

"Yes, that's me."

"Your wife is doing fine and you can go see her in just a couple of minutes. But I thought you would like to meet your new son."

I jumped up and looked at him and I was stunned, "Geez, are you sure this is mine?" I know most people will tell you that every newborn baby is beautiful, but very few would ever say that about young William. He looked like something out of a horror movie. He seemed to have huge hands and feet, like a newborn lamb. His big hands also seemed to have another layer of skin that was coming off and hanging down in strings. And what's that on the side of his head about the size of a tomato? "Is he supposed to have a big lump on the side of his head?"

The nurse said, "The doctor will talk to you and your wife about that, and I'm sure he will tell you there is nothing wrong and that it will go away in a short time." Thank God. My heart was still pounding.

When I saw Jeanne I said, "I can see him now as a wide receiver on a football team or maybe a first baseman. He won't even need a glove."

The birth of a child has to be one of the great miracles of life. It is also a miracle to one minute see this poor woman writhing in labor pain, while you can do nothing but stand there and wring your hands, and a few minutes later you see her smiling face, all relaxed, very proud and beautiful. Your respect for the female role in life increases about one-thousand percent, because there would never be more than one baby born in a family if this was the man's role.

Life in our little rambler on Thomas Avenue changed rather dramatically, especially for Jeanne. It was now August, a very hot August, and we had no air conditioning. I was still doing some traveling, although not as much, but regardless, the burden of maintaining the household and being a mother was entirely hers. I was of little help.

It was almost a year later, but it seemed a much shorter time, that Jeanne announced, "Would you believe it? I think I'm pregnant again."

"Oh my gosh! What's causing this? I'll bet it's the polluted water in Richfield we have been hearing about."

Number two child seemed to be much easier. Jeanne probably could have gone on to produce an entire football team after the first one, but we sort of agreed, if this one is a girl, maybe we should try and find out what's causing it and see if we can put a stop to it. Fortunately for everyone concerned she was a girl and I was especially happy because my father and mother never produced a girl and my brother produced only boys. I had done something, or I had better say, *we* had done something that they did not accomplish.

Baby Jennifer was a chubby and truly beautiful girl right from the beginning. Even as a newborn, she possessed some amusing personality traits and other characteristics that made her a very entertaining child. This included a big strawberry birth mark on her butt, but we were told it should go away as she gets older. I don't know if it did or not; I haven't checked since I stopped changing her diaper.

Having a boy and a girl only eighteen months apart couldn't have been more perfect, a rich man's ideal family, so they say. I agree. I was a very lucky rich man, and to this day, our children have provided us with much happiness over the years.

One of the major regrets I have about my early family life was that I didn't spend enough time with my children when they were growing up. It seemed like whenever something memorable occurred, and it only happened once, I was out of town. Like the first step, the first word, the first lost tooth or the first anything, I was never around to witness it and Jeanne had to fill me in with the details when I got home. In addition to missing all the fun stuff, I also wasn't there for the trips to the grocery store, to the doctors office, to the school events and the many chores and headaches of raising two small children.

When I was home I did some things I thought I deserved, like playing golf, having a beer afterwards, helping to coach a kids' football team, and joining a wiseman's club that was connected with the YMCA. As a fund raiser, the wiseman's club sold Christmas trees during the busiest time of the year when I should have been home spending time with Jeanne and the children. This disturbed Jeanne a great deal, especially when we had made plans to go out and I was consistently late getting home from the Christmas tree lot. I thought these community involvement things were something I should do because executives at Sears were expected to be active participants in their neighborhoods. I'm afraid it was more of a selfish interest on my part.

I suppose I could have put my foot down with Sears and said, "no more road work," and I'm sure they would have given me some kind of job. But I never did test this possibility because I was already much further along than the average non-educated flunky and all my new family responsibilities now made me more cautious about taking the risk of going backwards. Besides, other than being gone so much, I really enjoyed working in the field where you made decisions like you were your own boss. Many of the field units were not well managed and they were desperate for someone to help them. This I could do, and the fact that they readily expressed their appreciation gave me a sense of accomplishment.

I'm sure there are dozens of stories I could go into about interesting adventures on the road, but I will only get into one which I will never forget, involving a train ride home from Montana.

I was scheduled to board my train in Glendive about eight o'clock on Friday evening, bed down in my usual roomette sleeper for a nice relaxing ride home, and arrive in Minneapolis early Saturday morning. The trains during this period, before Amtrak, were truly a luxury, with a great deal of personalized service in the first-class Pullman sleepers. They even had a compartment for you to store your shoes in your room and when you woke up in the morning they were expertly shinned for you by someone during the night.

This particular train however, had some kind of accident coming across the mountains and the Pullman car and the lounge car had been removed from the train, meaning I would have to ride in a coach seat all the way back to Minneapolis. I didn't like the snoring passenger next to me so I got myself a pillow and a blanket and went up into the dome above the coach to sleep, even though it was a bit chilly up there. There were only about a dozen seats in this dome which were very similar to the seats in the coach, and I also discovered that I was the only person up there. This was great. It was a very dark, peaceful night and I could curl up in one of these seats and get a good night's sleep. This plan would change.

Shortly after the train made its stop in Dickinson, North Dakota, a woman walked up into the dome and took a seat two seats behind me. She did not see me curled up in the forward seat. A little ways down the track, a man made his way up into the dome and took a seat directly across from the woman. He did not see me either. The conversation that takes place from this point on may not be word for word, but it is essentially correct as I recall it.

"Excuse me ma'am," the man said. "Would you by chance have a light for a cigarette?" There were no restrictions on where you could smoke on trains at that time.

"Well, yes. Here, you may use my lighter."

"Thank you. Do you prefer riding up here rather than in coach?"

"No, I was supposed to have reservations on a sleeper, but it was canceled for some reason, and I didn't like the seats in coach."

"Where are you going?" the man asked.

"St. Paul. How about you?"

"I'm going to Chicago so we both have a long ride. It's kind of cool up here isn't it?"

"Yes it is," the woman replied.

"Do you mind if I move over and sit by you so that it will be easier to talk?"

"No, that will be fine." she said. The man moved into the seat next to the woman and offered her a cigarette. Now they were blowing smoke up my way and I was trying not to sneeze.

"Where are you from?" the man asks.

"Dickinson."

"Oh, I thought I knew just about everybody in Dickinson, and I don't think I would miss an attractive girl like you."

"Actually I'm from the little town of Gladstone just east of Dickinson."

There was more small talk, and then he asked, "What are you doing in St. Paul? Is this a business trip?"

"To tell you the truth, I don't know what I'm going to do. I'm sort of running away."

"Oh, are you married? I didn't see a ring on your finger."

"Well that's what I'm running away from. About six months ago I caught my husband in bed with another woman and I'm just now getting up the nerve to get away from him."

"I can't understand that. You're such a beautiful lady."

She giggled. "How can you tell that, it's so dark up here."

"Oh, I can tell. And you couldn't have been married very long because you're still young."

"I'm thirty-two. How about you?"

"I'm forty-five and I'm sort of doing the same thing you are. I should be leaving my wife but she won't give me a divorce, so I'm just going to Chicago for a few days."

"Too bad you're not stopping in St. Paul," she said. "Tell me about your wife." In between the clacking of the train wheels, I was now listening very intently and they obviously still didn't know that I was sharing this private dome car with them.

"My wife is six years older than I am and we're just not compatible anymore. I think it has been a year and a half since we have had sex and here I consider myself in the prime of my life."

"You should be thirty-two and go without sex. Since I caught my husband, I refused to sleep with him anymore, but that's tough. It was easy for him because he was getting it someplace else."

"I take it that you enjoy making love?"

"Ha, does a bee like honey?"

"I like sex best in the morning. How about you?" he said.

"Yes, I like it in the morning and in the afternoon and in the evening."

Then he said, "Do you mind if I kiss you?"

"That's okay."

Ye Gods, man, does she have to draw you a picture?! This girl is ready. Go for it. Now!

There is more talk about sex, or about how often she and her husband had sex after they were married.

"It's dark up here isn't?" he said.

"Yes, and thank goodness we're alone."

Yeah, that's what you think.

"You certainly kiss very nice," he said. "May I do so again?"

More kissing and very quiet now. Maybe they're finally getting into it.

And then, "Would you care for another cigarette?"

"Okay," she said. "Are you comfortable in this seat? Should we lean back more? You know, they recline so they practically turn into a bed. Would you like to share some of my blanket?"

More kissing. By now everybody on the train is sleeping except the sex-hungry female and the jerk she is with. Oh yes, old Floyd is staying up for the late night attraction.

"How long have you been married?" the man asked.

"Well I got married very young. I got pregnant and then I lost the baby, but we got married anyway."

There was more intimate talk about each other's sex life, but still no action. If they would just get it over with then maybe I could get some sleep. They would be quiet for a while and I would think *This is it*, but it would always end up with, "Would you like another cigarette?"

This all-talk-but-no-enchilada went on for hours and all of a sudden the train is slowing down and it's getting light outside.

Crap! We're coming into Minneapolis and I haven't slept all night. What a waste!

As we got closer to the station, I rose up from my seat, grabbed my blanket and pillow and walked by the hopeless couple. Their eyes as well as their mouths dropped open as if they had seen a ghost. I wonder if I looked as bad to them as I felt. As they watched me walk by I just shook my head in disgust.

Jeanne met me at the station and said, "My God, what happened to you? You look awful."

"It's a long story," I said, "about five hours long, but I first want to go home and get some sleep, with you beside me. Then I'll tell you the story. And let's pretend that we're riding a train all by ourselves."

Life is what happens to you…

…while you're making other plans.

Chapter 19

After spending a few years on the road having fun and doing a little work now and then, it should be about time for you to once again fall into that "right place at the right time." What was the big break that launched the second phase of your career at Sears?

SHORTLY AFTER OUR SON was born, I did fall into what I guess you might call a good break that was not of my own making. More and more I was permitted to direct my responsibilities in the field from an office in Minneapolis working alongside Robbie and the collection manager that Robbie brought in from LaCrosse, Clem Beeker. We ended up with an excellent year in profits, good growth, and better than average collection results. Robbie got credit for it, even though I thought I was doing most of the work and decision making, but that is the way a good manager is supposed to operate. He let me run with the ball.

One of the reasons we got along so well may have been that he liked to drink beer as much as I did. In fact, he liked it so well it turned out to be a reason he died quite young after he left Minneapolis. For some reason, he could not control his lust for alcohol and it eventually got him.

I don't think I intentionally contributed to this, but one hot July day I invited him over to our little Richfield pad to sample a new batch of home brew I was ready to uncork. Making home brew was becoming a fad among a number of us guys at Sears and I seemed to have a pretty good recipe. I made the mistake of giving my recipe out only once and it came very close to causing a divorce with one of my friends because he made the mistake of bottling it too soon and it all blew up on him. It didn't just didn't blow up at once, it blew up one bottle at a time starting at two o'clock in the morning until all twenty-four bottles had exploded before breakfast. Glass was imbedded in the walls and ceiling and the stench of the green fermented beer was a well-defined scent in their house for months afterward. Divorce was considered.

Floyd's home brew blew up once, for the same reason of bottling it too soon, but fortunately that happened in the garage and could easily be cleaned out.

The label designed for my beer was "Harmless Killer Brew from the Land of Richfield's Polluted Waters." That, of course, was in honor of the Minnesota Twins baseball slugger, Harmon Killebrew, and the Hamm's Brewing Company that used a slogan of "From the Land of Sky Blue Waters."

On this particular hot July day I had the beer cooling on ice, and after Robbie took one taste he couldn't leave it alone.

"But Robbie," I pleaded, "this is very powerful. stuff. Two glasses is all anyone should drink."

I quickly realized it was a mistake to invite your boss to sample your home brew, but it may be a more serious mistake to deny your boss a third or fourth glass when he especially liked it.

I lost count of what he actually drank, but before I knew it he was vomiting on the lawn outside our back patio. This incident haunted me for some time after that because it took about three years before I could grow grass on the four-foot circle where my boss uncorked his bellyfull of beer.

In spite of getting my boss sick on my home brew, I got another big break, this time at the expense of the general credit manager of the company who died of a sudden heart attack. This set up a chain reaction of promotions that resulted in Robbie going to Chicago to take over the international credit operations.

Because of the traumatic and sudden shift in management, there didn't seem to be anyone beating the drums to get their man to fill the vacancy in Minneapolis as there was when old Mac retired. I sat in the wings but didn't have the faintest idea that I might be considered for this job. After all it was just a short time ago it seemed that I was telling my new boss, then MacLaughlin, that I didn't know the difference between a debit and a credit. I learned quickly though. (I learned that the debits were always on the side towards the window.)

I wondered who my new boss would be and whether I would have to break him into the catalog systems as I had to do with Robbie. I didn't care as long as he was as considerate as Robbie. I didn't have to wait very long.

Lou Regan's secretary called and said, "The boss wants to meet with you in his office."

The fifth floor sanctuary. Wow! This would be only the second time I have ever been called to his office and I remember the first time very well. It was when I got everything all riled up down in Winona. *What have I done this time?*

"Come on in, Floyd, and pull up a chair," Regan said. After a bit of chit-chat, Regan said, "Floyd, the folks in Chicago don't believe I should have a lot to say about who our credit manager is because it is such a specialized job these days and they don't think I know anything about credit. They may be right, but I know people and I believe you are the kind of guy who could handle this job."

"Me?"

Regan ignored this and went on. "Right now they are so busy playing musical chairs that they don't know who's on first. So if you are agreeable I would like to put your name up there as the top banana. I know they will fight me on this but you're one of our boys now. Besides, Robbie has given you a hell of a recommendation and our controller thinks you, as much as anybody, were responsible for getting our mess straightened out."

"Gosh, I don't know what to say. You know I don't have a college degree, don't you? I believe most of the credit managers now have degrees in accounting or maybe business administration." I didn't think Regan knew much about me other than the Winona affair over three years ago. Yes, he would remember something like that and that was a plus.

"I'm aware of that and that doesn't bother me unless it bothers you. Most people know that you have been going to school, but we don't need to broadcast the fact that this was not a school where you could get a degree in accounting or any other degree. But I'll bet there isn't another credit manager who has completed a three- or four-year term of art school. Let's not sell that short." He would have made a good Godfather.

"Half of my life I have spent on a hopelessly poor farm in northern Minnesota, you know." I don't know why I said that. Thank God I didn't tell him about the chicken coop.

Regan said, "Well your farm background should be good experience for you in dealing with our rural customers." *Yeah,* I thought, *my dad will never buy another thing on credit.*

"Well I think I can handle the job, but aren't they going to think I'm too young? I won't be thirty-six until March. I don't believe there is another manager in our business that young." I couldn't have done a worse job on an interview. If I was the interviewer rather than the interviewee, I would have turned this rookie down before he could finish wiggling in his seat.

It wasn't that I lacked confidence in myself, it was that this was so totally unexpected. I was just off the wall with my responses which were completely wrong for making a good impression. Actually I had never interviewed for a job before, at least not a meaningful one, but this was definitely the "How not to do it" in any job search class for management trainees.

Regan went on. "Of course you will become a member of my staff."

This consisted of the operations manager, merchandising manager, sales manager, personnel manager, and the controller. They were all older and a level above the two previous managers I had worked for outside of credit, sort of like the board of directors of catalog in Minneapolis.

"In addition," Regan said, "you will be expected to eat in the executive dining room at the big round table."

The dining room was a good example of the segregation that went on at Sears at that time. You could only eat lunch in the dining room if you had checklist executive status. If you were a manager, you sat at a specified area in the dining room, but if you were a member of Regan's staff—the board of directors—you sat in the same chair every day at the big round table in the corner of the room.

I made the mistake of sitting there once when I was first given the checklist status, and boy, you would have thought I had just farted in front of Martha Stewart. I was hustled out of there in a hurry. There were only four or five women with executive status in the entire building and they were required to eat at a table by themselves.

Eating at the big round table were some other dignitaries also that I didn't even know and they had never heard of me, but apparently, as long as I was one of Regan's boys I must be all right. He was indeed the Godfather. My biggest disappointment was that I would have to give up playing bridge on my lunch hour with some of my warehouse buddies. On those days when I was in town I would either bring a sandwich from home or go without lunch.

"Now Floyd," Regan went on. "If there is any reason you don't want this job, don't worry, you can still go back to what you were doing and no one needs to know about this except you and me, but you know, we have a lot of faith in you after what you did in Winona. That showed the kind of courage and good judgment we like to see in young men."

He can't forget how lucky we were in Winona. On the other hand, that is the only thing he really knows about me, so it all comes back to that one episode I blundered in and out of in Winona.

"Well I think Winona was a case of being in the right place at the right time, Mr. Regan. It could have happened to anyone."

"It may have been," Regan said, "but some people have a knack for being in the right place at the right time. I think you might be one of those individuals."

I had never met a more positive person in all my life, and I learned something from that. He was positive and he was the general manager, whereas the former assistant credit manager, John Powers, was clearly negative and he was long gone.

"Well, if you really want me sir, I would like the job."

"Good," Regan said, "As soon as I cover this with Chicago, I will get back to you."

I left his office on the fifth floor and didn't even need an elevator to float all the way up to the twelfth floor where the credit department was now located.

When I officially got the job I wasn't going to gloat over it too much with Jeanne. She really had her hands full with two babies in diapers, with little chance of getting a promotion for herself or an increase in pay. I did advance the thought of moving to a bigger house.

Her response was, "But I like it here. I like my neighbors. I know my way around. I don't want to move out in the sticks where it will take me an hour to get to the grocery store or to the doctor."

Guess we had better drop the subject of moving, even though we had purchased a beautiful wooded lot way south on Cedar Avenue called Palomino Hills, which is now a part of Lakeville. True, it was a long ways south where not much development was going on at the time, and the road to get there, old Cedar Avenue, was hampered by a little old swinging bridge crossing the Minnesota River. But it was a beautiful location where you could even own your own horses, and the salesman said this would be a booming neighborhood in just a couple years with improved roads, bridges, and so on. I was bubbling with excitement and bought right away, but Jeanne never did get very enthused. She was right as usual.

Even though I was pretty sure we would never live there, one Saturday we took a ride to see our lovely lot in Horsey Hills. On the way home we drove down Highway 13 in Savage (now Burnsville) and saw some model homes with a sign about river bluff home sites. We stopped just to take a look. The father of the developer was there, an elderly gentleman who was not a pressure salesman, and invited us to take a ride around with him and look over the potential home sites. Jeanne immediately fell in love. The land was beautiful and rolling, and up very high overlooking the Minnesota River Valley. It also happened to be a clear sunny day which allowed you to see the entire Minneapolis skyline perfectly.

We walked through a pasture where some cows were grazing, over a barbed-wire fence, to a spot where some stakes were pounded in the ground to mark the roadways and the lot lines. Our escort said, "We could locate your house right here with a picture window in the back, giving you a view of the whole area."

"Could we have a walk-out basement?" I asked.

"Sure you could. Our L-shaped model would be ideal for a walk-out basement on one of these lots."

The L-shaped model was the one Jeanne liked the best. "The first ad for this development will be in the Sunday paper tomorrow and with a fifty-dollar deposit I will hold the lot for you. But if you change your mind just call me tomorrow and I won't even run your check through." We had nothing to lose.

The next day we went back to make up our minds and there were dozens of people there buying property like kids in a candy store. We decided to keep it and completed the contract. Actually we were the second buyer in the entire project, but we think we got the best location of all.

We really felt like pioneers staking a land claim in a new frontier and even more so when in the process of carving out roads and digging basements they ran into some old Indian graves. According to the archaeologists, the Indians were estimated to be from a period between two-and three-thousand years ago, when they buried their dead at the highest point along the river bank. That is exactly where our lot was located.

It took several weeks for the University of Minnesota archaeologists to recover all the remains, which was very interesting indeed, but it delayed the house completion about three months. That worked out just right because it gave us time to get our house in Richfield on the market and sold, which we did ourselves without the help of a realtor. Actually the first couple that looked at our house bought it, but it took over four months to close the deal. The buyers were a young minister and his wife who didn't have much money and it was extremely difficult to find a mortgage company that would finance them with only a small deposit and not much else to back it up.

It finally was done and we netted about three thousand dollars profit which all went into the new house. But now our monthly payments were going to be $148 a month, over three times as much as on our first house. How were we going to make it? Well, once again Lady Luck would come to our rescue.

In the meantime everything was going much better than I had a right to expect at work. It was February and the new fiscal year had just begun, so 1962, make or break, would be my first full year as the catalog credit manager. I chose to make Clem Beeker, already on the job, as my assistant manager, older than I, considerably more experienced, but very conservative, slow end colorless. We were a good balance.

I needed another man as a collection manager but didn't know another soul in the credit business so I relied on Chicago to send me whoever they selected. His name was Bob Noel from Lexington, Kentucky, and he had never been farther north than Chicago in his entire life. Bob was picked up at the airport and after a ten minute interview, he accepted the job and was introduced to the employees.

His very slow talking hillbilly jargon made a number of people chuckle, but he had enough charm and smarts to win over the troops. I liked him immediately.

That evening I gave Bob a ride to the motel on my way home. The poor guy had nothing but a thin rain coat, no hat or mittens, and this particular night in February was one of Minnesota's best beautiful blizzards. My car was in the employee parking lot located across the railroad bridge on 28th and Elliot. I still hadn't been given my staff executive privilege parking space close to the front entrance.

As we walked out the front door and faced the forty-mile-an-hour northwest wind, which undoubtedly meant the windchill was at least fifty below, I said to Bob, "You may want to consider investing in a pair of earmuffs or a stocking cap and maybe some galoshes on your feet because this sidewalk is always a sheet of ice. And what kind of a car do you have? You know it's going to be sitting out here in the open on these cold windy days and you had better have it winterized with a good battery." He never answered me.

When I looked to see why there was no response, Bob was not there. I had been walking alone and talking to myself. Back there about ten yards I finally saw Bob through the blowing snow clinging to a lamp pole for dear life. The wind had caught Bob, who only weighed about 130 pounds, and slid him backwards on the ice. He simply grabbed a light post and hung on, a most amusing sight.

The next morning one of Bob's friends called from Kentucky to ask him how he liked the great Northwest. Bob's reply was, "As of this morning they have just changed the name of this region. It is now called The Great F-ing Northwest."

And from that day on the men in our business always referred to our location as the GFNW, a most appropriate name in the middle of February.

One of the problems that continued to frustrate us after I took over as the new manager was the horrible billing irregularities and out-of-balance condition we were experiencing in the process of producing monthly statements. This was obviously before the age of computers. Each day before the customer statements could be mailed out we were expected to balance the amount billed with the amount of the controls, but because of our volume and because of the unusual and varied types of catalog documents the process was very difficult and time consuming.

Because we couldn't hold up releasing the customer's statements, we ended up making large adjustments to the controls in order to balance, all of which had to be approved by the catalog controller. Each time he had to do this he would become more irritated and chew us out, but he didn't know how to resolve the problem.

One day one of my employees came to me and said, "You know, Mr. Wachs, if we just had smaller controls we wouldn't have any problem balancing. We always balance the XYZ cycle immediately."

I said, "Are you suggesting that we break down the *S*'s for example, into like fifteen or twenty separate controls?"

"Sure, why not?"

"Well, you know you may have something here." I said. "But before we go any further, I want you to go over by the time clock and get one of those suggestion blanks and fill it out just like you suggested it to me. If we end up doing what you have suggested, you should get a good reward."

"Nah, I don't want to do that."

"Yes, I insist." But she never did.

We implemented the idea almost immediately and it worked wonders. To begin with this took a couple more people, but we were now balancing to the penny with each statement release and customers were assured of accurate billing. The employee morale improved considerably because they were now doing something right for a change, but more importantly the damned controller got off our butts. Politically, it probably saved my butt.

The one person I was supposed to be in awe of, or more correctly perhaps, scared shitless of, was Joe Hood, my Chicago boss, who recently took over, replacing Linden Wheeler, the man who became the company general credit manager when Frank Ross died. I had not met Mr. Hood, yet all the other credit managers warned me that he was one tough cookie who could chew you up and spit you out before you could say, "Joe Who?" I would soon give him the opportunity to do just that.

Joe, I mean Mr. Hood, and I had been in our respective jobs about six months when his secretary called and said Mr. Hood would be making his first trip to visit my unit in Minneapolis the following Tuesday. She gave me no further information other than that she would make his hotel reservations. I had never had a headquarters visitor before, so I didn't know what to do. As a result I did nothing.

The first mistake I made was not meeting "The Hood" at the airport. He arrived at my office while I was out to lunch and ran into the Kentucky funny man, Bob Noel. He must have guessed this guy was not Floyd because he asked where I was.

Noel, trying to be cool with a little slow talking Kentucky humor, said, "God, I don't know. I haven't seen him all morning. He said something about going fishing and if you showed up I should show you around until he got back." The Hood was not smiling.

Very shortly I arrived back to my office and met Joe Hood for the first time. The first thing he said was, "Was the fishing good?"

I didn't know what he was talking about, but I thought he must have been talking about my lunch, so I said, "As a matter of fact it was delicious. Someone had brought in some smelt from Lake Superior and the chef deep fried them in a beer batter and they were outstanding. How about you—have you had lunch yet?"

"Well I was hoping that we might have lunch at the airport before I came out here but I couldn't find you at the terminal."

"I'm sure we can still get something in the dining room if you would like."

Unsmiling Joe said, "It looks like I will just skip lunch today."

Oh shit. He is going to eat me for lunch. "I suppose I should have met you at the airport, but I didn't know what you looked like and I may have picked up the wrong guy." I thought that was kind of funny, but obviously it wasn't according to jolly Joe.

"I suggest you take a good look at me," he said. "I have a feeling I will be back and I hope you will be able to recognize me at the airport terminal." He seemed to emphasize the word *terminal* and I wondered if that also applied to me and my job.

I did take a good look at him and his very neat appearance, his clean-cut black hair and his dark, beady little eyes that seemed to look right through you. He had an intimidating technique of asking you a question that only required a yes or no answer, but then he would continue to stare at you without saying a word until you couldn't stand it any longer and you would end up nervously blurting out a whole bunch of things you really didn't want to talk about. After a few times of being trapped this way, I made up my mind I wasn't going to let him get to me and I just ignored his stares.

We spent the afternoon going over some reports and then Joe wanted to shake hands with some of the employees. I tried to pick out the ones that wouldn't say something embarrassing and those who I could remember their names, but at the point of introduction I still forgot who they were anyway. I was getting more nervous by the minute.

Before leaving the office he wanted to make a courtesy visit to Mr. Regan's office, without me, and then he asked me to make reservations for the two of us at a good restaurant downtown. I was told beforehand by some of the managers who tried to scare me, it was typical for Hood to invite you out for a nice dinner and then fire your ass over dessert. If this was going to be the end, I wanted to make sure I had a good dinner so I made reservations at the very best restaurant in Minneapolis at the time: Charlie's Cafe Exceptional. And I wouldn't have dessert.

During Hood's visit to the general manager's office, Mr. Regan fed him a line of flowery phrases on what a great job I was doing, flowery like the proverbial rose you come out of the brown stuff smelling like. Some of it was true but about ninety percent was jazz. It also helped that the regional controller was there and told him about how I had solved the problem of the large out-of-balance adjustments and our billing irregularities, but he didn't tell him it was really not me but one of our employees that came up with the idea.

When we left for dinner, Jolly Joe was in a much better mood than when he arrived off the airplane and met me for the first time. After skipping lunch, he really enjoyed Charlie's and insisted that we go there every time he came to town. This was the first clue I had that I might survive for another day. I was actually getting to like this guy, and although he was hard to read, I had the feeling that he may even be getting to like me. In fact I think he respected me more because I didn't genuflect, or kiss his ring (or kiss a few other things).

We had just completed a record first half of the year in profits and the year-end was even better. It came at a time when catalog merchandise profits were down, but more people were beginning to buy on credit and pay our huge finance charges. The fact that our credit department profits exceeded that of all the other merchandise departments combined was a little embarrassing to all the other staff members, but it didn't bother old farmer Floyd.

The following year I was rewarded by being selected to go to Chicago and attend a management staff school, or a "Charm School" as they called it, representing all of catalog from the Northwest, or should I say the GFNW. It was two weeks of intensive ego pumping by all the officers of the company from the chairman and president on down, who were all well qualified experts at slinging BS. They were much better than my big brother who thought he could sling cow manure further than anyone.

Out of a class of about forty, one-hundred-percent white males, all in dark suits, white shirts and dark ties, the "Charm School" was supposed to represent the future top executives at Sears. I traced the track record of most of these guys some time later and found that only three or four made it to a VP position, but considerably more dropped by the wayside for one reason or the other. So as a class we were not all that successful but we had a lot of fun and I went away believing I could smile and charm the skin off a snake before he could bite me.

During the next couple of years we enjoyed profit performances along with exceptional collection results and I readily give my collection manager, Bob Noel, credit for our success. But Bob had a knack for getting me in trouble once in awhile, and I unfairly gave him credit for that also. Bob would on occasion say as we were leaving the office, "Boss, you have been so darned busy today and I hated to bother you, but there is something I need to talk to you about. How about stopping for a beer on the way home so we can talk?"

Maybe it was something important he needed to discuss with me, but it usually wasn't. But how could I turn down an invitation to have a beer? I seldom did. "Sure, Bob. Why don't we stop over at Sunny's across the street?"

I expected it would be no more than one or two beers and we would be on our way, but Bob was a slow talker and it took a while for him to get around to what was on his mind. We had both worked until nine-thirty this night and I thought we deserved a few minutes at Sunny's. My big problem was that on these occasions I would forget to call Jeanne to tell her just how late I would be. Sunny's had a telephone but it was back in a corner by the pool tables where all the ruffians hung out and I didn't want to go back there and get mugged.

After about an hour or so, and three or four beers, I started home. To cross the Minnesota River to get to Burnsville at that time, there was a swinging bridge that opened up when there was barge traffic on the river, and it seemed like every time I was in a bit of a hurry, the bridge was open and I could not get across.

I arrived home about 11:30, but something was wrong: the garage door opener was not working. So I parked the car and went to the front door but the storm door was locked from the inside and I couldn't get in. Next I went to the back door on the garage, but Jeanne's car had been pulled up against it and it would only open a couple inches. I then went to the basement door to our walk-out basement, but that was also bolted from the inside and I still couldn't get in.

I was now getting pretty upset and went back to the bedroom window to wake up Jeanne. She was already awake and had the crank-out window opened a small crack. She said, "Do you have a problem?"

"I sure as hell do. What's going on here? I can't get in."

"Really? Maybe you should call me to make sure it is okay to unlock the doors."

"I'm sorry. I know I should have called you, but come on now and let me in."

"No," Jeanne said. "I want to make sure you know how to use the telephone."

"You've got to be kidding. Of course I know how to use the telephone. Now I don't want to stand here and talk to you through the window any longer. Let me in or I will break the damn window." I thought of doing that, but that would have just made a big mess and I would have had to clean it up and fix it.

Jeanne said, "Just go find a telephone to show me you know how to use it and I am sure we can work this out."

I got in my car and stormed out of there. I was really pissed, in more ways than one because I now had to go to the bathroom so bad my teeth were floating. I first had to find a dark side road where I could relieve myself and then find a pay telephone. There were no bars or all-night gas stations in Burnsville at that time so I had to find an outside pay telephone. I finally found one way out on Highway 13.

Now I can get this crap over with and get home to bed. Oh shit! I don't have a single coin in my pocket!

At that time a local pay telephone call was only a dime, but unless you first deposited two nickels or a dime the telephone would not operate. I had to drive in to Minneapolis to find some place just to get change for a dollar. By this time Jeanne probably thought I had checked into a motel someplace, which crossed my mind, but at the same time, I was definitely in the wrong so I desperately wanted to get things straightened out with her as soon as possible. I had been given a good lesson in communication, just like when I failed to call and find out if I should pick up my boss at the airport. I was learning the hard way.

I finally got to a telephone and demonstrated my ability to use that most complicated instrument.

"Very good," said Jeanne. "Why don't you come on home now?"

We are thankful...

For the sun that shines, especially on cold days.

For our body that keeps going in spite of our careless ways.

For friends who really know you and still remain loyal,

For our ability to forgive others when they cause our blood to boil.

For the motorist who is acting all impatient and mean,

But doesn't blow his horn just as the light turns green,

For all the children that need our true love and care,

For a wife who still loves me even when I'm more than she can bear.

Chapter 20

Not many executives at Sears could expect to move ahead in the company unless they agreed to accept a transfer to wherever you were sent, although Minneapolis may have been an exception because an unusual number of people seemed to be promoted there from within the ranks. You were an example, but now that you were in the specialized field of credit, any promotion would surely necessitate a move. You were dead set against moving to Chicago, a logical destination, but you went there anyway. What made you change your mind?

IF SOMEONE WOULD HAVE said to me, "You may have a contract with Sears to stay in your same job as the catalog credit manager until you retire, never move and receive only the bare cost-of-living pay increases," I believe I would have been happy to accept that. I was cruising, we were happy in our new house, our kids were enjoying our new neighborhood and making new friends, and I couldn't ask for a better arrangement at work. Remember, when things are too good to be true, there must be something wrong. But wait, they did get better.

In the early and mid-sixties it became virtually impossible for Sears to manage the tremendous growth in credit business using manually operated billing equipment. Sears Revolving Charge was now the largest provider of credit cards, larger than Mastercard, Visa, or American Express. We simply had to do something to mechanize our service. Sears also had many smaller locations all over the country that were not ready to make the best use of such equipment even if it was available.

Only the large locations such as Chicago, Atlanta, Philadelphia, and a few others had the volume sufficient to justify the huge expense of the early stages of mechanization. Lack of management experience was also a major problem.

Minneapolis was one of the smaller areas in comparison, but Minneapolis also had one of the largest toll-free calling area codes in the country. If all the accounts in this area code could be consolidated, and also combine retail and catalog together, it would be in the 400,000- to 500,000-account range and that would be on the edge of a cost-justifiable size. Our catalog credit department was only about 110,000, including all the little catalog stores in our five state area. The retail credit unit was over 300,000, and by adding in some of the surrounding stores, it would be well over 400,000.

The retail center manager, Tom Nieses, I thought, was one of the rising young stars in the credit business, so when the decision was made that Minneapolis would be consolidated and mechanized, I could see the handwriting on the wall. I would not likely be the tail wagging the dog and Tom would be the logical choice as the manager. But sometimes the dog with a wagging tail gets the bone anyway.

Joe Hood's assistant, Frank O'Reilly, called to tell me he was coming to town to see me. I made sure I met him at the airport. I already knew what he looked like, he was a tall handsome Irishman with a crop of snow-white hair.

When we got to my office to talk, O'Reilly said to me, "You know Floyd, we're getting a lot of pressure from up above to get on with this mechanization of our accounts. We've picked Minneapolis as the next location in our territory to get a computer because we think we can gather up enough accounts in this area to justify the expense."

"That sounds great," I said. "Do the accounts all have to be in one location?"

"Yes, to do a proper job at the lowest cost, the records all have to be together where the computer is located. By pulling together everything from the six metropolitan stores, the mail order accounts, the accounts from the fifty or more catalog stores and all the revolving charge accounts, we will have at least 450,000. But that's not enough. Headquarters says that we have to have at least a half a million before they will bring in a computer."

Why is he telling me all of this?

O'Reilly went on. "If we then bring in the retail stores of Mankato, St. Cloud, Wilmar, Owatonna, and Eau Claire and LaCrosse out of Wisconsin, it should easily be a half million."

"That sounds like a big plateful," I said.

"Well it is, and what I'm leading up to is that we would like you to oversee this conversion and manage the unit when it is all in one place."

"Holy shit." But my first question was, "What's happening to Tom Nieses?"

"Tom will be taken care of," O'Reilly said

The way he said it sounded like the Mafia talking, so I said, "What do you mean, 'taken care of?'"

"We'll move him back to Chicago where he originally came from and he'll be given a job there. You know he has really never liked living in Minneapolis."

If O'Reilly had come there to tell me I would not be getting the job, I might have been a little disappointed but would not have been at all surprised. In fact I was questioning whether or not they had picked the right guy for the job.

I asked, "Where would this facility be located? The retail credit operation is already overcrowded and there isn't any room here in the catalog plant."

"We have the property people here in town right now looking for space," O'Reilly said. "Don't worry, it will be a completely new location someplace in this area with all new fixturing."

"What about the employees? Will they all be new also?"

"There will need to be some new employees, but we should try and keep as many of the employees from both the retail and catalog units as we can, and perhaps there will even be a few from the stores being consolidated."

"Now let me be sure I understand this. Are you saying that we are to bring in the accounts from all of these units, both catalog and retail, interfile them into one A to Z alphabetical file, move our present operations with the people into one new consolidated central credit office, and mechanize everything to a computer system, all at the same time?"

"Yes, that is essentially correct," O'Reilly said. "Plus, we must make sure we provide the ongoing service to our customers and the stores involved as if there was nothing different taking place."

"Boy, I don't know. That is going to be one hell of a logistical challenge. If you want me to be a part of this I am going to need some good professional help. I hear that the Chicago conversion after nearly two years is still in a mess."

"I think you have to look at the Chicago situation as a different kind of animal. First of all it was a much bigger undertaking and because we were the first to mechanize we had no one to look to for experience. Now in your case we plan to have three or four experienced men from Chicago transferred here to help you get started. You will pick up all the executives that are now working for Tom Nieses, the two that you have, and perhaps there will be two or three credit managers coming out of the stores. All together it appears you will have a staff of about fourteen or fifteen. Oh yes, and it would be good if maybe you could find a woman to fit into that group. Some liberal thinker up in personnel thinks we should start developing some female executives."

I was still skeptical. If these three or four men from Chicago were all that good, why was that place still in a mess?

I don't ever recall saying directly that I would accept the job, but before I knew it, I was being introduced to the two hundred or so employees of the retail credit office, as their new boss. I was greeted with a deafening silence. It seemed quite apparent that their morale was not too good. I don't think they were too fond of their present manager, Tom Nieses, and now here was another young punk, from catalog of all places, they were going to have to put up with. Had there been a union representative around that day, I am sure he could have signed up a dozen or more new members.

I decided to make my introduction very brief and stated that I would come back tomorrow morning to cover in detail all that I knew about what was going to happen and then begin interviews with each individual employee on how they could be a part of the new credit operation. An employee once told me that she felt like a mushroom on her job because she was always kept in the dark and fed nothing but a bunch of bullshit. That made an impression on me, and since then I have always tried to make a point of keeping our office employees well informed with straightforward, honest information.

Tom Nieses had left immediately after he was informed that I was taking over. Even though he was not fond of Minnesota, he was very bitter that he did not receive the promotion that I was now getting. Later on in his career he would move up to be one of the two assistants to the general credit manager of the company, and I would be instrumental in helping him achieve this position. Right now, however, he was not offering any congratulations to me.

I was also introduced to the retail group manager and he immediately invited me to be a part of his weekly meetings that he had with his merchandise staff and store managers. This was time consuming but very good because the communication between these people and credit management was apparently less than desirable before. Now I was the one person that attended the meetings of both retail and catalog top management and soon realized that maybe I was being maneuvered by both sides to spy on the other.

Later on I learned, much to my amazement, that neither catalog nor retail management would even speak to each other unless it was absolutely necessary. This problem to some degree existed company-wide, and I believe this was eventually a factor in the downfall of the catalog business at Sears.

Sears had just opened a public relations office for the Minneapolis area, and no doubt looking for something to publicize, the manager sent a press release about my promotion, along with my picture, to all the newspapers of the area. Only one paper picked it up, the one in Dakota County covering the area where we lived, now Burnsville, but at that time a part of Savage. A brief story and my picture appeared, along with a headline that read "SAVAGE MAN NAMED CREDIT MANAGER AT SEARS." Boy, did I take some jabs about that!

The property people at Sears decided they could not find suitable office space for our credit operations, suitably cheap that is, so a decision was made that the best solution would be to add another story on to the building at the Sears Lake Street location. The one section of the building facing Lake Street only had three floors and it would be quite a simple process to build a fourth level to house our credit central. The property people assured me they could have it all completed and ready to move in by April 1, 1965, the date we projected for getting the computer installed to begin training and start our conversion.

Prior to that date I was sent to Chicago to spend some time learning about mechanized credit operations. About all I learned was that I sure as hell did not want to adopt what they were doing because they were still in a bloody mess with poor service, off-schedule conditions, unhappy customers, and disgruntled store managers. I interviewed the four men that were selected to work for me and assist with our conversion. I rejected one but I got the other three to report to Minneapolis the next week, to look for housing and begin setting up shop.

When I got back to Minneapolis I found that the telephone people were installing some very fancy, high-tech switching equipment like they used in Chicago, which in my opinion was causing them all kinds of problems. I told the telephone people to go back to a simplified individual phone system and had them rip all the other fancy stuff out. I suppose I could have lost my job over this, but I made up my mind that if they had faith in me enough to let me run this thing, they better start letting me make some decisions. I got away with it.

The three men, Jim Jacobs, collection manager; Frank McManus, accounting and processing manager; and Otto Brantley, operating manager all arrived from Chicago and wanted to know what area in the city would be a good place to look for housing. Since they all had children, I recommended they consider the area we lived in where there were some spec houses or models still for sale.

The men and their wives loved the place and all three families moved in quickly, a most unusual situation, but a great advantage in many ways. They said, "We can all carpool together." I didn't go along with that but the other three guys did. Except for one snow-stormy day which seemed to affect our high river bluff area more severely, all four of us couldn't make it to the office even though all the other employees did.

Naturally, the construction people didn't get everything completed on schedule so we had to set up the big cumbersome computer, all the key punch equipment, plus a number of other new machines, back in the dirty old warehouse. But I insisted we spend an entire month training our employees and simulating the complete processing of all the detail from start to finish just as if we were on line.

All during this first month we hired an outside firm called the Service Bureau, in north Minneapolis, to do the file maintenance work of key punching and converting all our existing records to the mechanized file, a mammoth job because all these records still had to be available to take care of our day-to-day business.

We rented a van to transport these records back and forth on an hourly basis and hired a sharp young man, Bob Storemoen, a University of Minnesota student who was between semesters, to drive the van. I insisted that he wear a shirt and tie to work to emphasize the immense responsibility of his job, but unfortunately the poor kid had never had to wear a tie before and didn't know how to tie one. So each day when he came to work someone had to help Bob with his tie. He did such a good job on this assignment that before he finished school, I hired him as a management trainee. I am proud to say that he is now a top executive with Dean Witter and the Discover Credit Card Company, formerly managed by Sears.

I ended up getting two women into the role as staff members and it was not surprising to find that they were a lot better than most of the men. One in particular, Barbara Johnson, became our personnel manager, and she was a Godsend. She had the uncanny ability to find good loyal employees, the sturdy Minnesota Scandinavian type, where you couldn't find enough work to keep them busy. We had the best employees of any place at Sears.

We were finally ready to move into our new facility, the fourth floor on the south side of the Sears Lake Street building, but I was a little disappointed in what I saw. Everything was brand new, but it was painted a very bright white with a lot of bright ceiling lights that made it too sterile with a hospital-like atmosphere. They installed more lights than for a normal building because there was not a single window in the place. The office work area was very good sized and wide open with maybe thirty or so support pillars holding up the ceiling about every twenty feet.

I got together with the painters and said, "We have got to do something to counter the stark white look of this office. Can you come up with some different shades of blue for all of those posts, I mean a different shade for each post?" I learned in art school that blue was a relaxing color and I thought the no-window, bright white look may drive some employees bonkers. "Now don't tell me you have to check with Chicago first, or I'll kick you out and get someone else to do it." Once again I got away with something I perhaps should not have.

Right at the peak of our conversion schedule Joe Hood, my Chicago boss, decided to pay us a visit. That's all we needed. Do I dare suggest that he stay home? No, I'll pretend like everything is under control, and I'll even pick him up at the airport. But when I got his suitcase and opened up the car trunk to put it in, there were my golf clubs and shoes lying in the trunk. He looked at these and reached down to pick something off from my shoes. He rubbed it in his fingers and said, "That's fresh grass isn't it?"

"Yah," I said, "I played golf last night. In fact, I had a pretty good round."

Hood, in a very firm, unsmiling voice said, "No one plays golf during a conversion."

"Oh, I didn't know that." It was as if I had broken one of God's Ten Commandments and I was now going to go to hell for sure. I said, "The guys in catalog have started a league and invited me to join them. We play every Tuesday night."

Hood the Horrible didn't say much from the airport to the office, no doubt contemplating how he was going to rip me apart when we got to my office and found the slightest flaw in the work we were doing to get our accounts on the computer. On the way into the building we happened to run into one of the catalog golfers and he says to me, "Hi Floyd. Hey don't forget, next Tuesday we're going to start at four-thirty instead of five."

Oh shit, why did he have to say that?

Hood gave me a look, and now he couldn't wait to get me in my office.

Prior to Jolly Joe's visit, I cautioned all the managers in our office that we must display super confidence in everything we're doing and not admit to anything that is not just going perfectly. I said I would doubt that Mr. Hood would recognize it if there was anything wrong in the first place, but just in case, let's not get into any conversation about any area that is a problem or not on schedule.

I had asked Frank McManus to hang around the front door when we came in and immediately invite Hood to have a tour of the office to see what we were doing. Frank was one of the few people that Hood could not corner into saying something stupid and in addition, he knew more about mechanization and the work we were doing than Hood would ever know in his lifetime.

Frank outdid himself. He said, "We're ahead of schedule on this phase, we're waiting for work over here, we've completed the mailing of new credit cards and if we don't get some more volume pretty soon, we may have to consider laying some people off." He even had a couple of employees primed to say, "Hey, I thought this conversion was supposed to be tough, but it's a piece of cake."

Things were not nearly that good, but Mr. Hood was impressed and never brought up the subject of golf again.

If there ever was a time when I feel I let my family down and devoted a disproportionate amount of time to my job, it was during that period of about a year and a half that it took to get the new credit operation off the ground and running smooth. The entire staff and I worked long hours six days a week and often on Sunday. The rest of the men wanted this to be a success as much as I did and they didn't mind the long hours particularly when I was working along with them to achieve the same goal.

I hope that Jeanne and the kids understand that it was the only way I knew how to do it. I was a hands-on kind of manager and hadn't learned yet how to delegate as well as I should. The three hours of golf once a week was my only escape from the office other than going home to bed, but I feel this was just as necessary as anything else I could have done.

The balance of the year following the conversion was a little rough but it was getting better every day. We could see that we would be ahead of our business plan projections by the end of the first year, and then another good break was about to occur.

The Sears management people of both catalog and retail were preparing for a visit from the company president, a fat, good old boy from Texas. I don't know the reason for his visit, unless it was the opening of duck hunting season in Minnesota, or something like that. I was informed about his schedule but was told that it was unlikely that he would want to visit my office.

However, at some point when he was with Mr. Regan, the big old Texan said, "I was told that I should take a look at the new credit office you guys have here with the crazy looking purple pillars."

A phone call was put through to me immediately that the president, Crowdus Baker, and a few of his staff lieutenants were on their way to my office. When the big cheese walked in the first thing he said was, "Hell, those damn pillars aren't purple, their blue. They look damn nice." He then turns to one of his boys and said, "Remind me to call our property people and tell them what a good-looking office they have put together here with all the blue pillars."

I wanted to say, "Hey, you big shit, those blue posts were my idea, not your property people." Of course I didn't say anything like that and after a quick tour of our office complex, the president left, but he first invited me to join the group of catalog and retail executives to a very plush state dinner that night at the Minneapolis Club downtown.

About a week after the president's visit I was informed that the general credit manager of the company, Linden Wheeler, another tall Texan, was coming to look at our office. No doubt the president told him to get up there and take a look at this new modern office. This was a big deal because Wheeler normally did not get out into the field that much.

After giving him a tour of the place, he told me to call all of our central credit executives and supervisors together in our conference room so he could have a little talk with them.

He was a long-winded Texan and I didn't listen to everything he had to say, except for one thing. He said, "Of all the credit operations we have now undertaken throughout the company to convert to a mechanized system, Minneapolis was completed in the smoothest manner, and in just one year's time is already starting to be profitable." I watched all of our people listening to him intently and could see they all were very proud of what they had accomplished and had heard it from the top credit man in the company, but at the same time I was hoping they didn't swell up too much because they were not used to hearing things like that.

When Wheeler left after this meeting, I said to the operating manager, "Go out and find a bakery that can make up a couple of big sheet cakes. Have them all decorated up and on one put 'Happy Birthday' and on the other put something like 'Thank You for Our Success'. Then before the employees go home today, get on the loudspeaker and tell them that we will have a birthday party starting at noon tomorrow and then they can have the rest of the day off with pay."

The operator said, "But boss, are you sure we are allowed to do that?"

"No, it probably isn't in the book, but not all of our people got to hear what the big boss had to say and I want them to know we appreciate all their hard work. Besides, do you think anyone could find a reason to fire us now?"

The next day we not only had cake but also some *hors d'oeuvres* to snack on along with coffee and soft drinks. The surprising thing was that only about half the employees took advantage of our offer to take the afternoon off. That's the kind of dedication these people had, or maybe they were concerned that the management staff left behind would not know how to handle the work and get everything screwed up. They were probably right.

Shortly thereafter a decision was made by the company to insert another level of management in the credit organization. It would be called a regional credit manager along with a staff of regional credit supervisors with the country being divided up into about thirteen different regions. Because of the tremendous growth we were experiencing and the difficult task of centralizing all customer accounts on to a mechanized system, it was the right decision to make, just like it was the right decision to make when the regional offices were abolished about fifteen years later.

This new regional manager position would not have two bosses to report to like all the other credit managers did. His line of responsibility would be strictly credit through the territories and on to headquarters.

Charlie Carrol would be the regional manager covering the five-state area of the northwest including Minneapolis and our credit central. Charlie was an older fellow, well experienced, but a little on the nitpicking style of management. He wanted to look for the fly shit in the pepper, and by George he could find it. Since our unit made up at least a fourth of his region, his bottom line depended a great deal on what we did. He said, "Floyd, as long as you keep on turning in good results, my boys and I will leave you alone." But that was extremely hard for him to do.

Charlie's office was also on the fourth floor a little ways from mine and whenever he was in town he had to walk by my office to go to the washroom. He could not make that walk to the washroom four or five times a day without stopping to point out something that wasn't just perfect in his eyes. "Floyd, why are those girls standing around that file over there laughing?"

"I don't know Charlie. I'll look into it."

On the next trip, "Floyd, the washroom soap dispensers are out of soap."

"Okay Charlie, I'll check into it."

On the next trip, "Say what is the dress code around here anyway? There's a girl over there that's got a skirt on that's so short her buns are almost sticking out."

"Really Charlie? I'll check into that right away."

After about six months had gone by, Charlie called me into his office one day and said, "Joe Hood just called and wants to offer you a promotion in Chicago."

"Oh, did he say what the job was?" It didn't really make a lot of difference. I wasn't too excited about moving to Chicago.

"I don't think I'm supposed to tell you, but I'm quite sure he wants you to take over the Chicago Credit Central."

Even though the Chicago Credit Central was the largest in the company and I should have been honored to be considered, I was now even less excited about moving to Chicago. I said, "Do I have to go for an interview?"

"Well that's the customary procedure if you want the job."

"What if I don't want the job?"

"You've got to be kidding. This is a darn good opportunity. I would think you would be jumping at the chance."

I thought a while and then said, "I'm sorry, but Chicago is the last place I want to move to. Furthermore, I don't know a lot about the Chicago operation, but from what I hear, it would be a friggin' nightmare. We are just now getting this place to run the way I want it to and in spite of your spyglass watch over us, I like it here. Now if you would rather replace me, please let me know."

"What do you mean? I didn't think we were pushing you too hard. You'll get a decent job performance rating from me. Quite frankly, what Hood has in mind, I believe, is to send the Chicago manager to Minneapolis, and from my standpoint, I would rather keep you here. In other words, he just wants you two guys to trade jobs."

It was typical of the way Sears did things. I was flattered, but I said, "If I turn the promotion down, will that kill my chances for anything in the future?"

"Well you know how the company looks at things like that. What I think I'd better do is have Mr. Hood call you and explain what he has in mind and give you some indication of the consequences if you turn it down. Are you saying no to the job or even an interview?"

"I see no point in going for an interview if I plan to turn the job down anyway."

I'm sure Charlie Carrol relayed my sentiments back to Joe Hood, but I never got a call from him. From this I got the message that Jolly Joe was no doubt pissed at me, and in fact, I didn't hear from him again for several months. I went home and told Jeanne about the events of the day and said, "I hope you don't mind staying where you're at because my chances for anything in the future are probably next to zero, that is if I can just hang on to the job I've got."

Jeanne was very supportive and was happy to continue living in Burnsville.

It was almost exactly one year later to the day when Joe Hood called me personally to make me another proposition. He was very brief and said, "Jim Getzendanner, you know Jim, wants you to come to Chicago and be his assistant. Because he has the largest region in the company, we have made an exception and granted his request to add an assistant regional manager to his staff. Jim has asked for you. There's no need for you to come in for an interview. Just talk it over with your wife and give me a call on Monday."

There is no doubt in my mind that this rather off-handed manner of offering a promotion, not too great a one at that, was all by design because of what happened a year ago. I believe Hood fully expected me to turn the job offer down again, so then he could clearly highlight it in my record that Floyd never wants to leave Minneapolis and there is no need to consider him for any further promotions. The fact that I would not need to report to this new job until the first of the year, over six weeks later, also made me suspicious, because that would give them ample time to line up another candidate.

That Friday night I discussed my frustration and anger with Jeanne over the way I thought I was being manipulated into turning another job down. "What do you think I should do?"

"You know the kids and I are willing to go along with whatever you think is best. Just do what your instincts tell you, but maybe this is a good promotion. Who is this Jim whatever his name is?"

"Oh, he's not one of my favorite people, but he's okay. He's a real bull-headed German that will work night and day on a two-bit problem if he can't find the answer."

"Sounds a lot like you."

We made lists of the pros and cons for moving to Chicago or staying in Minneapolis and they always came up very heavily in favor of just staying put. Our kids were getting used to their new school in Burnsville, with Bill in the third grade and Jenn just starting first. I said, "This isn't very fair to them, so let's see what they think."

We discussed it with the kids and we decided that they should have an equal vote on whether we move or stay. I suggested that we each take two pieces of paper, one blue and one white and in this little box we should put in the white piece of paper if you want to move to Chicago or the blue piece if you want to stay where we are. That way we won't know which of us wants to move or which of us elected to stay. After everyone had voted we opened the box and all four pieces of paper were blue meaning we all wanted to stay where we are.

Most everyone in the family seemed happy about that, but that Sunday night before going to sleep I said to Jeanne, "You know I just would like to screw up their little plan in Chicago and accept this job that they're expecting me to turn down and see what happens. What do you think?"

"Okay, let's do it." Jeanne said. "But from this point on now we've got to look at it in a positive manner and act excited and grateful that you should be given this opportunity, regardless if it is a good promotion or not. I will take care of the kids and make sure this is an adventure for them."

So much for the democratic process in the Wachs household.

Make it another martini

There once was a young couple who longed to have a child of their own and after many months of empty frustration and heartbreak they were finally blessed with a newborn son. There was a problem, however: the baby was born without any arms or legs or even a body. It was just a head.

Even though it was just a head, it was healthy, had a smiling face and they loved it dearly. They reasoned it might be best for all concerned if they not expose their unusual child to the outside world, so they kept the joy of raising him all to themselves. He grew older and provided much happiness to his parents, but still never developed beyond just being a head.

Time went by and eventually the head turned twenty-one years old. The father said, "I cannot allow this secret to continue any longer. I don't care what people may say, I want my son to learn about life in the outside world."

So on his birthday the father wrapped up his son and carried him under his arm to a local bar. As he set his son down on the bar, he said to the bartender, "I would like a double martini and I want you to make one for my son here, too." The head sipped the martini and discovered that he liked it.

The father was ecstatic and said, "He really likes it. Mr. Bartender, give us two more martinis." As he drank the second martini the head started growing a body and arms and legs just like a normal person. The father said, "This is absolutely amazing. You must make my son another martini."

The head, now a full grown person, jumps down on the barstool and finishes his third martini. But all of a sudden he falls over backwards onto the bar room floor. He was dead!

Very concerned people in the bar all gather around, but the bartender just leans over the bar, looks down at the still body on the floor and said,

"He should have quit when he was a head."

Chapter 21

Chicago, the Windy City, the City by the Lake, the City that Works—even Frank Sinatra sang, "My kind of town, Chicago is." Many people think Chicago is one of the greatest places in the US to live, but you were dead set against moving there. Yet this was going to be your home for the next fourteen years. When did you make up your mind that Chicago really wasn't all that bad, or did you ever?

"Is it official? Are we moving to Chicago?" Jeanne asked.

"Yes, I'm afraid so. I had a long talk with Getz today—everybody calls him Getz rather than Getzendanner—and he explained the whole program to me much better than Joe Hood ever did. He said he has been trying to get the approval to bring me in for some time. That made me feel better, but I don't know. I wish I was smart enough to know if this was the right decision or not."

"Oh don't worry about it," Jeanne said. "Remember now, we're going to think positive about this from now on. Besides you usually come out smelling like a rose anyway."

"Yeah, but why do I have to get into the shit in the first place?"

"So what do we do now?" Jeanne asked.

"I guess we go ahead and put our house on the market. We've got all of six weeks before I have to report, but we might as well get on with it. It may take all of that to get it sold."

We called Bermel Smaby, the biggest realtor in the city at that time. An agent was out the next evening and drew up a listing agreement, although he thought we were out of line in the amount we were asking for our house. Maybe that's what the realtors tell everyone regardless of what they ask. The next morning carloads of other realtors, involved with the multiple listing service, paraded through our house. By the end of the day there were even some lookers.

On the evening of the third day our agent called us and said, "I can hardly believe this but I've got three bona fide offers for your house on my desk already. I haven't looked them over yet, so why don't I run on out and we can look them over together."

Jeanne and I sat down at the kitchen table and looked over the details of each offer. The first two came in with a slight reduction from the asking price, but still very reasonable and no apparent flaws. We opened the envelope of the third offer and was astounded to see that the offer was the exact amount of our asking price, along with a very sizable earnest money check.

The realtor said, "I have never seen anything like this before. And the strange part about this, I am told that the people are from Houston, Texas, and only the wife has seen the house. The husband doesn't plan to be here until the closing."

I was suspicious that there might be something wrong so I had the manager of the Minneapolis credit bureau do and investigation of the buyer. It would be illegal for him to do that today but at that time we could still get away with a lot of things. The report showed an excellent credit rating, that he was employed by IBM, where there was a large office complex in Minneapolis, but more important, he regularly maintained enough money in his checking account to pay cash for our house. We also learned that he was transferring with IBM from Houston to Rochester and not Minneapolis. Why were they moving to Minneapolis?

We still went along with the deal and we didn't see either the husband or the wife again until the day of the closing. But there is a bizarre ending to the story.

A year later at Christmas time we received a letter from our next door neighbors in Burnsville, the Punts, stating, "You will never believe what has taken place in your former house. One night about midnight the entire circle where we live was lit up with lights and powerful searchlights down in the ravine behind your house. Police and FBI agents were all over the place and dozens of squad cars had the whole area blocked off. I can tell you now that for the past two months the FBI has been using our house as a stakeout. It seems that your buyer was involved with importing drugs from Mexico while living in Houston and since he moved to Minnesota, he is suspected of being the largest supplier of drugs for the entire Twin Cities market. Both the man and his son are currently in jail but we have no idea where his wife is."

When it comes to buying and selling houses, I guess drug money is just as good as any other money.

The buyers of our Burnsville house wanted to schedule the closing about a week before Christmas, meaning that we had better hurry up and find a place to live in Chicago or we could be out in the cold. And I mean it was cold that year. We spent a couple nights in a Howard Johnson Motel on Highway 100 and I remember that the temperature dropped down to twenty-seven degrees below zero the week after moving out of our house.

Thanksgiving weekend was coming up and the kids would be out of school so we all drove to Chicago to do some house hunting and if possible make a fun trip out of it. The realtor from the western suburbs of Chicago met us on Friday morning and we started out looking in Hinsdale, where Maggie Dixon, a girlfriend of Jeanne's, once lived and thought it was the Camelot of Chicagoland if there could ever be such a place. It was Camelot all right if you were also the president of A&P as Maggie Dixon's father was. No way could we afford any decent house in Hinsdale, and those that we possibly could afford were pieces of junk. It sounds like we were being a little high and mighty here considering our background, but really, if we were going to maintain a positive attitude about Chicago, we had to do better.

The realtor kept us moving one village after another west of Hinsdale, looking at one little shack after another until we landed in Downers Grove. There we ran into a rather new development called Prentiss Creek that was almost completely built, but there were a couple model homes and a spec home that were still for sale. We went through three homes and could have settled for any one of them except for one in which six-year-old Jennifer said, "I'll never move into that house."

"Why not?"

"Because I saw a spider in the bedroom."

That was immediately crossed off the list and we concentrated on the other two even though I thought Downers Grove was much too far west to commute to the city. Our choice was narrowed down to two houses and Jeanne really liked the four-bedroom English Tudor, the most expensive of the three, but everyone seemed to be happy with it. It was very spacious, with a nice backyard that backed up to some very expansive common ground, ideal for a kids play area. In this common area there was also a swimming pool and club house, but because it was winter and now closed we didn't inspect it. We would let that be a surprise to the kids after we moved in.

We made an offer to buy and the realtor told us we should not have a problem getting the builder to accept our offer and we should surely be able to close on the deal before Christmas. We drove back to Minneapolis quite pleased that we had gotten everything pretty well buttoned down for our move to Chicago. As my Grandpa would say, "When you are warm and happy and filled with laffa, be prepared for some cold and kriffa." We were not prepared.

The next thirty days went by fast and after a couple of going-away parties with our friends in Minneapolis, the movers were there with a big semi and loaded everything from the piano to the dirty breakfast dishes to the garbage can filled with garbage. The people buying our house were there the next morning with a similar semi full of stuff from Houston.

It was now just a couple days before Christmas and our plan was to drive to Chicago in one car, leaving the kids with Lois and Doug, my brother and his wife, while we closed on our Downers Grove house. We planned to meet the movers, unload our furniture, sleep in our new house the night of December 23, and fly back to Minneapolis to spend Christmas with our kids. The plan was good, but execution left a little to be desired.

After signing all the papers at the bank, and realizing for the first time that our new mortgage payment would be over three times as much as we were paying on our Burnsville house, and also realizing that I still did not know how much money I would be making on my new job—I wasn't thinking very clearly at that time—we drove out to 2148 Oxnard Drive in Downers Grove to wait for our moving van. We waited and waited, sat in the middle of the living room and had crackers and cheese for lunch and then waited some more until about three in the afternoon to investigate what was wrong.

We went to the neighbors, Bill and Mary Field (who are still our very good friends today), to telephone the moving company only to learn that the moving van had been caught in a snowstorm in Wisconsin and wouldn't be there until sometime the next day, December 24. But we had a plane to catch the next morning in order to be with our kids on Christmas. So after a couple of hurry-up phone calls to Sears, we finally convinced Sears and the moving company that we could not accept our furniture until January 2. This meant that everything had to be unloaded, stored in a warehouse, and reloaded again on another truck before it could be delivered a week later, creating a real mess.

Between Christmas and New Year's some medical problems Jeanne had been having came to a head necessitating some surgery which we thought was going to be minor, but it left her with some lingering disorders. Although I had planned to drive to Chicago on January 1 with Jeanne and the kids, Jeanne's doctor advised against riding such a long distance in a car. So Jeanne flew to Chicago while the kids and I drove and as we went by O'Hare Airport we picked up Jeanne and drove to our house.

Somehow the movers got the key to our house and unloaded everything on New Year's Eve. No doubt in a hurry to begin celebrating the coming of 1969, they left the place in a chaotic mess. There were boxes of dishes in the bedroom, living room furniture in the basement, and a burst water softener sitting in the middle of the kitchen leaking water. It couldn't have been worse. Jeanne, not in the best physical condition, to say the least, could only break down and cry and I could only damn myself for being so stupid and making such a horrible mistake of agreeing to the move to Chicago. It was becoming increasingly more difficult to remain positive.

After we found all the bedding I set up the beds, went to the grocery store to buy bread, fruit, milk and cereal for breakfast, and then to a take out fast food place for our first dinner in our new home. The movers were supposed to come back the next day and get everything put in its correct place. Their contract called for them to put dishes in the cupboards, make the beds, and even hang pictures if we so desired, but Jeanne was so mad that she never wanted to see the damn movers again and told them they had better stay out of sight. "I'll unpack only one box every day for the next six months if I have to," she said, "but I don't want those movers in my house ever again."

I ended up writing a long letter to Sears along with my claim forms for damages, and to my knowledge Sears never used that moving company again.

That night there was a forecast of a mild snowstorm for the next morning and not wanting to be late the first day on the new job, I said I had better allow about an hour and a quarter to get downtown. I had mapped out exactly what route I would take, down the Stevenson Expressway to Lake Shore Drive and then into the hotel garage where I was told the executives of the State Street building had free parking. It looked very simple.

There was one more thing that was going to be a rude awakening: Chicago traffic. True, it was the first snow of the season, when half the people are scared to death and the other half will give you good reason to be scared to death. It was the beginning of the most depressing work day of my life. As I inched along the expressway—they should call it depressway—I cursed myself a hundred times for being sucked into this Chicago transfer. I could have stayed in Minneapolis and been to work in thirty minutes, snowstorm or not.

I arrived at my office at about ten minutes to ten and met my new boss, Jim Getzendanner. "I'm sorry I'm late the first day on the job Jim, I thought sure I left early enough to be here by eight."

"Looks like you're going to have to get up and leave for work a little earlier," was his only response.

Getz introduced me to the field supervisors who were all there on Monday morning. I had only met one very briefly once before, but they all seemed to know who I was. A secretary was already hired for me, a very young and very shy Polish girl but still very capable. We then went to my office which was supposed to have a view of State Street but the windows were so dirty it looked more like a back alley.

Getz outlined my responsibilities. "I'm usually only in the office on Monday and traveling the balance of the week, so I want you to stay on board here and run the office, no traveling, at least for a while." Let's see, was that a plus or a minus. "I also want you to work with the Chicago Credit Central management here and give them the benefit of your expertise from Minneapolis. This will be your baby and no one else will interfere." The "Baby" was a nine-hundred-pound gorilla, getting bigger and meaner by the day.

We discussed this a bit longer and then Getz said, "By the way, I don't believe we have ever talked about what your new salary would be. Because there is no Assistant Regional Credit Manager title in the company, there is no salary bracket for this job, so we had to classify you as a Credit Field Representative. The best we could do under the circumstances is give you a fifty-dollar-a-month increase."

I couldn't believe what I was hearing. *I gave up my cushy job in Minneapolis, left our beautiful home in Burnsville, forced my family to move to Chicago against their wishes and buy a home with monthly payments three times as much, all for a measly fifty dollars a month, about thirty-five in take home pay.* How could I be so stupid not to get that cleared up before I accepted the job? I was really disgusted with myself but now even more disgusted with the bureaucracy of this friggin' company.

"Getz," I said, "That is pure chicken shit." Getz didn't respond, so I got up to leave and then said, "And I do know chicken shit."

I drove home that night ready to cry and apologize to my family for being such a dumbass, but when I got home Jeanne was actually kind of bubbly. She outlined in detail the events of her day.

"The kids and I took off in a taxi this morning to find their schools. They're actually going to school in Woodridge you know, not Downers Grove. I got Jennifer enrolled okay, but Bill goes to a different school. The taxi dropped us off at what we thought was his school, but it was the wrong one so the school principal, would you believe, drove us both to the right school, got Bill enrolled and then drove me home. He was a very nice man, and a big, former football player for the Philadelphia Eagles, I believe he said. Does a football player named Leopold mean anything to you?

"The kids liked their schools and there are three girls in the neighborhood in the same grade as Jennifer and a girl and a boy the same age as Bill. I also met some of our neighbors and they are really nice. One of them helped me clean the cupboards and unpack some dishes. And we're even invited to a party. How was your day, honey?"

"Well the good news is, I won't be traveling. I think that's good news, and the bad news is.... No, I don't want to talk about it."

"If it's that bad," Jeanne said, "Then I don't want to hear about it either."

It was definitely a partying neighborhood. I don't remember the reason for the first party, but the one on St. Patrick's Day was a blockbuster. When I woke up the next morning I said to Jeanne, "Have you checked on the kids? Are they all right?"

"Yes, they're still sleeping"

"But what about Laura, the babysitter? Did she have to walk home by herself?"

"I don't know, didn't you walk her home?"

"You had better call Laura's mother sometime this morning and apologize and then I will walk down and pay her."

Jeanne did call Laura's mom, Mrs. Mellahan, and apologized for me—she was much better at those things than I was. Mrs. Mellahan was very understanding and said that Laura wasn't home, but she would have her call when she came back.

Laura called back later and Jeanne apologized to her as well.

"But Mrs. Wachs you have no reason to be concerned," Laura said. "Mr. Wachs walked me home, he paid me for five hours which was a little more than necessary and then he even gave me a tip."

I had no memory of any of this. I made a late New Year's resolution to myself never to let this happen again.

Work began to settle down to a routine, even though it was a rather hopeless routine. Getz would be in the office every Monday and then would take off for either Detroit or St. Louis, the other two large credit centrals in the region. I would spend my days in the Chicago Credit Central. I always made sure I was in my office before eight o'clock every Monday morning and sometimes I wouldn't leave until six-thirty or so at night, because that is how long Getz hung around. But on the other days I concluded the long hours were unproductive and kept a more normal schedule.

I got the driving routine down to one hour in the morning and about an hour and fifteen minutes at night if the weather was good. On snow days it could be as much as an hour-and-a-half longer each way.

Working with the Chicago Central manager, Ed Lay, and trying to overlay a Minneapolis style of operation in Chicago was a bad idea, but I couldn't convince the stubborn old German, Getz, of that. Ed Lay was a very hard working individual, but with an accountant's approach to problems more than a people approach. He didn't necessarily resent my presence in his office every day, even though I tried to stay out of his hair, but if I were in his shoes, I wouldn't have been too receptive having somebody always looking over my shoulder and suggesting a better way of doing things. More often than not I agreed with Ed that the Minneapolis system just would not work in Chicago.

The lack of any improvement in the performance of the Chicago operation during the past six months that I was on the job was trying the patience of Joe Hood as he, in turn, was getting pressure from headquarters.

Finally, one Monday Getz said to me, "Hood called and wants us to provide him, once and for all, with a complete analysis of what is wrong with the Chicago operation and exactly what needs to be done to make it competitive with the other units of the company. He said he would listen to any recommendations regardless of costs, personnel, or other factors that may have been off-limits before."

"Great. I welcome that opportunity, but do you really think he is offering a blank check?"

"I doubt it, but why don't you write down your thoughts as if that were the case. Spend the balance of the week on it and have it on my desk by next Monday so we can discuss it when I'm back in town again. Whatever you come up with, lets make sure we keep it to ourselves. It may be best that you use my secretary to limit the number of people involved."

This is what I had been wanting to do for several weeks—a complete overhaul; throw everything out that isn't working and start all over again. I had discussed bits and pieces of my ideas with Getz but we never seemed to have the time to sit down and put everything together. I wasn't very good at verbally communicating such things anyway and found it easier, if I had the time, to make recommendations in writing

Together with Getz's secretary we worked at this all week, writing and rewriting paragraphs, digging up reports and copying other records. It was a very detailed review of the entire credit central performance with all the T's crossed and the I's dotted.

Essentially it was my recommendation that the Chicago operation be separated from the comparative reports of all the other units in the region, or even from the total company if possible. It was the Chicago mess, which was supposed to have been the headquarters model for all mechanized credit centrals, that was undermining the standards for the rest of the company. I also recommended that the huge Chicago operation be broken down into four separate units and relocated in suburban mall stores. The present unit covered the entire eighth floor of the building, a full city block long, where an employee could get lost doing nothing for days and no one would even realize it.

I knew the personnel folks would have a problem with moving everything to the suburbs, but there was no reason whatsoever that we should be located downtown other than that it was very cheap rent in the old State Street building.

On Friday afternoon the presentation—a three-page typed letter with all the supporting documents—was in Getz's confidential file for his review on Monday morning.

Monday came and went and Getz didn't say one word to me about my letter. Well, maybe he was too busy to talk about it, but the following Monday it was the same thing, nothing was said. Finally, after Getz had left town again, I asked his secretary, "Whatever happened to that letter we prepared for Getz that we worked so hard at a couple of weeks ago?"

"Oh, I thought you knew," she said. "Mr. Getzendanner just wrote a two- or three-line cover letter and sent your entire file on over to Mr. Hood."

Damn, I didn't know he was going to do that. There were a few things I would have liked to explain before it got to Joe Hood, because if you wanted to read between the lines, in a couple of places it might be implied that Hood was part of the problem. *Oh well, it's too late now. We'll soon find out when the fit hits the shan.*

But nothing happened. Weeks went by and no word from anyone and no further discussions about the Chicago Credit Central. My report and all my work connected with it must have found its way to file thirteen, that round file on the floor under the manager's desk.

It was a short time later on a Friday night that Getz called me at home. That was strange. He had never done that before. "Floyd, this is Jim. There are some rather important developments taking place that you should know about. As of today I am no longer the regional manager. I have been reassigned to a job in headquarters."

I was about to say congratulations, but then I wondered. Is this really a promotion or is this one of those occasions where a guy gets booted upstairs because he doesn't deserve to be fired and they don't know what else to do. "Holy cow, Getz, that really is a shocker. But there must be more to it than that. Who is taking your place, and are you okay with all this?"

"I'm being taken care of. I've been getting a little sick of traveling every week like this and headquarters staff work is not what I always wanted, but the change I think will do me good. I can't tell you much more but I understand Hood is going to get in touch with you over the weekend."

Hood did not call me, but on Saturday morning his secretary did. "Mr. Hood and Mr. Hall would like you to meet them at seven-thirty Monday morning in Mr. Lay's office on the eighth floor at State Street. Mr. Lay is on vacation."

Another weekend ruined thinking about what all this meant. I hope they were not planning to replace Ed Lay also. At least that was not one of my recommendations. But I knew that Lou Hall, Joe Hood's assistant, wanted to be the next regional credit manager so bad that he would be willing to shoot his own grandmother if it would help his cause.

So I had it figured out that Lou would be taking Getz's place and I would be working for him, but why did they have to make me come downtown at seven-thirty in the morning just to tell me that. I liked Lou Hall okay but he was another one of those good old boys from down south and all the southerners seemed to be taking over all of the good jobs at Sears. I was not too anxious to be his "gopher boy."

On Monday I was at the designated location bright and early. Joe Hood, with Lou Hall by his side, was straight to the point. "We have decided to separate the Chicago Credit Central from the rest of the region and make it a new region by itself. Lou here will be the new Chicago Region manager and he will set up his offices in Skokie where we are located. As you already know, Getzendanner is going to headquarters and Dan Spencer, whom you may not know, will be coming from headquarters to take Lou's place as my assistant. There will be no other management changes as it relates to Chicago, but later on it is our plan to set up three separate centrals outside the city. Keep that under your hat."

Well I'll be damned, that's coming pretty close to what I recommended in my letter about two months ago, I thought, but not one word was mentioned at this meeting about my letter, nor would there ever be in the future.

Hood went on to say, "And Floyd, we want you to take over the balance of the region after removing Chicago and be the Midwest Credit Region Manager."

Holy shit! This was totally off the wall. I had not given one thought as to how this opera might play out and I certainly didn't expect to be one of the principal players. Was this in the cards all along when I was pulled out of Minneapolis? I would never know.

After a bit of silence, Hood said, "So what do you say to that, Floyd."

What the hell do I say? Was I supposed to jump up and say, "Yes," or "No," or "Let me think it over." No, I don't think there needs to be any options here. So, after listening to my stomach growl because I left home in a hurry without any breakfast this morning, I said, "Do you suppose there is some place around here where we can get a cup of coffee?"

Attitude

The longer I live, the more I realize the impact of Attitude on life. Attitude is more important than education, than money, than circumstances, than failure, than success, than what other people say and do. It is more important than appearance or giftedness of skill. It will make or break a company, a church, a home. The remarkable thing is we have a choice every day regarding the Attitude we will embrace that day. We cannot change our past. We cannot change the inevitable. The only thing we can do is play on the one string we have, and that is our Attitude.

I am convinced that life is ten percent what happens to me and ninety percent how I react to it, but we are totally in charge of our own Attitudes.

Chapter 22

After about a year of frustrating activity working in Chicago, you obviously were not prepared for this sudden change of events in your career. As one of your jibing business friends would say, "At what point did you first come to the realization, Floyd, that you were in totally over your head?"

THE PAST TEN OR TWELVE years of my working life at Sears have whizzed by like a raging river, a little rocky here and there, but for the most part very rewarding. I'm afraid, however, that what was supposed to be a story about my life, has turned into a tale (perhaps too many a boring tale) of my career at Sears. That was not my intention when I started this whole thing. In telling the story of my life I didn't want to talk about my work that much, but on the other hand, my job was my life, and unfortunately, during this period there wasn't much I was doing other than, as they say, keeping my nose to the grindstone.

Everyone used to say, "Life is what you make it." But nobody ever said making it was easy. Jeanne, while working at the little travel agency in Downers Grove, used to have a pet saying when things got screwed up with an airline, a tour company or some other supplier making her job frustrating. She would frequently grind her teeth and say, "Nothing is easy." She said it so often that when she quit her job to move back to Minneapolis, the other employees presented her with a plaque made from a neatly polished pine board with the words NOTHING IS EASY etched on the front. It was very innocent looking hanging on the wall in the family room, but if you should turn it over, there were also three words etched on the back: IT'S FUCKING HARD.

I might even go one step further and suggest that life is war. Whether the battleground involves your personal life or your workplace, everyone in their lifetime has a war to fight, a hill to climb, an objective to conquer. My war was now going to be my job at Sears, and even though I may have been in over my head, I had to go at it with a "must not fail" attitude. I could not, as I did during my youthful days in the Navy, just go halfway up the hundred-foot tower and then quit. I had to now go all the way, even if I was scared to death.

I was one of those people who had to work much longer than eight hours to complete a day's work. I envied others who seemed to be able to accomplish just as much with half the effort. But that didn't mean I was going to let anyone else get ahead of me. Whatever it took, I was too stubborn not to try to be the very best. This meant, I regret to say, not spending as much time with my family as I would have liked. I knew I could make up time with Jeanne as things settled down and we got older, but the kids, they leave the nest so quickly it seems and you cannot go back and pick up the lost time.

I hope that I have not made my life history sound like a rags-to-riches sequence of events, the tale of a backwoods farm boy who crawled out from under a pile of chicken shit and became the savior of Sears. I may not have done a very good job of relating my story but that is not the way I want it to read. What I want to get across, I repeat again, is that I was very lucky. I was fortunate enough to be in the right place at the right time and I took advantage of the opportunities that were out there. In this regard I may have been the luckiest guy on earth, but anyone else could have accomplished the same thing given the same good luck. True, even with my luck I had to work very hard, and who was it that once said—was it Jackie Robinson or Willie Mays—"The harder I work the luckier I get."

Now that I am away from Sears and don't have to face my peers, I will also admit the competition for executive positions in credit was not all that great. Careers in credit were started, in many cases (yours truly included) because the company didn't know what else to do with a particular employee. In fact, an individual may have failed in merchandising or sales or some other job, but because credit was growing so rapidly and needed manpower, he or she may have been thrust into one of these positions rather than be fired. I would soon meet some of these individuals.

I cannot think of a single person at that time who would have set out to be a credit executive. A banker, an accountant, a lawyer, or something in business administration maybe, but never specifically as a credit manager. So if a young trainee, after spending four years in college, ended up in credit, it was not necessarily a positive outcome in their mind. In my case, not having a college degree or any specific goals in mind, I was very grateful to have been given a shot at a credit career.

The meeting that early Monday morning with Joe Hood and Lou Hall was very brief, but I suppose it was my interview, more or less, for the job to be the new regional credit manager. Someone did eventually round up some coffee, and since a yes or no answer didn't seem to be necessary, I excused myself to go to the bathroom, something else I didn't have time to do before my early departure from home. There in my private stall I had a little time to collect my thoughts.

I was about to take on a rather high-powered job, a job with a lot perks and discretional latitude coveted by just about everyone in my field. Holy shit! It would still be one of the largest regions in the company, even after taking out Chicago to form the region that Lou Hall would get. It would consist of Detroit and St. Louis, two very large markets, and then all the stores in Michigan and Illinois outside of Chicago, plus South Bend, Indiana. Although I only knew about half of the fourteen other regional managers in the company, I knew I had to be one of the youngest. I'll admit to being a little frightened, but I was determined and confident that I could do as good a job as Lou Hall, and for sure I should be able to beat Getzendanner's record.

Once again I failed to ask what kind of salary went with the job, but this time I got lucky. The outside firm that Sears employed to evaluate the salaries of all executive positions in the company placed the regional credit manager's job at a relatively high value in comparison with other Sears executives because of its accountability, its wide area of responsibility, and the affect it could have on the bottom-line performance of the company. They had to pay me at least the minimum salary in the bracket for this job and as a result my salary nearly doubled overnight.

I was also given a company car and I didn't have to answer to anyone for my expense account other than the local auditor who only wanted to make sure I documented everything and followed the rules for the IRS. I could now take someone out to lunch or dinner with cocktails without telling them they could only order off the left side of the menu.

Hood indicated that I would now be given stock options and the relatively new supplemental profit sharing plan for higher ranking executives. This was something the company started in lieu of bonuses in which only a limited number of executives would participate. My motor was racing at a dangerous pace and I would have to visit the bathroom two more times that morning before I settled down.

I knew Jeanne would want me to call to tell her what happened following Getzendanner's departure, but I decided to wait until I got home that night. We could open that special bottle of wine someone gave us. I was concerned about how she would accept the fact that I would have to do more traveling again. "But, I will be getting a new company car," I said.

"You mean I'll have to get rid of my little F-85?"

At that moment it seemed to be her only concern. It was a cute little navy blue Cutlass with white leather seats. She still says it was the best car she ever owned.

The first task I had in my new job was to quickly hold a meeting to inform the office staff and field supervisors who were all in on Monday. The only thing they were aware of was the fact that Getzendanner was gone and his office door was locked. But the grapevine at Sears was so fast and blatantly accurate, that I was willing to bet everyone knew what was happening before they were told at the meeting. I learned for the first time that most of the field supervisors hated Getz's guts, so they were quite pleased to be assured he was really out of there.

Of the six field supervisors, I was to retain three and three would be assigned to Lou Hall. I would also keep the two secretaries and the statistician. Since I knew the supervisors better than Lou Hall I was able to pick most of the ones I wanted first.

I don't know if it was to my advantage or disadvantage that I knew virtually no one in the area who would now be working for me. I had met the credit managers at Detroit and St. Louis at a meeting some time ago but I didn't know much about them and I doubt that they remembered me. I had also met the group managers, the top Sears executives, of each of these two cities, but otherwise I hadn't met a single store manager in the entire region. It was like starting from scratch, but I liked that.

My first trip on the road was to Battle Creek, Michigan, because they had won a collection contest some time ago and nobody had gotten around to present them with a trophy or any recognition. It was the next day on the job when I called Battle Creek to tell them that I would be there on Wednesday to present their office with a trophy and take their collection department out to dinner or something. It was here that I met the credit manager, Larry Roumell, for the first time. He would eventually work for me at three different locations. Later on, after retirement, I would help get him started in his own collection agency business and he would become my lifelong friend.

Larry the Greek, as he was known, was a perfect example of someone who lives on the edge. He was a very outgoing sort; he was a little short on the details of his operation, but he was an excellent bill collector and definitely a people person. I liked this about him, along with his uncanny ability to delegate responsibility to the point that his employees worked their butts off, and to top it off, they loved him for it. I wish I had some of those characteristics.

Larry was from Detroit, where he learned the credit and collection business among Detroit's wonderful inner city clientele. He had big city ambitions and lots of guts, but if you asked him to explain his P&L statement, he was lost. Regardless, I could see him as a major credit central manager some day.

After my trip to Battle Creek, I realized it would take the better part of a year to get around to all of my units in the region. I decided to bring everyone into Chicago to meet them all at once and give them a chance to have a look at me. We were all more or less starting off in the dark.

Meetings were something Getzendanner had little time for, and Joe Hood and Company thought they were just expensive parties where people just came to eat and drink and have a good time. So it took a bit of arm-twisting to convince him it was something I had to do. Then, of course, I was forced into inviting him and some of his staff to the meeting. Next time I would know better than to ask his permission.

Most of the credit managers in the region had never been to a general meeting with their peers before, unless they had been around for ten years or more. About thirty-five or forty attended, all male, of course. I made arrangements at a hotel close to O'Hare so it would be convenient to either fly or drive in the night before, stay for a two-day meeting and then go home the afternoon of the second day. Above all I wanted them to have a good time.

I planned an informal, less structured agenda, giving everyone the opportunity to loosen up and get acquainted. I had no idea how uptight everyone was. I was disheartened by the fact that so few people chose to participate in the discussions and even more disheartened by the few that did. At the next meeting, I decided, we would have some entertainment, play some cards, and maybe arrange it so we could get a round of golf in.

I invited the general credit manager of the company to speak to us the afternoon of the first day and then stay for the cocktail hour and dinner to follow. During his speech he found some way to let us know that he was also an ordained Mormon minister, which I guess gave him the opening to talk about the virtues of a good Christian and how that all could be applied to everything we did in our daily work. Of course, he wouldn't drink a drop during the cocktail hour, and even though that did not inhibit me, a lot of the guys held back in their tight little shells. Based on what I learned from this first meeting, there was indeed a lot of work to do.

Detroit and St. Louis made up about sixty percent of the region in volume, and they were both dragging down the overall results, so if I was ever going to make any progress, I definitely had to focus on these two areas. Getzendanner had been doing this, but no improvement was evident.

I made my first trip to St. Louis the following week. If I was discouraged before, I was really depressed after this trip. The major credit operation was located in a Sears building in the inner city. It was a rats' nest, but like many other locations, it reflected the mentality of Sears at the time: "We have a store only occupying half of the building so we must utilize the space by having some non-selling function installed to help pay the rent." Credit was always the logical sucker.

Whenever I made a trip to a Sears market I always made a point to visit or at least call the top man to let him know I was in town, available to discuss any matters of concern he may have about credit. Greg Gingell was the Group Manager, the Mr. Sears of St. Louis. At one time he was in Minneapolis and I knew him there but he no doubt did not remember me.

On about my third trip to St. Louis, I called Mr. Gingell and said, "I would like very much to spend a little time with you to discuss some credit matters that I think are important, but your secretary says your day is completely filled. Might you be available for dinner tonight?"

"Well I think I could be, if there is a martini involved." It was obvious the only food he was interested in was the anchovy-stuffed olives in the bottom of his martini glass.

"I assure you there will be at least two." I was about to be introduced to a magical martini drinker who could make them disappear faster than a raindrop in the Mojave Desert, but still never lose his sense of direction.

After about the fifth attempt at getting the bartender to cut down the amount of vermouth in the next glass, while I was still nursing my second beer, we finally got down to business. I said, "Mr. Gingell..."

"Damn it Floyd, I told you to call me Greg."

"Okay, Greg, I have a proposal to make to you; in fact I have two proposals."

"Shoot."

"I think if you would pin down some of your store managers, you would get them to admit that they are having a number of unnecessary problems with credit. I'm afraid most of this, although not all of it, reflects back on the central manager. Marv seems to be well liked as a person, but as a manager he may be burned out and it may be necessary to make a change."

Marvin Peak was the central manager. Marv was the perfect example of the management type that we referred to in the staff school as "the Peter Principle."

The Peter Principle came from a management psychologist named Peter Drucker, who advanced the theory that many corporations were guilty of promoting rising young executives to a point of at least one step beyond their level of competence. They would then either come crashing down or flounder in an atmosphere of frustration for both management and the employee. There were a lot of Peter Principle people in management at Sears. Would I be one of them?

"You've got to be shittin' me," Greg said. "I've been trying to tell Getzendanner that Marv was in trouble ever since I've been here, but he tells me it's not Marv's fault and a change wouldn't make that much difference. Besides, he said Joe Hood wouldn't go along with it."

"Well Getz is partly correct. Marv is not the entire problem, but I had a long talk with Hood this morning and he is now in agreement that Marv needs a new environment and he would work out another assignment for him, providing you are in agreement."

Greg said, "I don't want to see the guy get hurt."

"I've been assured he would not lose any pay, and quite frankly, I think he will be greatly relieved to get out of St. Louis."

"Who would we get to replace him?" Greg asked.

"I haven't got the answer to that for sure but the guy we have in mind you may already know because he was in Minneapolis at one time also. His name is Bob Vedvig."

"I don't remember him but if you say he's the right man, let's do it. Do you want me to call Hood?"

"No, not so fast. I wouldn't even recommend that we move Marv out and replace him until we consider another matter. Remember I said I had two proposals."

"Now what? I think I better have another martini." That would be number six, and not just the bar-type martinis, they were Tanqueray's. *Man if I can get this pink sheet past the auditor, I should be able to get away with murder.*

"Mr. Gingell, I mean Greg, like the rest of your business here in St. Louis, your stores deserve a first-class credit operation, but until we move out of that rats' nest, that inner city location where those poor people are beating their heads against the wall day in and day out, it will never happen."

Greg swallowed hard and then said, "I'm not surprised that you would suggest that. Maybe this gives me an opportunity to solve another problem. We have a restaurant along with an employee cafeteria right here in our St. Ann Mall that's doing a piss-poor job and losing money by the buckets. It might be the ideal space for your central."

Indeed it would be, a nice suburban community where we should be able to attract some quality employees with a slightly greater interest in working than collecting welfare checks.

I was sure the Martini Man would forget everything we talked about the next morning and we would have to go over everything again from the top. At least he had sense enough to let me arrange for a taxi cab to run him home. I was mistaken however. The next morning I stopped by his office, not expecting to find him there. I was surprised to see that he had already started the ball rolling on what we had talked about. How does he do that?

By the end of the week Marv Peak was scheduled for an interview in Cleveland, and the man I wanted for St. Louis, Bob Vedvig, was scheduled for an interview with the Martini Man. Even though it took nearly another year before everything was put in place to move the central to the suburban location in the St. Ann Mall, it eventually got done and we were well on our way to getting a fix on St. Louis.

This was a slam dunk, man, easier than I expected. Now all I have to do is pull off a similar stratagem in Detroit and I'll have this thing whipped. Or would it whip me?

Detroit was very similar to St. Louis, except that the credit manager there grew up in Detroit, went to high school and college there, worked in one or more of the same stores his entire career, and ended up as the Detroit Group Credit Manager for fifteen years or so. He was as much a fixture in Detroit as the bronze cornerstone in the first Sears store here forty years ago, or Henry Ford's first Model T off the assembly line now in a local museum.

Chet Phillips was no doubt at one time a very good, productive manager for Sears, but as often is the case when you have been in the same location so long, you become complacent with your results, and as the market begins to deteriorate you slide down right with it believing there is not much you can do about it.

Detroit's main similarity to St. Louis was that the credit central operation was located at the Grand River store, definitely within the ghetto region, literally a war zone. Following the assassination of Martin Luther King, race riots were commonplace in most of the major cities across the nation and Detroit's was a dandy. The Michigan National Guard used the Sears parking lot on Grand River Boulevard to stage their riot-squelching maneuvers. They had machine guns mounted on the roof of the Sears building, while our employees, those brave enough to come to work, watched the tanks moving up and down the streets outside.

This is all the people wanted to talk about when I made my first trip to Detroit in 1970. They seemed very proud of the fact that they had even survived and were able to carry on with serving the customers and the stores. However, they were woefully inept in the area of collections. But who was I, a total outsider, to come in there and tell them we should expect a better performance?

Yes, I could be sympathetic with their plight in trying to stay afloat, and even with the manager who threw up his hands when the only employees willing to work there were barely beyond the beginning reading and writing level. I sensed however that the manager didn't seem to be pushing very hard to get his operation moved to a better location. After all, how could he be blamed for the miserable results he was turning in once you saw the working conditions he had to put up with? His hands may have been tied, but he wasn't making a big effort to free them.

The number-one Sears man in Detroit, Woodrow Culp (called Woody by most everyone), was a sharp, highly respected executive, perhaps among the fifteen to twenty people in the company who could have made it to the presidency if he had the political ambition to do so. Woody was not the type to go out for dinner with a bunch of martinis lined up and talk business. Oh, he enjoyed his happy hour, but his rule was, once you took your first drink you no longer talked business. I had only a limited acquaintance with him previously, but I knew he was the type that would listen to reason if I could spend enough time to thoroughly review the problems we faced.

When we finally had the chance to sit down and talk without interruption, I thought I was well prepared. We first talked about the difficulties of trying to function as a credit central at the inner-city Grand River location. Woody was quite understanding of my concerns on the subject and said, "I'm not surprised. When I first got here and saw the condition of that building I wondered how long we could force our employees to go to work there. Someday soon I predict that we will have to close all three of our inner city stores, but right now the city fathers would have a shit hemorrhage if we did that."

After a bit more discussion Woody said, "The property people out of headquarters are supposed to be in town next week and we're thinking of extending the third floor out over the store here at Troy. We were going to use the space for something else, but maybe this would be better suited for the credit central. I think there should be enough space."

Man, I really liked this guy. Troy would be an ideal location. It was not that far out, there was bus service from the city out to the mall and we should be able to retain most of our good employees. We seemed to be clicking on the same wavelength, and then I dropped the bomb.

"After making several visits here, I am convinced that we need to replace the credit central manager." This brought a sickening frown to Woody's face. Not many people at Sears relished the idea of putting someone's head on the chopping block.

There was a long pause and then Woody said, "Is this Joe Hood's idea? Is he making you do this? If it is I'll tell him to go screw himself."

Very few people liked Joe Hood so this was a natural reaction. "This is not Mr. Hood's idea, although if I had involved him beforehand I am sure he would be in agreement. In fact, if there is any way I can give him credit for this decision I would gladly do so because I am already starting to get a reputation as a hatchet man." Following the change of managers in St. Louis, we had to release another manager who admitted to some hanky-panky with one of his employees, and I talked another man into retirement rather than be fired because of a miserable performance. So I definitely didn't need another notch in my gun barrel.

"How do you know that Chet's poor report card is not just the result of the location where he is forced to operate?"

"I don't know that for sure, but I am asking you to accept my judgment on the matter. Even in an ideal environment, I am convinced we could only expect a mediocre performance from Chet at best, and I know we can find someone else to come into Detroit and do a much better job."

"Hell, there is always someone who might be able to turn in better results. There's probably somebody that could replace me and do a better job, and yourself as well, but that doesn't mean we have to fire every man that ranks on the bottom of the list."

"Oh, I wasn't thinking of firing him. Chet is a very likable guy; he's lived here all his life and he plays poker with your store managers every month. I was hoping you could place him in another assignment here in Detroit where he would not have such a dramatic impact on the overall results of your group."

We discussed other possible jobs for Chet but nothing was popping out as a suitable solution. I realized my proposal was weak, but Detroit was such an important market for my region and Chet Phillips was still a few years before retirement. If anything was going to be done it would have to be done now. If we waited until after we moved the office the picture would be all muddied up.

"I understand your concerns and right now I'm not sure that I agree with you," Woody said. "But give me a week or so to think about it and I will let you know."

I left feeling that I had not made a good impression or come close to accomplishing my mission. I followed up with a letter outlining everything we had talked about and said I would wait for his reply.

Three weeks went by and I had not heard a thing from Woody Culp, nor did I contact him. I was hoping he would at least call me. Finally I received a letter.

> Dear Floyd,
>
> You should know that the property people were here and looked at the possibility of extending the third floor on the Troy store. It can be done but because of the way the building was constructed there would have to be some weight restrictions on the third floor and with your big file cabinets and other equipment it might not be suitable for a credit central location. We can discuss this further but right now I don't have another alternative.
>
> In regard to the matter of Chet Phillips, I am totally against relocating him in any other assignment outside of credit here in Detroit. I am sorry, but at the moment I don't have another suggestion to offer you on this subject as well.
>
> Very truly yours,
>
> W. Culp

Damn! That was certainly to the point, along with being a complete bust. The response from the group manager in Detroit, even though I respected him a great deal, was certainly a lot different from what I received in St. Louis. I concluded it was much easier to deal with martini drinkers.

At the first opportunity I discussed Woody Culp's letter with Joe Hood. His only response was, "It looks like you have a problem." And then he added, "I hope you don't view this as an excuse for your region not performing up to the level of your competitors. We will continue to expect above average results regardless of the circumstances in Detroit."

The SOB was not about to cut me any slack and I didn't want any. Somehow I would find a way.

The results in Detroit continued to deteriorate, and about two months later I received a phone call from The Hood: "I just learned that Woody Culp will be in the territorial office next Monday meeting with the personnel manager and they want to talk about Chet Phillips. They have invited me to participate but I have an important meeting downtown that day, so I think you should come over and sit in."

The following Monday I went to the personnel manager's office in Skokie. Woody Culp was already there. "Where is Joe?" they asked.

"He had a meeting someplace and asked me to fill in. I think I am as familiar with things in Detroit as he is."

We discussed the results in Detroit from a credit department perspective, and I painted as dismal a picture as I could. Then out of the blue Woody said, "I have just submitted a recommendation for a salary increase for Chet Phillips. I know that Hood has to sign off on this also before it goes to the vice president for final approval, and that's why we wanted him here at this meeting. It's been over a year since Chet has had any salary adjustment, and regardless of the quality of job he is doing he deserves a cost-of-living increase. Besides I'm not sure he is not doing as good as anyone else could under the circumstances."

Once again I was dumfounded. "I am almost positive that Mr. Hood would never go along with this."

"Well then to hell with him. We'll get the vice president to put it through whether Joe approves it or not."

I went back to Hood's office. He had been in his office all the time, so he really didn't have a meeting downtown as he told me. The chicken just didn't want to meet with Culp and the personnel director. "Did you come up with a plan on what to do with Chet Phillips in Detroit?" he asked.

"Hell no. Would you believe they want to give him a pay increase?"

"You've got to be kidding."

"No, I'm not," I said. "But I told them you would never agree to that. You wouldn't, would you?"

I left Hood's office as quick as I could, now even more frustrated over my situation in Detroit than I had ever been.

About three weeks later I got to work on a Monday morning and one of the field supervisors met me. "Have you heard the news?" he asked with a smile on his face.

"No. What's up?"

"Joe Hood has just been canned."

"I don't believe that. You're joking. Sears just doesn't fire people at that level. Unless maybe he was screwing his ugly secretary."

That news occupied just about every circuit on the grapevine for several days, and practically the entire credit organization of our territory was jumping with joy. I did not realize just how much they hated this guy's guts.

It took me a few days to find out what really took place causing Joe's demise. I was flabbergasted. Apparently there was a bitter dispute between Hood and the territorial vice president over a position of authority on approving or denying a salary increase for Chet Phillips. This perhaps was not the only reason the vice president had for jerking Joe's job, but it may have been the convenient straw.

Joe Hood was not one of my favorite people and I was learning about his stubborn, arrogant management style, but I was still distraught over the fact that I may have put him in a situation where he had to stand up to these high-powered people just to support my position on holding back a salary adjustment for Phillips.

Ye Gods, if I had realized what was going to happen, I would have said to give him the damn raise. It still wouldn't change my opinion about his performance. Does this mean I am in trouble too?

A new territorial credit manager was selected to replace Hood immediately. He was the assistant general credit manager of the company out of headquarters, Jimmie Brasher. No not Jim or James, it was Jimmie. It was not uncommon for people from the South to be christened that way, though I was never comfortable calling him Jimmie. I had met Mr. Brasher once at a meeting but I'm sure he did not know me from Adam. He, on the other hand, was well acquainted with the other three regional managers of our territory. I learned that he had been in contact with the other three men but for a period of about two weeks he had not called me. Were they trying to figure out what to do with me—this maverick who helped get his boss fired and couldn't get things straightened out in Detroit?

When Mr. B. finally called, he apologized for not getting to me sooner and then said, "When I was called to take over this assignment a couple of weeks ago, I had about a ten-minute interview with the vice president and he told me I should come in and carry on with the business in my own style. But there were two things that were left up in the air before Hood left. They both concern your region."

Oh-oh, here it comes. "Maybe I can guess what they are but perhaps you better tell me."

"No, why don't you come out to Skokie some day this week to have lunch and we can talk them over."

Oh shit, he is going to make me sweat for a couple days. Having lunch usually doesn't mean you're getting canned, but it still could mean a butt-chewing.

The luncheon meeting a couple days later was very pleasant, but for an hour nothing was mentioned about the items to be discussed. It gave me a chance to size up my new boss and I suppose vice-versa. Jimmie Brasher was a slight built, extremely well-polished individual with a full head of salt and pepper hair and a Cary Grant look that the girls thought was especially charming. He was very meticulous about his dress as he was about everything he did in his work. Every T must be crossed and every I dotted. He was equally meticulous at home about his house and his car. He is the only person I know who would not only clean his gutters every fall, but carefully paint them on the inside to be sure they would not rust. When he bought his new Cadillac he refused to drive it to work because it would be left out in the open and it might rain. He could obviously see that I would not be a threat to his classy style.

What intrigued me the most about his appearance was the way he parted his hair and the way he tied his necktie. Both were absolutely perfect and every chance I got I would sneak a look to make a closer examination. The part in his thick hair left a very visible line of his scalp with every hair carefully separated so that it was on the proper side of the part. It interested me so much that I had to ask my barber about it the next time I got my hair cut. He said Mr. B. undoubtedly had his scalp plucked each time he had his hair cut so there would always be a permanent part.

The necktie also left such a vivid impression that I went home and practiced in front of the mirror trying to duplicate it. I soon gave that up, right along with the part plucking. My part was gradually becoming a pavement anyway.

When we got around to talk about business, Mr. B. said, "The vice president tells me there is a plan to consolidate all credit offices in Illinois outside of Chicago into one central location. What do you know about this?"

"Gosh, this was a proposal that I had made to Hood some time ago but since I didn't hear anything, I thought it just went into the round file."

"You know that this is something that headquarters has talked about for the future for our smaller markets after we reach the level of computer and communication technology that we need. So do you think this is a workable plan that we can put together at this time? If you really believe we can, then here is what you're going to have to do."

We discussed this at length and Mr. B. asked me to prepare a whole raft of charts, graphs, maps, budgets, and profit projections. These were things I was confident about doing, but I knew they had to be very crisp and professional looking. He then took all this material and presented it to the vice president and his staff (and me) in a special meeting. I learned that he was not only very professional in his appearance but he was also a super professional salesman. All I had to do was answer a few questions. Later I would have the job of selling this to the store managers, but with the vice president already behind it, the store managers all fell in line and it soon became a full-speed-ahead project.

I was much less enthused about the second subject we had to talk about that day, which was the matter of Chet Phillips in Detroit. Mr. B. said, "You know the vice president is still holding on to the salary increase request for Mr. Phillips and wants my approval before he puts it through. What should I do?"

Wow! He wants me to tell him to put his neck on the chopping block like I suggested to Hood? No way.

"I think you had better go ahead and approve the increase," I said. "That's not going to help the situation in Detroit, but I am just going to have to find another solution to my problem."

That ended my first meeting with my new boss and in spite of some of his quirky ways, I definitely liked the guy. It appeared as if he would let me steer my own ship.

A month or two later I called Mr. B. and said, "I have a proposal I would like to discuss concerning my problems in Detroit."

"Fine, can we do it over the telephone?"

"Hear me out," I said. "Chet will be eligible for early retirement with full benefits in less than a year. If I offered him a job traveling on my staff, which would require him to move to Chicago, I am certain he would not like this and would choose to take early retirement instead. Mr. Culp believes that whatever we do with Chet he should stay in the credit field, but if he knows that Chet has turned down an assignment in credit I think he would give him a salesman's job or something for the balance of the year until he is ready to retire."

"But you don't have an opening on your staff," Brasher replied.

"The man who I would suggest we send to Detroit to replace Chet is Jake Mayes, who happens to be on my staff now. So if Chet should accept the transfer, I would then have an opening. Jake has worked with Woody Culp before and I know Woody would be very pleased to have him as his group credit manager."

"All right," Mr. B. said. "Woody and I go back a long ways, so why don't you let me run this by him and see what he thinks." Great. I knew Brasher was a salesman.

Mr. B. called me back and said, "Mr. Culp thinks you've got a hell of a good idea, but he insists on making this look like a promotion with a salary increase and the whole bit, even though he just got a pretty good bump."

"My God," I said. "He'll be making more money than I am."

"Does that bother you? If he turns the job down, as you predict he will, there won't be any promotion anyway."

It was all set up that Chet would fly into Chicago and I would meet him at the airport and interview him for the job, so to speak. I would outline the whole package of another salary increase and all the other things the company would do for him in connection with an executive relocation. I also told him that if he turned the job down there would be another assignment for him in Detroit that he would have to accept, although at the moment I did not know what it would be. Chet went home and was to call me about his decision the next day.

I was totally unprepared for what happened next. Chet called and said he would be very pleased to come to Chicago and work for me. He said he and his wife Lucy were really happy about the prospect of getting out of Detroit. I was dumfounded and had no earthly idea on how I was going to make this work.

As it turned out, I was pleasantly surprised. Chet was a very loyal staff member, and with his credit knowledge and experience, he became a worthwhile asset in the supervision of the smaller units he would be calling on in the field. He loved to play golf and moved to a golf course community in the suburbs—he could now afford it—and continued to work for several years beyond what I thought would be his early retirement date. Much to my surprise he turned out to be a creditable supervisor and a fine addition to the staff.

In addition to taking care of my management problem in Detroit we also decided to split the credit central into two separate units. In that way, with the reduced size, we could utilize the third floor addition at the Troy Mall. The second unit would be located at the Novi store, a new facility that was under construction.

The consolidation of all the smaller credit departments in Illinois was set up in Peoria, one of my favorite cities in Illinois (and not because I had been propositioned a couple of times by the hotel prostitutes). It turned out better than I expected, with a satisfied group of store managers and even a greater profit picture than we had projected.

After a few years, and a lot of dedicated effort, collection and operating results were improving each month, even at the two sore spots of the region, Detroit and St. Louis. and I was starting to feel like I belonged in my job. I was at the peak of my career and for the first time I thought I could really win this war.

To know me is to love me. I must be a hell of a man.
Oh Lord it's hard to be humble, but I'm doing the best that I can.

But as my grandpa would say, "When you feel like you could jump up and fly, be prepared for a hard fall. Because you know, God didn't make you with wings."

The hard fall was coming. After laffa comes kriffa.

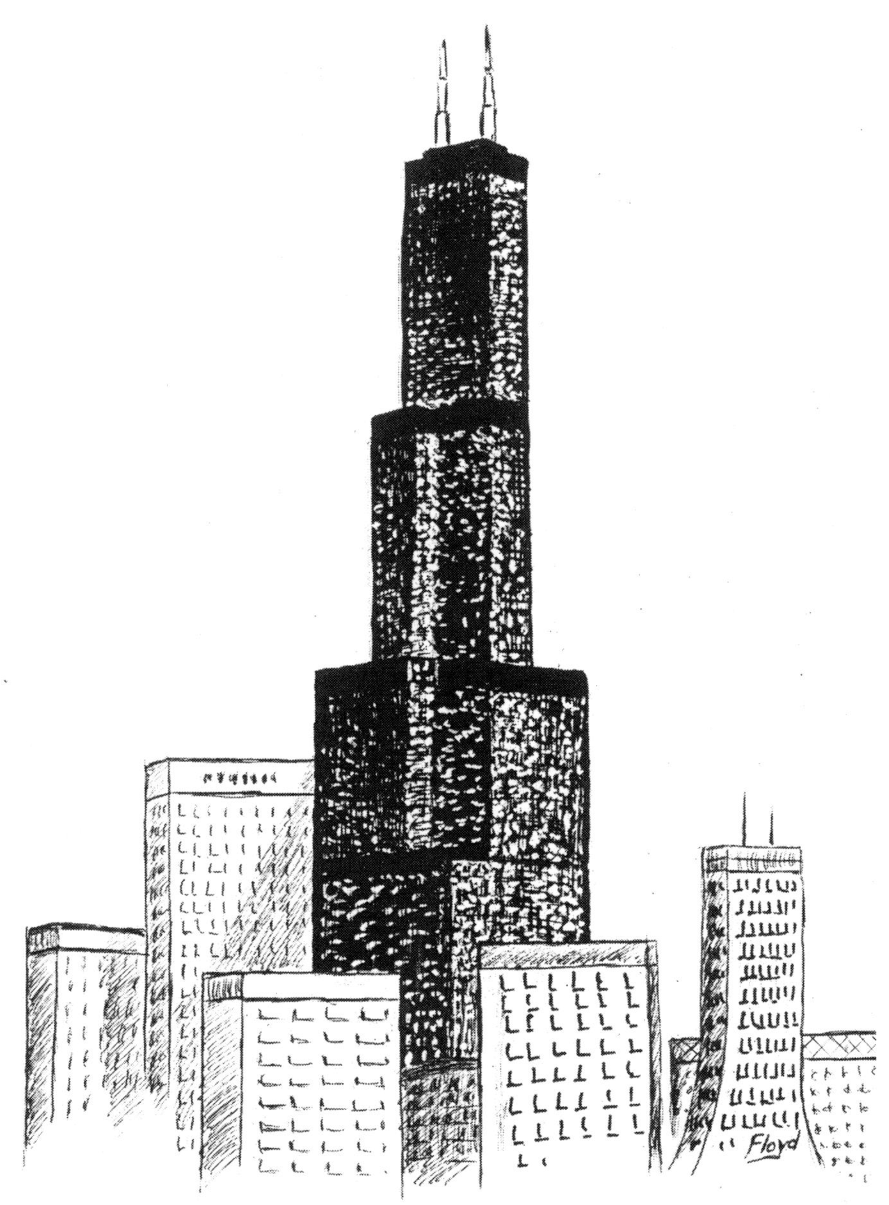

THE SEARS TOWER

Life Begins at Eighty

I have good news for you. The first eighty years of life are the hardest. The second eighty are a succession of birthday parties. Once you reach eighty, everyone wants to carry your baggage and help you up the stairs.

If you forget your name, or an appointment, or your own telephone number, or promise to be in three places at the same time, or can't remember how many grandchildren you have, you only need to explain that you are eighty.

Being eighty is a lot better than being seventy. At seventy people are mad at you for everything. At eighty you have a perfect excuse no matter what you do. If you act foolishly, it's your second childhood. Everyone is looking for symptoms of softening of the brain.

Being seventy is no fun at all. At that age they expect you to retire to a house in Florida and complain about your arthritis. You ask everybody to stop mumbling because you can't understand them. Actually your hearing is about fifty percent gone.

If you survive until you are eighty, everybody is surprised that you are still alive. They treat you with respect just for having lived that long. They seem surprised that you can walk and talk sensibly.

So please, folks, try to make it to eighty. It's supposed to be the best time of life. People forgive you for everything, even for something as dumb as this.

LIFE SUCKS AT EIGHTY.

Chapter 23

You are now in your late forties and at the crest of your mountain, but even though the credit segment of the business was doing well, Sears as a company was struggling. What affect did this have on your career and your life in Chicago?

It is true. Without the income generated from credit in the merchandising end of the business and the income generated from Allstate in the insurance branch of the company, Sears may have been in serious trouble. It is hard to conceive that the largest retailer in the world could allow itself to reach these depths. Some of it had to do with the overall economy in the mid- and late-seventies, but as often is the case, it had more to do with management than anything else. Top management at Sears was flying high without realizing that the absence of wings might cause them to fall.

For years, Sears had control of the middle class market: the farmers, the factory workers, people on welfare, and young homemakers. Sears management wanted more. They envisioned a new, higher class of customers that were currently more likely to find their way into Marshall Fields, to Neiman Marcus, to Saks and others. Why shouldn't Sears be their shopping choice? They overlooked the fact that another group of thrifty-minded customers, perhaps a more rapidly growing group, was drifting off in another direction, to the K-Marts, the Wal-Marts and others. Why should Sears worry about them with their warehouse-looking stores and their cumbersome checkout aisles? After all, everyone knew that Sears was the original discount store.

During this period of negative sales results and an even worse profit picture, management took a survey of a selected group of lower-ranking executives seeking their opinions and suggestions on what they thought should be done to revitalize our business and rebuild our customer base. I was one of those whose opinion was solicited, a clue perhaps that they must have been desperate.

I talked to quite a number of my friends and neighbors about this, but obviously it was not a very scientific market analysis. Nevertheless I did submit a rather lengthy report about the thoughts of these people as well as much of my own. I felt that we should not discount the other discounters in what they were doing, but to meet them head on and beat them at their own game. I didn't feel that we should abandon our beautiful mall stores, but instead create a totally new store for the new breed of budget-conscious baby boomers coming on the scene. Rather than close some of our unprofitable units, I wanted to see them made over, expanded and reopened under a new name. The name I suggested for these mass merchandise thrift centers was Roebucks, to bring back that portion of the Sears, Roebuck and Co. name that had been abandoned some time ago. I felt the name would lend itself well to a marketing concept for this new group of customers with very modest incomes that should be our future target.

Speaking of Target, that is the name the Dayton Company hung on their new discount chain that was just starting out about this same time. Currently this happens to be the tail that's wagging the dog for Dayton's, but it just as well could have been, should have been, Sears. The headquarters hierarchy simply couldn't conceive of selling pickles and potato chips alongside perfume and purses as Wal-Mart is doing today. We had everything all over this crazy upstart—Wal-Mart—with our mass merchandise buying and distribution system, but the geniuses, who have long since retired, are now wondering how this simple little store out of Arkansas got to be nearly three times the size of Sears. I'm sure my neat proposal never got beyond the mail reader's outbox. I never heard another word about it, but that's okay. This was not my war.

Some of the other casualties of my war very well could have been my wife and two children. They were abandoned four or five days out of every week while I went back to the trenches. Thank God for Jeanne, who had to be tough and once in awhile went bonkers being alone with the kids. But I am also proud of my son and daughter. I'm sure they had a chance to sample all the bad things that went on in their schools. They were definitely not nerds but they seemed to know right from wrong without a lot of fatherly counseling.

We did have some great vacations and travel together, even camping, but that was only a temporary escape from day-to-day life. Oh, I made an attempt at being a good father by attending the Little League games, the swim meets, and Jennifer's stage performances, but I was not there for the many daily trips to the practice fields and other places. In spite of not inheriting many good athletic genes from Mom and Dad, Bill was an adequate Little League ballplayer and more than an adequate member of the swim team in high school. And I dearly wish that Jennifer would have continued on with her participation in the drama field where she was a natural talent.

At the same time, I was a bit selfish and still wanted to do the things that other guys did that were home every night, like playing golf every Saturday morning. I thought it was a macho thing in which I had to participate, but I also felt I needed an outlet, to once a week get completely away from the battlefield. I didn't realize that the game of golf can get even more frustrating. It's a war by itself.

Regardless, every Saturday morning at the break of dawn, Bill Field, John Fontana, Ray Ward, and others would join me on the links, trying to be the first ones out of the fog to tee off.

One of the more memorable occasions relating to these golfing events was when John Fontana and I, as a result of some door prize, a drawing or something, had each won a free lesson from the club pro.

The golf pro, Howie Johnson, may have been a good golfer, although I had never heard of any tournaments that he had done well in, and he may have been a good teacher, but I would soon have some serious doubts about this too. You see, Howie had the personality of an African warthog and he also had a harelip, which made for an interesting combination.

The day John and I scheduled our free golf lesson, Howie the Harelip met us on the driving range. Howie said, "Kay Foid, you tay ear and whing at a few baws while I go over dare and ook at Yon whing is cub."

"Which club should I use?" I asked.

"I down care. Use a ive, ix, or even. Dey all whing da ame way."

While John was taking his cuts at the balls in front of Howie about twenty feet away, I listened in to see if I could pick up some pointers.

"Kay Yon, now eep yo eft arm twaight."

"Okay Howie. Oops, I almost missed that one," John said.

"Ell, yo damn fool, yo eep ifting yo ead up." John took another swing.

"Ey, I toad yo to eep yo eft arm twaight. Doan yo isten?"

"I guess I must have misunderstood you, Howie."

"Kay Yon, eep whinging." Having run out of patience with John, Howie walks over to where I was standing, trying not to laugh.

"Kay Foid, ets see yo whing."

I wound up and took a wicked swing at a ball.

"Oh Yesus Quiest!" was Howie's immediate expert analytical assessment of my golfing ability.

That was my first and only lesson in the art of playing golf. I decided there wasn't any need to go on with any more lessons when I was already a superstar comparable to Jesus Christ.

Many businesses were feeling the economic crunch in the 1970s and were reacting to it by downsizing, cutting out the fat, and closing down the poor profit-producing segments. Sears was slow to react. They first tried to reduce the selling organization in the stores and make an attempt at adapting to a K-Mart style of service. This backfired, with reduced sales and unhappy customers. They next started closing the profit-losing inner city stores. As a result the NAACP did a pretty good job of blasting Sears with a lot of negative publicity, making Sears look like the bad guys in most of the major markets.

One more brainstorm was adopted which called for the closing of a number of reduced-volume stores in the smaller markets. All this seemed to do was invite Wal-Mart to come into the same towns where they did a tremendous job. There is no reason in the world why Sears could not have done the same thing if they had put a different name on their existing stores and started acting like a discounter.

Finally, Sears began downsizing by reducing the number of management levels and cutting out some high-salaried executives. It was definitely the right thing to do, except that it should have been done about five years sooner. Credit would not be excused from this effort even though we were practically the only area of the company, outside of Allstate, that was producing a healthy profit and growing. But it still was the right thing to do, and it would soon affect me personally.

It was on a Friday while on a trip to Peoria that I would get the word. I was getting ready to make the four-hour trip home after being gone all week, but at the last minute I decided to go out to lunch with the manager. When we returned his secretary said, "Mr. Wachs, there is going to be a conference call for you from Mr. Brasher in about a half an hour and he asked that you be sure and stick around."

Damn, why didn't I take off before lunch?

Well, it was more like an hour before the conference call got hooked up and then it took Mr. B. about another forty-five minutes to tell us all one thing. The position of regional credit manager was being eliminated throughout the company. Now why couldn't he have waited until Monday to tell us that rather than ruin the entire weekend? But it seemed like a custom at Sears that if anyone was going to be released from the company, it had to be done on a Friday afternoon.

We always used to joke that if you made it to three o'clock on Friday, you had it made for another week.

We all had a lot of questions about this crushing announcement but Mr. B. could not tell us anything more. "Just continue on in your jobs as if nothing has changed. Headquarters wanted you all to know about this at the same time so that you wouldn't hear about it on the grapevine. We will have to wait and give you more details at a later date." Thanks a lot.

It was now about three-thirty before I started my trip home, and hoping to make up a little time, with a lot of things going through my mind, I probably drove a little faster than I should have. It was a two-lane highway out of Peoria for about forty miles before connecting with the freeway, and as I passed an eighteen-wheeler and pulled back into my lane, there was a highway patrolman coming up over the rise. He immediately turned his red lights on and blinked his headlights. I wondered why he did that, certainly that was not for my benefit.

I kept on going. About five miles down the road there again was a highway patrolman, only this time in my rearview mirror, with his red lights blinking and also a blaring siren. He was after me.

"What's your hurry, buddy?"

"You really don't want to know," I said.

"I clocked you about five miles back going sixty-nine miles an hour in a fifty-five zone."

"But you were coming down the road towards me. How can you clock me that way?"

"Step back in my vehicle and I will show you." He demonstrated his little radar gun.

"But you saw that I was passing a big truck and I had to speed up a bit to avoid hitting the car in the left lane."

"The car in the left lane was my patrol car."

"Well then, it's a good thing I speeded up, otherwise I would have hit you head on."

The patrolman looked at me in disgust and proceeded to write me out a ticket. "You have your choice of either appearing in traffic court in Springfield in three weeks or paying me thirty-seven dollars now."

Thirty-seven dollars, damn, that was a lot and I don't want to go to Springfield.

"Can I write you a check?"

"No, it must be in cash."

I looked in my wallet and all I had was two twenty-dollar bills.

The patrolman said, "I don't have any change."

I think he would have gladly accepted the entire forty dollars but damned if I was going to let him get away with that. I said, "I saw a Seven Eleven store about three miles back. I can make change there."

"All right, I will follow you back there."

I got the thirty-seven dollars in bills and handed it to the patrolman. I noticed that he had a pre-addressed envelope in which he stuck the cash and his copy of the speeding ticket. He licked it shut and then got a stamp out of a folder and stuck it on the envelope.

I said, "Would you like me to mail that for you?"

He responded with another look of disgust and drove off. I later wondered if that thirty-seven dollars ever made it to the traffic court. I never heard another word about it.

When I arrived home about eight-thirty I was greeted with more than just the look of disgust. "Have you once again forgotten how to use the telephone or do I have to hit you over the head with it?"

"You might as well. Nothing much worse could still happen to me today."

Jeanne's demeanor changed. "What happened? Are you all right?

"Well in addition to being hit with a traffic ticket, I think I just lost my job."

"Oh dear, I'm sorry. I don't think we can make it on my salary."

On the day Jennifer turned eighteen, February 5, 1980, Jeanne applied for a job at a little travel agency in Downers Grove. Without any experience or training she got the job because of being a stewardess a long time ago and because she made a good impression with her enthusiasm.

The travel business was right up her alley and she has been working at it off and on ever since, allowing her to travel just about every place in the world and providing some good travel benefits for the two of us together as well.

Even though I was a lame duck, my job as a regional credit manager continued on without change for nearly four more years. In fact, it even got bigger. One of the other regional managers of our territory retired and was not replaced, so my region grew to include Michigan, Ohio, Kentucky, and Indiana minus South Bend. The Illinois units I had before, plus South Bend and St. Louis, were given to Lou Hall. This new region was a much more interesting area which I enjoyed very much, but I was anxious to move on to my next assignment, if there was ever going to be another assignment.

We were told that the company would try to place us in a job of similar capacity, but we could not take advantage of the early retirement package with a golden handshake that was being offered to executives whose units were closing.

Eventually I got around to tell my boss, Jimmie Brasher, that I was sick of traveling in this awkward position where the job no longer existed and that I would be willing to go back to being a credit central manager at any large market any place in the country where there was an opening, providing I didn't have to take too big a cut in salary. I said I would even move to Detroit.

He said, "Are you sure? Would you consider going to headquarters? You know you have not had any experience there and this would be good for you. I know Ray Kennedy likes you and as this whole reorganization shakes down there could be some good jobs opening up at the headquarters level."

Ray Kennedy was now the general credit manager for the company, a super guy and there had been a few occasions, both business and social, where we had been together. I know we hit it off very well and it would have been a joy to work for him. I didn't give Brasher a flat out "no" to his hint that I should remain open for a headquarters assignment but I did imply that I much preferred field work to those desk jockey staff jobs.

Had I known that Ray Kennedy was quietly putting together the Discover Credit Card package for Sears at the time, I may have pursued something in that direction. I would have loved to have been involved in launching that new credit card. As it turned out, the Sears chairman pushed Discover over to Dean Witter rather than Sears at the last minute, and a lot of would-be Sears executives got left out. Still, I was able to get three men promoted to positions with Discover based on my recommendation, which made me feel good.

During this period of time, Jennifer, who was now a student at the University of Illinois, had the opportunity to go to school in Dijon, France, for a year in connection with her French major. She would be finishing her semester in the spring of 1983, so Jeanne decided to take off for few days and go see her. Her job at the travel agency allowed her to work out reduced travel fares and sometimes she could even travel free.

On the day that Jeanne was to leave for France, Brasher called me and asked me to stop by his office in Skokie. "I have something I want to run by you."

It didn't sound too important so I said, "Fine, as long as I can get out of there by two o'clock." I didn't tell him that Jeanne was going to France and I wanted to take her to the airport.

At our meeting in Skokie, Brasher said, "You told me some time ago that you wanted to cut down on your traveling and would be willing to accept an assignment at a major central. Well, the manager in Minneapolis just resigned this morning. Does this sound like something you might be interested in?"

Minneapolis? I couldn't believe what I was hearing. Of all the places in the country where I might have gone, Minneapolis was the furthest from my mind. It was difficult to hide my overwhelming joy and I said, "When do I leave?"

"Not so fast now. I want you to go home and talk it over with Jeanne and make sure this is something she can live with and then call me in a day or two. No one else will be considered until I hear back from you." He always seemed to be more concerned about Jeanne's well-being than mine.

I left but I had already made my decision and I had no intention of talking it over with Jeanne, particularly when she was about to board an airplane to Europe. It would shake her all up and disrupt the enjoyable vacation she was planning with Jennifer. I wasn't even going to tell our son, Bill, but I had to talk to somebody about it and eventually spilled out the news to him with the threat of doing something that would change his voice about three octaves higher if he breathed a word to Mom or anyone else before I talked to her.

The problem was that I had committed to a rather important three-day meeting in Battle Creek that would take me out of town the day Jeanne arrived home. Bill would have to pick her up at the airport and somehow keep his mouth shut.

I called Mr. B. the next day to tell him that Jeanne was very agreeable to the transfer to Minneapolis. An announcement was made in his office and everything was complete except that a wife of one of Brasher's staff members went to the same hairdresser that Jeanne did. I knew that once you tell a hairdresser anything, you might as well tell the whole world.

The night Jeanne was scheduled to arrive home her plane was late, so I had to leave the poker table of our meeting and call home about every fifteen minutes to make sure I talked to her before anyone else did. When I finally reached her, I said, "Grab a chair and sit down."

"Why, is there something wrong?"

"Well no, unless you consider moving wrong."

"Where are we moving?" The excitement elevated.

"Where would you most like to go?"

Jeanne guessed all the places she hoped that some day Sears would move us. "Atlanta, San Francisco, Dallas, South America, Spain." Minneapolis never crossed her mind.

Needless to say we were all very happy about this prospect. To be able to move back to the community where you will eventually want to retire was totally unheard of, particularly at Sears where such things just never happened. No one deserved to be this lucky.

Jennifer was now finishing up her year in France and wanted to do a little traveling before she came home. Bill, also out of school and not committed to a job at the moment, arranged to go to Europe and also spend a few days traveling with Jennifer. Since Jennifer had not yet been informed about our move to Minneapolis, we told Bill to bring her up to date with this news and we also gave him a letter to give to Jennifer that would answer any questions concerning her future. In the letter we assured her that she could finish school at Illinois and then move to Minneapolis if she chose, or if she found a job and wanted to remain in the Chicago area, that would be all right too.

When Bill arrived back from his trip, we asked, "What did Jennifer have to say about our move to Minneapolis?"

Bill said, "Oh shit, I forgot to tell her."

"What about the letter? You gave her that didn't you?"

"No, I forgot to give her that too."

To this day Jennifer has accused us of attempting to move and not giving her our new address.

Similar to the other houses we had sold, it took about three days to get a satisfactory purchase agreement on our Downers Grove house. Then we had to go through the process of house-hunting in Minneapolis. But at least it was an area we were a little more familiar with.

We met the Minneapolis real estate agent at her office at Edina Realty on a very hot Sunday afternoon. This fat, frumpy female (I think she was a female) reminded me of a character out of the cartoon *Far Side*. When we climbed into her new Mercedes she turned on the air conditioner, pulled up her skirt and for about five minutes directed a blast of air to blow up between her legs. Since she had no stockings on, you could see the half-inch long hair on her legs rippling in the breeze. How could anyone have recommended her, but she was the top salesperson in the entire Twin Cities market and we would soon learn the reason why.

Off and on for nearly thirty days we looked at houses in the Edina/Bloomington area. We were amazed at the amount of junk there was on the market in what was supposed to be a preferred location. Only one house appealed to us but it was about twenty thousand dollars above our ceiling price. We gave up and decided to build a house on a very good lot by a lake in West Bloomington, meaning we would have to move, store our furniture, and temporarily rent space until our house was built.

On the Sunday night before I was to fly to Minneapolis to sign the papers for the lot purchase and meet with the architect, Jeanne was very upset and went to bed crying at the prospect of building a house that we would probably have to move into in the middle of winter, another big muddy mess. About nine-thirty that night I got a phone call from our charming real-estate agent. "Do you remember the house you looked at on Tanglewood Court in Edina?"

"Yes I remember it," I said, "But it was well above our price."

"What would you say if I told you the seller was ready to meet your price?"

"I would say that's too bad because we have decided to build a new house."

"Damn, I've been working all day on this guy to get him down to your price and now you're backing out. I think you would be making a big mistake if you don't consider this house. What would it take?"

"Two things," I said. "First of all we would have to be able to move in by the end of this month to avoid storing our furniture because that is when we have to get out of our house here."

"Oh, that would be impossible."

"Okay then, just forget it."

"What's your second unreasonable demand?"

"I want the taxes paid for the entire year."

"We don't do that here in Minnesota. They have to be prorated."

Again I said forget it. "But I think I know you well enough to believe you can twist arms and make the impossible happen whether it's done that way in Minnesota or not. How bad do you want your commission?"

"I'll have to get back to you," she said.

About a half hour later Miss Congeniality called me back. "It looks like you have just bought yourself a house. Somehow the seller said he will meet all your demands."

We moved into our house the same day the seller was moving out. It was a great house in a super location, twenty minutes from my workplace at Sears and ten minutes from Jeanne's fun place, Southdale. It also turned out to be a good investment since we sold the house after twelve years for sixty percent more than what we paid for it. Once again, have I mentioned that I am a lucky SOB?

The job also turned out to be the best I ever had. Since the credit regions had all been eliminated, I had some responsibilities for servicing the Sears markets tied to the Minneapolis credit central, which included some of Wisconsin, Iowa, Nebraska, and Montana, and all of the Dakotas and Minnesota. But rarely did I have to travel.

The credit central in Minneapolis was one of the best operating units in the nation, not because of the previous manager who resigned, but because of his assistant, John Nygaard, who was still there. John actually managed the operation and I quickly recognized that all I had to do was stay out of his way. In the Sears system of evaluating the performance of your subordinates, John was the only person I had ever given the rating "Distinguished," the highest rating to be used for only a select few.

The only weak spot in Minneapolis was in the area of gross income. Minnesota laws prevented us from charging the normal eighteen percent or higher finance charge rate that was being used in other states. After a considerable amount of effort to propagandize the consumer, a bill was finally introduced in the Minnesota legislature to increase the maximum credit card rate to eighteen percent.

We acquired the services of a lobbyist but it was still left up to the credit people at Dayton's, Penny's, Sears, and other places to work on the legislators to get this bill passed. I spent a few days talking to people at the capitol, taking people out to lunch, and making telephone calls, but I never thought I would end up making a personal contribution to a state senator for his reelection fund just to get his vote—a DFLer no less. We got the bill passed, meaning many more bucks for Sears, but it was a crappy business.

Shortly after arriving in Minneapolis I got a phone call from Jimmie Brasher in Skokie. "I need to ask a favor of you, Floyd. The credit central in South Bend is going to be consolidated into a larger unit and we need to do something with Larry Roumell since he is not quite old enough to be offered the retirement package. You, more than anyone else, have been able to get the best out of Larry, so I'm asking you to find a spot for him in Minneapolis."

Larry Roumell was the credit manager in Battle Creek when I first took over the region and where I made my first field visit. So how did he get to South Bend?

Larry is enough of a colorful character that his story deserves an entire chapter, but I will try to condense it into a few paragraphs.

During the beginning days while I was trying to solve the St. Louis and Detroit problems, the credit manager at South Bend, Gene Nisswonger, had a serious heart attack. After he was off work for about a month the store manager called me. "We all know that Gene, who is past sixty, will certainly retire after his heart attack, but he won't sign any papers until the doctor tells him he is ready to come back to work. I think we should just go ahead and bring someone in here to replace him without waiting another two months or more."

I agreed, we couldn't leave South Bend without a credit manager indefinitely, but the personnel people wouldn't let me make a permanent replacement. I thought of Larry, the Greek from Battle Creek. It was close enough that Larry could commute and not have to move his family.

"Larry, this will be a good promotion for you," I said. "But I can't give you the job permanently until Nisswonger retires." Since Battle Creek was a small unit without any other assistants, I had to transfer in another man to replace Larry immediately. This would be permanent.

After three or four more months of dragging out his recovery, the doctor finally said that Nisswonger was able to come back to work. But instead of retiring as everybody expected, Gene wanted his old job back, which according to personnel policy he was entitled to. Now what do we do? Larry could no longer go back to Battle Creek and there was no other place open where he could be sent. The only option I had was to make room for him on my staff, meaning he now had to physically move his entire family into the Chicago area.

We had to invent a job for Larry, so I made him a credit marketing specialist. This was right up his alley. He could go out into the stores, hold meetings with the employees, and bullshit about the tremendous value of the credit card on sales and profits. But once in awhile he would get carried away and forget that he had other responsibilities.

One such example was when I sent him into some of the southern Illinois markets and told him to use my company car because I was not going out of town that week. I believe it was in Lincoln, Illinois, where he got a parking ticket and forgot to pay it, or more than likely just tore it up, since up to this point he had never paid for a parking ticket in his life.

Only this time, the Lincoln police decided to pursue this law-breaker and issued a warrant for the arrest of the car title holder.

Ordinarily that would have been me, except the company car I was driving formerly belonged to Joe Hood, my former boss, and was given to me when he left the company. I never got around to getting the title transferred, so the warrant went out for the arrest of Joe Hood.

About six months later after they finally tracked him down, the fit really hit the shan. The security people at Sears kept Joe from going to jail. When they eventually learned that I was now driving Joe's car, I told them, "There must be some mistake because I have never been in Lincoln, Illinois."

After a little research, however, I soon learned it was Larry who was using my car on the day the ticket was issued. This resulted in just one of several ass-chewings Larry received from me for some of his carefree behavior. Nevertheless, he was a productive, hard-working employee who continued to work for me for the next three years.

When Gene Nisswonger of South Bend finally got around to retiring, Larry was the logical choice to replace him on a permanent basis. This time Larry continued to work at South Bend for several years even after South Bend was no longer in my region, so when Mr. B. called to ask the favor of manufacturing a job for

Larry again, I immediately thought of all the narrow scrapes I had to get involved with to keep him and I out of trouble.

"Sure Mr. B., I'll work out something for Larry to do." Since I knew that Larry had always done a good job in collections, I gave him the assignment of overseeing the six collection division managers I had in Minneapolis, who were all immature and borderline qualified in their jobs.

Larry's wife, Jean Roumel, had a good job at the University of Notre Dame, working in the athletic department, I believe, so when it was learned that Larry was being transferred to Minneapolis and she would also have to move, someone in the athletic department at ND (it may very well have been the athletic director) called the University of Minnesota to see if a job could be made available for her there.

The person they called was none other than Lou Holtz, who had also just arrived in Minneapolis as the new Minnesota Gopher head football coach.

As everyone knows today, Lou Holtz really had his eyes focused on the head coaching job at Notre Dame, so he would do cartwheels to try and accomplish any favors he might be able to do for the folks at South Bend.

As it turned out Lou had a secretary's job open for one of his assistant coaches so he said to have Mrs. Roumell come and see him personally as soon as she got into town.

Larry came to me and showed me the flowery letter of introduction his wife had from the athletic director at Notre Dame. "You've got to show me how to get to the University of Minnesota and find Lou Holtz's office."

The next day Larry took Jean to see Lou for the interview and they both ended up spending about three hours with him. I think Holtz was thinking to himself, *There is a connection with Notre Dame here, remote as it may be, that I might be able to make use of some day.*

The interview ended up with Lou claiming Jean was over-qualified for his job, so he made a phone call to Harvey MacKay, one of the prominent Minnesota businessmen responsible for bringing Lou Holtz to Minneapolis. Jean ended up with a good job at Campbell Mithun, a big advertising agency in Minneapolis, and Larry ended up with a date to play golf with Lou Holtz at one of the prestigious country clubs, I think it was Interlachen.

I was a little apprehensive about this crazy Greek playing golf with our new coach, but Larry was something else. Larry said, "I told Lou my boss won't let me have the afternoon off unless he can come along, and Lou said by all means bring him along." That's how Larry got things done.

I was not able to keep my golf date with Lou and Larry, which is probably a good thing because Lou happens to be a very good golfer, but I did get a chance to have lunch with Lou at the U and you will never meet a more gracious man. He spent most of the afternoon showing us around the Bierman building and the renovations they were making in the athletic department.

There was a frantic effort at the U to rejuvenate everything relating to the new football program and Lou Holtz, including the redesign of Goldie the Gopher, the U logo. I saw the opportunity here to use the new logo in connection with some various premiums we were using as gifts to give customers who applied for a Sears credit card. It would be very well accepted at our stores in Minnesota.

At one of the visits that Larry and I had with Lou, I discussed the premium idea and using the Goldie Gopher logo. Lou said, "This would be great, but it is very difficult to do. Not only do you have to have the university approval but you have to get the approval from the Big Ten as well. But I'll take you in to see Paul Giel and he'll tell you what you have to do."

We met Paul Giel, the university athletic director, and I was surprised to see that Giel's office was much less pretentious than Lou's. Giel put us in touch with someone else and eventually we received a letter authorizing the use of the M emblem and the Goldie Gopher logo as long as it was used on giveaway items that would never be sold. I then got my friend in the premium business, Chuck Greer, to produce a selection of items at a cost of one dollar to a dollar and a half each and we were in business. Our sales promotion people at Sears were ecstatic over this new venture and they practically gave me a blank check.

The climax to all this was that we were able to get a Minnesota State Fair booth at a good location to hawk our premiums in exchange for an application for a Sears credit card. We opened thousands of new accounts. Lou Holtz even got excited about it and got his close personal friend Sid Hartman to interview Larry on his show at the fairgrounds.

Larry could have been President Clinton's press secretary. He was a showman and could stretch the truth as well as anyone including the fact that he had Holtz convinced that he had contacts with some top people at Notre Dame. This is exactly what Holtz wanted.

I did not maintain the close relationship with Lou Holtz as Larry did so I was taken aback the day my secretary walked into my office and said, "There is a man named Lou Holtz on the telephone that insists on speaking to you."

"Hello, Floyd. It's been a while since I've talked to you. How are things at Sears?"

"It's nice to talk to you, coach. What can I do for you?"

"Well I just got off the phone with your man Larry and I wanted to ask him a favor, but he said you would be the person to talk to. I hate to impose but I have a dear uncle in East Liverpool, Ohio, who has been a top salesman for Wards for about twenty years. But they are closing their store and he will be out of a job. He tells me that Sears is going to open an agency in East Liverpool and he would like a crack at it. Larry tells me this used to be your territory and maybe you would know some people that you could talk to that might give my uncle some consideration. I know you will not find a more honest hard working individual anyplace in the whole area."

"I don't know there is a lot I can do Lou, but I will try. What is your uncle's name? Is it also Holtz?"

His name was George something, other than Holtz, but I don't remember what it was. I had never heard of East Liverpool before so I looked it up on the map and found that it was right on the West Virginia boarder. For this reason it was in the Eastern Territory jurisdiction which I had nothing to do with. I still called the office in Philadelphia and eventually located someone who had something to do with setting up the agency in East Liverpool. The man knew who I was talking about but had never heard of Lou Holtz, which I couldn't understand. Must have been an Ivy League nerd. He told me they had the application from the man, Holtz's uncle, and were seriously considering giving him a contract for the agency. This was where I left it as I couldn't honestly make a recommendation other than to say he was the uncle of the football coach at Minnesota.

About a week went by and I received another phone call from Lou Holtz. "Floyd, I can't tell you how much I appreciate what you have done. I just talked to my uncle in East Liverpool and he was given the job of running the Sears agency there. Man, I can't thank you enough."

"Lou, I had nothing to do with it. Your uncle did this all on his own. I just..."

"Now, don't give me that. I know better. If it wasn't for you he would have never gotten the job. I shall forever be indebted to you for what you have done. If there is anything I can do for you just let me know."

I wasn't going to argue with him. Holtz did return the favor, although there was no debt to be repaid.

When the coaching job opened up in Notre Dame, Holtz was on the telephone with Larry every day. "What have you heard? Who is being interviewed?" And when the job was finally offered to him he was out of Minnesota faster than a scared rabbit. Minnesota football would go back into the closet where it had been for twenty years.

At about this time Larry Roumell was becoming disgruntled with his situation working for me with little chance of becoming a credit central manager on his own, or getting any other job where he could be his own boss. He decided to leave Sears, work for an independent collection agency for a while to get some experience, and then open his own business in a collection agency.

"But Larry," I said, "you only have a few years to go before you will receive full retirement benefits and it would be a shame to give that up."

"Yeah, well I think I was screwed when my unit was closed in South Bend and I moved to Minneapolis. I should have been able to retire then."

"Well why didn't you? I had no idea you were even considering it."

"Because they told me I wasn't old enough," Larry said.

That was not exactly true. The policy stated that you had to be fifty years old to be eligible for the unit closing retirement package, but if you were just forty-nine you could take a year's leave of absence from the company, come back when you were fifty, and then receive the full retirement package. Larry was only forty-eight so nobody bothered to explain the whole policy to him. However, he had a birthday before his unit was officially closed so he was, in fact, old enough to take advantage of the early retirement buy-out. He would not have had to move his family to Minneapolis.

I thought this screw-up by somebody in personnel was a terrible injustice. I suggested to Larry that he write to personnel in headquarters, review the complete circumstances, and see if he could still receive the same retirement package if he resigned now. I even composed the letter for Larry. The response was a one-line, flat-out "No."

This really ticked me off so I said to Larry, "If you would care to pursue this, I think you've got a strong legal position against Sears."

Larry had an uncle who was a circuit judge in Detroit and he lined him up with a good attorney in Chicago. The conclusion was a settlement offer by Sears consisting of full retirement benefits, a substantial cash settlement, and attorney fees. Larry then moved back to South Bend and went to work for a collection agency to learn the business and his wife got her job back at Notre Dame.

When I retired, Larry wanted to go into business with his own collection agency and he talked me into joining him. It was a big gamble, but it was fun for a while. I handled all the accounting work, paid the bills, and took care of the payroll, the IRS, and the state of Indiana, while Larry took care of the day-to-day operation. Larry even asked Lou Holtz to be on the board of directors for the company. Lou said, "I don't know if the university will let me do that."

Larry said, "You won't have to do anything, We just want to show your name on our stationery."

"What the heck then, go ahead," Lou said. "I owe you guys a favor anyway."

It was a struggle and occasionally I had to inject a little cash to keep us afloat from one month to the next. It took us about a year and a half before we started to produce a little profit. Our biggest problem was the long distance communication between South Bend and Minneapolis, and we couldn't afford a computer. I eventually opted out of the business. After all, I had already retired from one career and I didn't need another one. Larry bought me out, or should I say, paid back my investments plus interest and he carried on alone. He did exceptionally well.

There is one crazy sequel to the Larry Roumell/Lou Holtz saga that I must include here. It was eight or nine years later and Lou Holtz was in his last year of coaching at Notre Dane. I had gone to three or four Notre Dame games which were a lot of fun. We were planning a fall weekend in the Chicago area visiting our son and his family, and I thought it would be great if Bill and I could go to a Notre Dame game. I believe it was next to the last game Lou would be coaching and I called Larry to see if he could get a couple of tickets.

"Floyd, you're asking the impossible," Larry said. "But you know, if anybody can get tickets, I can."

About a week before the game Larry called me. "Guess what, Lou's secretary got you two tickets from his personal allotment. Apparently somebody canceled. They should be good seats and the best part is, they're free." They were not just good seats, they were about twelve rows up right behind the Notre Dame bench and smack dab on the fifty yard line.

Bill and I went to the game. I was curious about a cheer the spectators were doing which consisted of thrusting a hand in the air and shouting something that sounded like "You, you, you." When the game was nearly over, I said to Bill, "I wonder what that cheer is supposed to mean."

A lady seated directly in front of me, about my age or maybe a bit older, was attending the game with a young girl who possibly was her granddaughter. The lady turned around and said to me, "They're saying 'Lou, Lou, Lou' and you're supposed to raise your hand in the air and form the letter 'L' with your thumb and fingers." And then she added, "I ought to know because Lou is my nephew."

Nephew? Aunt? Uncle George? I said, "Are you by chance from East Liverpool, Ohio?"

"Yes I am. How did you know that?" the lady replied.

I didn't want to go into the whole story about my involvement in the job Uncle George got at Sears and fortunately I didn't have to. At that moment there was an exciting ending to the game that got everyone's attention and we split. There were about seventy-five thousand fans at the game so the chances of something like that happening are about seventy-five thousand to one. Is this a small world or what?

My tour of duty as the credit central manager of Minneapolis was perhaps the most enjoyable period of my career. I didn't have to travel unless I wanted to, the operation in Minneapolis was very clean and profitable, and I probably had the best assistant manager of any credit central in the company. I was able to take off when I felt like it without worrying about the job falling apart, and with Jeanne working part-time at the travel office at Dayton's, we had the opportunity to do some vacation traveling. Being back in Minneapolis and hooking up with our old friends again was ideal. Retirement was now on my mind.

At this time a big event was being planned in Chicago: the wedding of Angie Cominsky and Bill Wachs. Bill had met Angie before we moved out of Downers Grove. He had brought her to our house a couple of times to meet us, and it was pretty obvious he was really smitten with her. At the beginning I was not as overwhelmed with this girl as Bill was, more than likely because I was losing my only son and she was taking him away. She was the possessor and I was the dispossessed. I failed to see it like I was gaining a daughter as you are supposed to look at it. I already had one of those.

The idea of your firstborn leaving home in favor of a woman may be easy for some fathers to accept, but I had a bit of a problem. I hope it didn't show.

On the other hand, I soon caught on to the fact that this Angie person was making my son happier than I had ever seen him before, so she couldn't be all bad. And certainly he must have inherited some of my unquestionable abilities to judge people and to select the right girl to spend the rest of his life with. I don't know about that but I would have hoped that he at least received some of my good luck genes. In any event I am happy to say that I now admire Angie, a most charming daughter-in-law and a wonderful, loving, and enthusiastic mother of two very exciting grandchildren, Nicholas George and Bridget Jean. Angie, I should also mention, is probably one of the most positive people I have ever known. Yes, I think Bill did inherit some of my expertise in this area.

The Cominsky-Wachs wedding was something else. I thought the wedding of Jeanne and I was a bit unusual, but in comparison it made their wedding look like a Spielberg movie. It was on a ship (I believe that is what you would call it) that once was a passenger liner on the Great Lakes (or maybe it was a rubbish hauler, I don't know). It was now anchored, chained, cabled, and welded to the dock at Navy Pier in Chicago. I know, I checked it out very carefully before I would go aboard.

On board this "vessel," the setting for the wedding had all the appearances of being an otherwise traditional wedding: rows of chairs spread out on the bow, a staircase—or should I say a ladder—for the wedding party, I believe there was a dozen or more in total, to walk down the aisle with the usual wedding gowns and tuxes, flowers, music and a minister in a robe. It was a beautiful fall evening with the bright sun just setting over the Chicago skyline. There were even sea gulls circling overhead shouting their greetings of joy and searching for a nice, wide-brim, white hat where they could deposit their gifts. But wait, there is something wrong here. All the guys had deck shoes on, not necessarily all that clean, sticking out from the bottom of their tux pant legs. Okay, deck shoes I guess would be appropriate.

Finally the minister said, "I now pronounce you man and wife, before God, before all your friends and relatives, and let's not forget the sea gulls." I think he was happy to get through this wedding.

And then the girls in the wedding party, not wanting to be outdone by the boys, reached into their dresses someplace and pulled out sunglasses to don before they marched down the aisle. Yes, that would be appropriate also.

The good luck genes I had hoped to pass on to my daughter as well were not all that apparent in her life, although having missed the brass ring the first time around, I believe it is now available to her in the future. Jennifer's first marriage was equally as grand and fun-filled as Bill and Angie's mainly because it consisted of two weddings, one in Chicago and one in a quaint old village in France. As a matter of fact, I think they had to repeat their marriage vows a third time to satisfy some requirements to be married by a priest in France without a long delay.

The first ceremony took place at a large old house in Hinsdale, a Chicago suburb, that once was a private home but was later converted to a park building to be used for weddings and similar social events. It was a beautiful setting. All the furniture, kitchen, bar, and dining facilities were available and Chef Pierre, the groom, along with his work friends did a masterful job of preparing the wedding dinner. Although we had now been living back in Minneapolis, we still invited many of our Chicago-area friends and neighbors and some of my old Sears associates.

In addition there was quite a sizable group of friends from Minneapolis included on the invitation list, although we didn't expect that many to attend. But one of the more entrepreneurial guests, Bob Miller, decided there were enough people invited to the wedding out of Minneapolis that it would be cheaper and a lot more fun if they hired a bus and driver. As a result nearly everyone attended. Needless to say it was a good time for all of us.

Everyone was also invited to the second wedding in France as well, but only one couple, our good friends Kay and John Waters, were able to make the trip, probably because they were sort of planning a French vacation anyway.

Another couple, our good friends from Germany that I talked about earlier, also attended. Otherwise, everyone at this wedding were friends or relatives of Pierre's, and only a very few could speak English. Nevertheless it was a very happy time in this little neighborhood hall where the barrels of wine, beer, and what have you, plus about a thirty-foot table of French specialties, were lined up waiting to be consumed. The next day, as soon as everyone could raise their weary heads, it started all over again with more wine, beer, and leftover food.

Following all of this, Jeanne and I took off on the TGV, the two-hundred-mile-an-hour French train, down through Switzerland, Italy, Austria, Germany, and back to France, one of our very best vacations.

Taking marriage vows three times or three hundred times would not have made a difference to that marriage. It appeared to be doomed to failure very early on, and I am indeed happy that they did not sacrifice their lives to a trap of unhappiness just to avoid admitting to a mistake. I cannot possibly imagine the emotional trauma one must go through in a failed marriage, particularly for a woman and especially when there is a child involved. To have your trust, your faith, your hopes, and your self-esteem stripped from your soul and discarded like a banana peel has to be one of the most painful experiences anyone should be expected to endure.

Very possibly what made it all worthwhile was the one very gloriously beautiful creature this marriage produced, Claire Marie Gardien, our first grandchild. What a thrill it was to see her beautiful face only a few hours after she was born, and how lucky we are to have been living close by while she was growing up. Perhaps it is wrong to say this, but Jeanne and I are both amazed at how natural it was for Jennifer to assume the role of a delightful mother. I'm sure the close relationship she has with her daughter has been a lifesaver throughout the difficult divorce period in more ways then one.

Unlike Jennifer's first marriage, I have very positive feelings that she and her second husband Karl will have a long, happy lifetime relationship. He's an attorney, but let's not hold that against him. I almost think he is too nice a guy to be an attorney, but what do I know? I think I have already demonstrated my judge of character has been about ninety percent luck and ten percent warm feelings.

There is considerably more that I could write about my children and grandchildren. (Then again, maybe from their point of view I have said too much already!) But this should be their story told in their own way in their own time. Everyone without exception has a story to tell and I only hope that someday they will let others share their thoughts and feelings in the form of a book, a diary, an autobiography or something.

It was in the fall of 1986 when I made the formal announcement that I would be retiring from Sears. A lot of people had the idea that I had already retired, I just hadn't gotten. around to stop coming to work. It was also a letdown to realize that, unlike the other three or four times that I tried to quit Sears, no one tried to talk me out of it. Not one word was uttered as to whether I was certain about this decision. "Are you sure you want to continue working all the way into March of next year?" That was the only question.

Yes, it had always been my goal to retire before I was sixty, even as early as fifty-five, the earliest you could retire from Sears and receive full benefits. On March sixth I would be sixty years old, making it over forty years with the same company, something unheard of in today's corporate world. But I had enough vacation time coming that I could actually leave at the end of December so my replacement could take over at the beginning of the year. That seemed to make Pete Fisher, my boss and the current general credit manager of the company, a little happier.

Sears in Minneapolis had always been very big on retirements of long-service executives, with company sponsored dinners, open bars, gifts, and entertainment. Originally they were men only, because there were no female executives, and of course, spouses were never invited. But now we were starting to acquire some women in key jobs who would have to be included in the Good Old Boys Club, and that sort of put the damper on our frolicking parties.

There was a bit of an exception made in my case, probably because all the store managers in the northwest area had been called into Minneapolis for a year-end meeting, plus the fact that another manager in the group was retiring at the same time and they could roast two birds with one fire. It would be a first class, five-course dinner with wine, an open bar, gifts, the roasting, and so forth.

The days of "Goodbye, here's your gold watch," were not entirely gone because when it was my turn to open my gifts, I had six little packages, all the same and each one of them contained a watch, except that these watches were the cheap, under-two-dollar variety I had been able to acquire from my good friend and premium supplier Chuck Greer. I had the reputation of being the junk man or the trinket hustler at Sears because I was always trying to persuade the store managers to buy these cheap Taiwan trinkets to give away as premiums for opening a new Sears account. It did the job and at some places I see it is still being done.

Everyone had a good time seeing me embarrassed by all this, but I suppose it was their roundabout way of saying thanks for my efforts in helping to build credit sales.

Right after Christmas I said to Jeanne, "Don't you think we should go out for dinner or do something to celebrate my retirement from Sears?"

"Why, I'm still working, besides you don't officially retire for another two months yet. We'll do something on your birthday."

My sixtieth birthday came up on March sixth and Jeanne said, "Lois and Doug are coming over and they're taking us out for dinner."

"Good, where?"

"It's a place called 'It's Greek To Me' on Lake Street."

"Oh, I've been there for lunch. It's okay." I didn't want to complain too much, but it was hardly the place I would have selected to celebrate this milestone in my life.

When we got to the restaurant everyone seemed to be in a hurry and ordered just a sandwich or a salad. I had a lamb shank and ordered a bottle of wine. You couldn't even get a drink in the dumb place. As we left, Jeanne said, "Let's go back to our house for coffee and dessert."

Boy, is this all there is? After nearly forty-one years of busting your tail and on your sixtieth birthday you get to go to some cheap restaurant on Lake Street. I didn't complain and quietly drove home to our dark and deserted house in Edina.

As I drove into the garage, feeling a little sorry for myself, and popped open the back door, all the lights in the place seemed to go on at once and I was met by a noisy crowd of people singing "Happy Birthday to You." I know that a lot of surprise parties are organized where the recipient of the surprise has somehow found out what is going on and then he has to fake being surprised. That was definitely not the case here. I was totally in shock. I thought I might be retiring, having a big six-o birthday, and a heart attack all on the same day. There must have been seventy-five people there, everyone we knew in Minneapolis. And there in the middle of the pack was our daughter from Chicago and she was just home two months ago.

Our good friends, Mary and Al, Clayt and Elsie, and Dee and Rog had come into the house while we were out to dinner, decorated it, set up the bar, had the dining room table elegantly spread full of food, and made sure everyone parked their cars a block away out of sight.

While I walked around shaking hands and kissing and hugging the girls, I said, "It looks like everyone we know is here except our son and daughter-in-law from Chicago." I no more than got the words out of my mouth when the front door popped open. There stood Bill and Angie. What a party, and what a family I have that would go to such lengths to make an old man feel so good. Am I lucky?

There was one more event associated with my retirement that was difficult and heart-wrenching. That was saying good-bye to the office staff and a group of wonderful employees who worked for me and given so much for my success. You know, they too get to be like family. Some of the people of my office were there over thirty years ago when I started in credit. They were the teachers of this rookie; they were patient and didn't give up on me, although I'm sure they considered it, and I'm sure they never expected that some day I would be their boss. Saying good-bye would not be easy, but another party (I guess you would call it that) was planned for the first Friday in January, my last day to come into the office.

Most everyone shut down early that day to set up decorations, tables of *hors d'oeuvres*, a punch bowl and a big, well decorated cake. Jeanne was invited to come in. It was the first time she had ever been to my office. Bill and Angie and Jennifer were also invited to be in attendance, but they already knew they were going to be coming to my birthday party in a couple of months so Bill, understandably, said they couldn't afford another trip. Jennifer, however, said she would like to be there and would fly in that day.

At about three o'clock everyone gathered around the large open end of our office and I was expected to make a farewell speech. That would ordinarily not be a problem but I soon realized it would be one of the most difficult things I would have to do on this day. There were at least three hundred people gathered, most of whom were my employees but there were a few local store managers, former retirees, and some outside business people I had worked with in the credit community that had also been invited.

The committee of employees who organized this thought it would be fun to lighten things up with one of these entertainer types that come in and roast the boss in front of his people. The entertainer happened to a shapely, scantily dressed young lady who assumed the role of a French maiden and proceeded to tell dirty stories about her and I and several other females I had been involved with. I could have been another Bill Clinton. I swear I never saw her before, I mean I don't think I have, I mean I don't recall seeing her before.

All this smutty stuff did not go over at all with the employees, who were mostly female. I was embarrassed for the poor girl and I finally got the microphone away from her and let her disappear.

As I began to talk and relate some of my growing up experiences with Sears, I couldn't help but think about the time that I broke down and cried in front of the entire one-room school while in the third grade, about the time when I had to live in a chicken coop for three months with my dad and was scared someone would find out about it; about the time when I was in the Navy on top of that hundred-foot tower and didn't know how I was going to get down. What I was doing now was almost as scary, so when my voice started to crack, I suggested we all go have some cake and coffee and I would say my good-byes personally.

Jennifer had called my office from Chicago earlier and said her flight was delayed because of bad weather and she didn't think she could make it for my party. And then when we were winding things up she called again to say that the plane was now getting ready to take off and even though she would be late she wanted to come home anyway.

Jeanne told her, "Dad and I will be going out to dinner someplace when he is through here but I don't know where. When you get into Minneapolis, why don't you call my office at the travel department at Dayton's and I will leave word with them where we're at and you can take a cab and join us there."

At about five-thirty, while I was packing up my personal stuff in my office, there was a group of about eight girls standing outside waiting. Finally one of them came in and said, "Some of us would like to buy you and your wife a drink over at Sunny's before you leave if you would be willing to do that."

"Boy does that sound good. Jeanne, do you think we have time to go have a drink with these nice people when we leave here?"

"Sure, I think so," Jeanne said.

Sunny's was a well-known bar, but not for its family atmosphere. Over the years it has experienced a few stabbings, a gun brawl or two, numerous fights, and it probably transacts more drug sales in a week than the pharmacy at Snyder's across the street does all year. But it was the only bar within twenty blocks of Sears and it was kept in business primarily by the energized Sears employees who wanted to get the dirty work taste out of their mouths before they went home. Yes, on occasion I may have been one of those people. There was simply not another place between there and home where I otherwise could have stopped. Those Vikequeens in south Minneapolis did not want a trashy tavern stinking up their neat little neighborhoods.

Actually, Sunny's served some fairly good snack food if you wanted to take a chance on their buffalo wings, baby back ribs, greasy hamburgers, hot dogs, and French fries. The cheap beer, booze, and boilermakers were the main attractions, usually served in a clean glass. No girls would want to go there by themselves or in pairs. A group of six or more was a little safer.

When we all got to Sunny's, Jeanne said, "Oh, I've got to call my office and let them know where we're at so they can tell Jennifer when she calls. Her plane should be landing any minute."

Jeanne spotted a telephone right away. I'll be damned, I didn't know Sunny's had a telephone. If I had known that I certainly would have called Jeanne all those times I stopped here with Bob Noel or Larry Roumell to let her know I may be a little late.

At the airport Jennifer's plane finally got in. She first called Jeanne's office to find out where we were and then she picked up her bag and hurried out to catch a cab. Jennifer had on her full-length fur coat that she bought while working in Montreal, high-heeled shoes, jewelry, and a fresh hairdo. She looked like a million bucks.

"Where to ma'am?" the cab driver said.

"I need to go to Sunny's bar. I believe it's on Chicago and Lake Street across from..."

"I know where it is ma'am," the cab driver interrupted. Nothing more was said until they left the airport area and were headed toward Lake Street down Hiawatha Avenue. The cabby couldn't resist any longer. "Pardon me for asking ma'am. I know it's none of my business, but what's a nice looking lady like you doing going to a place like Sunny's?"

Jennifer, not one to miss the opportunity to be a little dramatic, put a little quiver to her chin and a crack in her voice, said, "Well, my mother's an alcoholic, and my father just lost his job. I was told I could find them at Sunny's bar. I just now flew in from Chicago to see what I could do."

"Oh, you poor dear. I am so sorry ma'am."

They drove all the way to Sunny's without any further conversation at which time the cab driver got Jennifer's suitcase out of the trunk and carried it up to the door of the bar. "This is the place ma'am. Are you sure you're going to be all right?"

"I'll be fine."

"Well, good luck with your folks ma'am." And then he added, "At least it looks like the next generation in your family has got it together."

A Prayer For When You Grow Old

Lord, you know I'm growing older.

Keep me from becoming talkative and possessed with the idea that I must express myself on every subject.

Release me from the craving to straighten out everyone's affairs.

Keep me from the recital of endless detail.

Give me wings to get to the point.

Seal my lips when I am inclined to tell of my aches and pains. They are increasing with the years and my love to speak of them grows sweeter as time goes by.

Teach me the glorious lesson that occasionally I may be wrong.

Make me thoughtful but not nosy, helpful but not bossy. With my vast store of wisdom and experience it does seem a pity not to use it all.

But you know Lord, I still want a few friends at the end.

Epilogue

WELL, I THINK we can say the book is now finished, but already I am contemplating a rewrite to eliminate some of the stuff that is unnecessary. At the same time there could be another one hundred or two hundred pages of memorable incidents that keep bobbing to the surface of my watery brain that might make the tale more interesting.

That's what I mean when I say that everyone should write a book about their life history because that is the only way these events, big or small, can be preserved and shared with your family and friends. Everybody has a story to tell and you don't have to be a professional writer to do this. (Have I not proven that?) If you can tell about some happenings in your life in conversations with others, then you can put it down on paper as well.

I apologize for the reality of the gross language and the verbal abuse scenes between my parents during my growing up years. Unfortunately, that's the way it was.

Looking back over your life generates heightened self-worth and fresh insights, and even provides for a cleansing of emotions. Taking the process one step further—committing your story to paper—forces you to analyze your life more deeply and systematically. Then there's the added benefit of handing down your history to your children, your grandchildren, great grandchildren and so on, linking the generations together.

Furthermore the entire project can be a lot of fun. This was a lot of fun, and the more I got into it the more enjoyable it became even though there is a little work connected with it. The work involved is not in putting down the words that form the sequence of events page after page. Once you get started this begins to unfold very easily.

I didn't even consider the three hundred plus pages of typing that much work, in spite of my inability to be more than a one-finger typist. I don't know what my words-per-minute speed might be, but I know I can now type faster than I can write and I'll bet I am faster than some of the so-called secretaries I used to put up with while working at Sears on the Chicago west side.

The work, or should I say the frustration, is all due to the damn computer and its brain-dead operator. Perhaps I am one of those old farts who doesn't think he needs to understand computers at this stage in his life. After all, I was only going to use it as a word processor. But there is more to it than that, like setting up the page layout, the page numbering, back up disks, remembering to "save" and much more. Three whole chapters disappeared on me once, never to be recovered, because I pushed a wrong button or something.

I finally went to a computer class put on by the Bloomington Community College but learned virtually nothing. It was filled with little old ladies who barely got beyond turning the computer on, or the other extreme, a couple of guys seeking out the porno displays on the Internet. I was someplace in the middle, the lower middle.

It truly is a fantastic piece of equipment and to think that almost all of it has been developed in the last twenty years. With its rate of growth and advancement, what is it going to be able to do in the next twenty years or the next one-hundred years? I'm not going to strain my simple mind worrying about it.

I would also like to express my deepest gratitude to a dear proofreader who I think found most of my mistakes, but if you should run across some misspelled words or incorrect punctuation, please don't be too critical. You see, she happens to be one of the principal characters in the story and she may have gotten all caught up in the yarn and forgot her purpose in reading it. I'm not going to complain, because in addition to being an adequate proofreader, my dear wife does many many other wonderful things for me that are just perfect.

To order additional copies of this book, please send full amount plus $4.00 for postage and handling for the first book and 50¢ for each additional book.

In Canada, add $6.00 for first book and $1.00 for each additional book. For international airmail, add $15 for each item, or $1.00 for each item for surface mail.

Send orders to:

Galde Press, Inc.
PO Box 460
Lakeville, Minnesota 55044-0460

Credit card orders call 1–800–777–3454
Phone (952) 891–5991 • Fax (952) 891–6091
Visit our website at www.galdepress.com

Write for our free catalog.